MW00778187

TO
THE END
OF THE
WORLD

TO THE END
OF THE
WORLD

Nathanael Greene, Charles Cornwallis,
AND THE Race *TO THE* Dan

ANDREW WATERS

WESTHOLME
Yardley

Dedicated to North Carolina, my native state.

Title page: A ca. 1779 sketch of the British 17th Light Dragoons charging. (*Anne S. K. Brown Military Collection, Brown University Library*)

Westholme Publishing, LLC
904 Edgewood Road
Yardley, Pennsylvania 19067
Visit our Web site at www.westholmepublishing.com

ISBN: 978–1–59416–348–7
Also available as an eBook.

Printed in the United States of America.

For my father, *R. Charles Waters*,
and son, *Eli*, whose love of history inspires my own.
And for *Anne*, my muse.

CONTENTS

———

PART FOUR: *Afterward*

MAPS

———————

(A gallery of illustrations follows page 82)

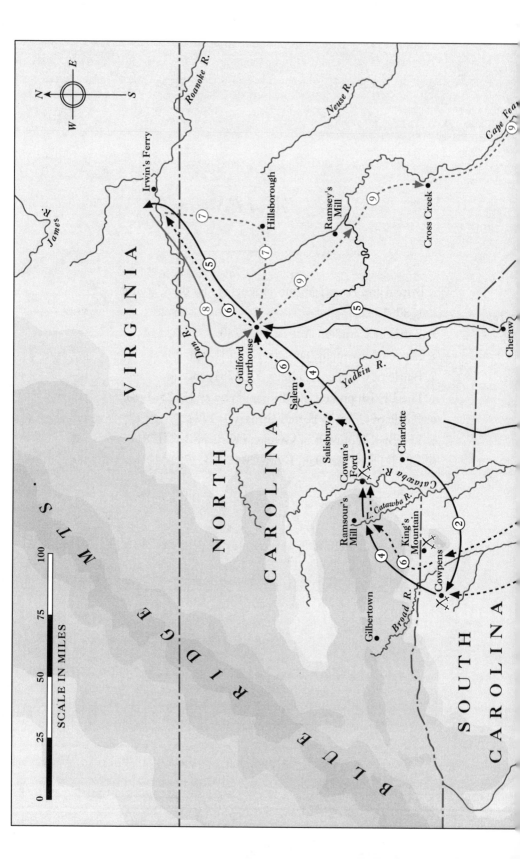

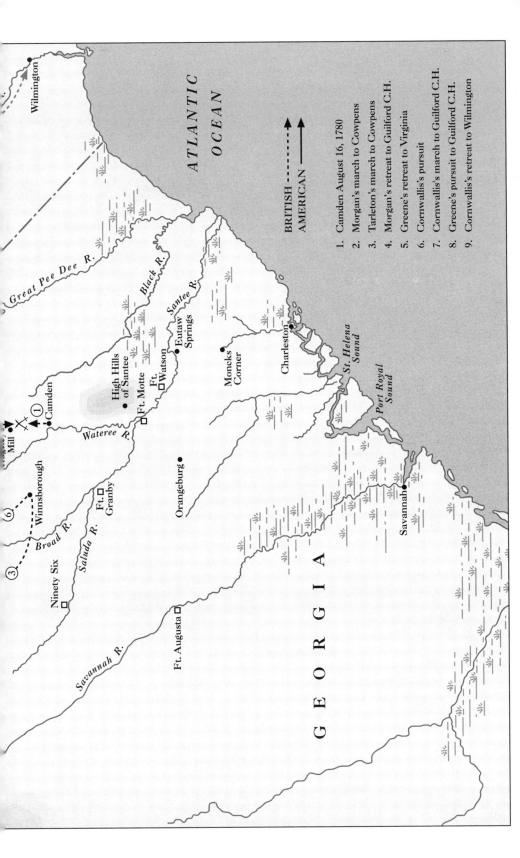

INTRODUCTION

———

Rivers ARE MY BUSINESS. As a land conservationist, my job often focuses on river corridors and watersheds. It makes sense if you think about it. Most of us get our water from the nearest river, and land conservation along river corridors helps keep water clean by providing natural filtration. So many conservation efforts focus on strategic corridors along these rivers to protect that most precious of natural resources. In fact, many land conservancies denote their service region as the watershed of a specific riparian area.

My land conservation career has centered on three of these watersheds. My first conservation job was at the Catawba Land Conservancy, focused on North Carolina's lower Catawba River Basin. From there I went to the Land Trust for Central North Carolina (now called the "Three Rivers Land Trust"), where our work focused on the Yadkin/Pee Dee River, centered around the Piedmont town of Salisbury, North Carolina. And most recently, I worked at the Spartanburg Area Conservancy in Spartanburg, South Carolina, where our focus was on South Carolina's upper Broad River Basin, including the Pacolet River.

Rivers were also Nathanael Greene's business, though in a very different way. As quartermaster general of the Continental army, the army's chief corporate officer in charge of transport, supply, camps, and troop movement, Greene looked to rivers for transportation. And as one of the army's most talented generals, he understood implicitly the strategic significance rivers could play in any theater of operations. When Greene took command of the Continental army's Southern Department, which I refer to as the "Southern Army" in this book, Greene hoped the South's vast network of rivers could alleviate some of the substantial supply issues facing these southern troops. Even before arriving in the South in late 1780, he had discussed strategies and designs for river transport with George Washington and others, including Thomas Jefferson. And as you shall read, he devoted considerable attention to studying three strategic river corridors traversing Virginia, North Carolina, and South Carolina: the Catawba River, the Yadkin/Pee Dee River, and the Dan River, a major tributary of the Roanoke River. And when Greene sent Daniel Morgan to the "west side of the Catawba" in December 1781, Morgan crossed into the Broad River Basin, setting up operations at a well-known location on the Pacolet River.

These four rivers—the Broad, the Catawba, the Yadkin, and the Dan—would go on to play a starring role in the "Race to the Dan," Greene's strategic retreat across the Carolinas into Virginia, just as three of them have starred in my own career. And though he would never use them as transport, as he originally intended, the study he devoted to them would reap strategic dividends in his conflict with Cornwallis.

BUT IT WASN'T THIS RIPARIAN CONNECTION that first attracted me to the story of the Race to the Dan. Like so much of my fascination with the American Revolution's southern campaigns, it was John Buchanan's book *The Road to Guilford Courthouse* that first ignited my fascination. As a native Carolinian, born in North Carolina and now residing in South Carolina, reading Buchanan to me was like revelation; through him I became aware of the incredible American Revolution history swirling all around me.

Before Buchanan there were hints. I remember Joe Morris, my colleague at the Land Trust for Central North Carolina, telling me the story of Nathanael Greene arriving alone at Steele Tavern in Salisbury, recounted here in chapter eleven. In it, Greene arrives at the Salisbury tavern alone deep in the night, after a solo ride across the war-torn countryside of North Carolina's Rowan County. As you shall read, it is a remarkable instance of Greene in isolation, traveling alone through an active war zone, hardly believable now and even less so then, as Joe is known for never allowing the facts to get in the way of a good story.

I lived in Salisbury for seven years, and outside of this office chatter, I rarely heard anything about the Race to the Dan, or heard it discussed in a cohesive context, though the city plays a central role in its story. As I note in a closing chapter of this book, wars aren't taught in American schools anymore, and if this shift to a study of culture and sociological movements from one of warfare is understandable in an increasingly diverse and politically sensitive world, it's unfortunate that campaigns like the Race to the Dan have been forgotten. In a place like Salisbury, you can live among its ghosts and still not know it's there.

Too bad. For the Race to the Dan is a remarkable tale, fit for cinema or an epic novel, and not only for its accounts of four narrow escapes across its four rivers. True, conflict is always a component of great narrative, and the Race to the Dan has plenty of it, but character and context also contribute. The American Revolution is not only the story of our nation's birth, it was also a revolutionary period of thought. Ideas about politics, philosophy, technology, law, and society were shifting rapidly, and warfare was no different. Thanks to writers like the Prussian king Frederick the Great and Maurice de Saxe, the illegitimate son of a Polish king who went on to fame as a European soldier of fortune, military theory was shifting from battlefield mechanics to the more nuanced craft of *petite guerre*, or partisan war—intelligence and sabotage, ambush, terror, and reconnaissance conducted with small detachments. And *petite guerre*'s tenets not only emphasized "light," or mobile troops, over the conventional soldiers of the line that had dominated European battlefield tactics for centuries but also a new brand of military officer capable of unusual self-reliance.

The Continental army lacked manpower and resources, but it was blessed with talented officers like Nathanael Greene and the Virginia backwoodsman Daniel Morgan, who embodied *petite guerre*'s doctrines. From early in the American Revolution, the Continental army had turned to these "partisan" tactics not out of intellectual curiosity but sheer necessity. Outmanned and outgunned from the beginning, George Washington relied on "light" troops and irregular militia led by talented junior officers not because he was a devotee of Saxe but because he had no other options. Washington was learning partisan tactics on the job, and under him was one of America's most talented military students, his protégé Nathanael Greene.

Born to a devout Quaker and Rhode Island merchant, Greene's training was in business, not war. But like so many young men of his era, Greene was consumed by the *rage militaire* fueling the American cause. Mentored by Boston bookseller Henry Knox, who would also go on to become a Continental army general and the United States' first secretary of war, Greene *did* read Frederick and Saxe as a young man, though they were but two of the numerous enlightenment writers that consumed him. It was probably family connections, not intellectual study, that garnered Greene his remarkable transformation from buck private to Continental army general in less than six months, but Washington recognized his potential at once even though Greene had his share of early setbacks in the war, notably at Fort Washington during the Battle of New York, when his decision to hold the fort in the face of a British assault ended up costing the Continental army over 2,800 soldiers, either killed or taken prisoner.

Born with an unusually facile mind, Greene learned quickly from these early mistakes and soon earned a reputation as one of Washington's most dependable battlefield commanders, leading with distinction at Trenton, Brandywine, Germantown, and Monmouth Courthouse, among others. It was during the dark winter of 1777, after the disastrous retreat from New York and New Jersey, when Greene first saw the partisan tactics he had read about as a younger man put broadly to the test. And there both Washington and Greene gained empirical knowledge of the underlying premise in those European texts: that it was the skill of the officer that mattered most in partisan warfare.

Greene's administrative talents were receiving attention as well, and when Washington needed a quartermaster general in 1778, he turned to his talented protégé, Greene, who reluctantly accepted the role, though he commented famously, "Nobody ever heard of a quarter master in history." Still he served the role competently, though not happily, finally resigning the appointment in July 1780 in a tiff with the Continental Congress. His reputation in disrepair over rumors of alleged self-dealing, Greene was in the right place at the right time when Washington needed to appoint a new commander to the Southern Department in the fall of 1780, following Continental general Horatio Gates's humiliating defeat at Camden that August.

Though the upbringings of Nathanael Greene and Charles, Lord Cornwallis, were vastly different, their military careers in the American Revolution shared a symmetry. They were born just four years apart, Cornwallis in 1738, Greene in 1742. Both developed important patrons: for Greene it was Washington; for Cornwallis, King George III and also Lord Germain, the crown's American secretary. Both Greene and Cornwallis earned reputations as dependable fighters on the battlefield, facing one another in battle many times, most notably at Monmouth Courthouse. And both were unhappy in secondary roles. For Cornwallis and Greene, the southern theater represented independent command, the chance to define themselves away from their superiors, the type of opportunity by which military careers and historic legacies are made.

Despite the similarities, they were vastly different men, leading vastly different organizations. If the Continental army was poor and undermanned, though intellectually creative, the British army was built on a bureaucracy that ably administered a global empire but often was bound by convention and tradition. It would be unfair to say the ideas of *petite guerre* had not infiltrated the British army—certainly talented junior officers like Banastre Tarleton and Francis, Lord Rawdon, embraced its principles. But for a senior officer like Cornwallis, raised at the upper levels of England's class system and trained on the battlefields of Europe, the unconventional tactics of war in the southern frontier could challenge his sense of propriety.

But Cornwallis was not completely convention bound. His plan to conquer the American South by invading North Carolina and Virginia was a bold one. Too bold, as we shall soon see, though his masters in London were eager for a decisive strike. In its execution, he commanded his soldiers' respect and devotion, one of his great strengths as a military leader, yet he never shared with Greene the relentless attention to detail such strategies demanded. Like Greene he recognized the fate of the American South lay in the fate of Greene's army. Destroy it, he believed, and Patriot sentiment throughout the region would soon crumble.

Yet Greene's strategies vexed him. Almost immediately upon taking command of the Southern Army, Greene realized it could not continue to operate as a single body. In its current condition—morale, discipline, and organization decimated by the outcome at Camden—the army could not stand in opposition to Cornwallis's invasion. Outmanned and outsupplied, his own troops desperately hungry and poorly equipped, Greene turned to the most potent weapon in his arsenal, his mind.

Greene's decision to send a "Flying Army" into the Broad River region in late December 1780 defied military convention by splitting an inferior force in the face of a superior enemy. "I am an independent spirit, and confide in my own resources," Greene would famously explain, yet he was acting from experience as much as instinct, for the lessons of New Jersey were not lost on him. In this dark moment Greene turned partisan tactics into a game of chess, positioning his pieces across the Carolinas not as a coherent offensive strategy but in an effort to disrupt the strategies of Cornwallis. And Cornwallis would come to understand it was a game in which he was overmatched and destined to lose.

IT IS AT THIS MONUMENTAL MOMENT—Greene's decision to detach Morgan's "Flying Army" west—that I begin the narrative thread of the "Race to the Dan." Some historians might argue with this distinction. By strict definition, the Race to the Dan has been regarded as the portion of Greene's strategic retreat from Guilford Courthouse to the Dan River, what comprises only the very last portion of this narrative. But from my perspective, living now in the upstate South Carolina countryside of its origin, the Race to the Dan begins after Daniel Morgan's momentous victory at Cowpens on January 17, 1781. With the dead and wounded still littering the Cowpens plain, Morgan realized immediately that Cornwallis with the remainder of his British invasion force would soon be in pursuit, eager to regain the seven hundred soldiers Morgan had taken prisoner. Later that very same morning, Morgan began his retreat into North Carolina, anxious to reunite with Greene and move out of Cornwallis's way.

It is at this moment also that the Carolinas' rivers take center stage, for Morgan needed to escape across the Broad and Catawba Rivers as soon as possible. If Morgan is mostly remembered today for his victory at Cowpens, and also his service at the Battle of Saratoga in September and October 1777, his retreat from Cowpens may be one of his most underappreciated feats of the war. Instead of moving due east toward Greene, Morgan crossed the Broad to the north, moving into modern-day Rutherford County, North Carolina. Either by luck or deliberate deception, probably a bit of both, Morgan's move fooled Cornwallis, leading to a delay of several days that allowed Morgan to safely cross the Catawba River on January 23.

Cornwallis would not cross the Catawba until February 1, pausing at a frontier meeting place called Ramsour's Mill for a dramatic bonfire, then facing Patriot resistance at Cowan's Ford. With Morgan's health failing, Greene had raced across the Carolinas to take command of the "Flying Army" and gather Patriot militia on the east side of the Catawba. At

Cowan's, Greene pushed the Patriots' capacity for partisan warfare to its limits, attempting to rally local militia even as he ordered the Flying Army toward safety in Salisbury. It was a mixed success. Though the Patriot militia did bravely withstand the British charge at Cowan's, General William Davidson was killed in the process, leading to a breakdown in command that seriously undermined Greene's efforts to organize central North Carolina's militia. It is at this moment, when Greene realizes the Patriot militia he has ordered to rally to him are not coming, that we have Greene's solo ride across the war-torn fields of western Rowan County, arriving in Salisbury alone late that evening, a vengeful British army not far behind. If the story my friend Joe Morris told me of Nathanael Greene's escape sounded too good to be true, the truth is even more remarkable, for in it we see Greene acting with a bravery bordering on recklessness, the independence and innovation of the partisan soldier taken to an extreme degree.

Two rivers, two escapes, including British and American heroics at Cowan's Ford. But the story only gets more tense from there, with yet another near-miss escape at the Yadkin River, the British vanguard arriving at the Yadkin's famous "Trading Ford" only to find the Flying Army just reaching safety on the other side. Then a dramatic council of war at Guilford Courthouse, where Greene's officers agreed to abandon the state of North Carolina for the sake of saving Greene's now reunified army. The desperate five-day push to the Dan, with Otho Holland Williams serving ably in the partisan commander role now abandoned by Morgan due to his failing health. And it is at the end of this desperate race, the British vanguard and Williams's light corps within reach of one another day and night, that Greene's insight pays its ultimate dividend; the boats waiting for the Continentals on the Dan River were the result of his careful prescience and planning over two months before.

THE HISTORIAN Charles Heaton attempts to contextualize the Race to the Dan in this broader context by dubbing the period from Cowpens to the crossing of the Dan as the "Piedmont Campaign."[1] Though this interpretation may satisfy the American Revolution's dogmatists, who insist the Race to the Dan was only the last chapter of this period, I think the translation loses in narrative drive what it gains in objective accuracy. Yes, the "Race to the Dan" remains obscure, but there is alchemy in the phrase, a certain intrigue in people's eyes when I describe its particulars to friends and family during the course of writing this book. And so for these story-telling reasons, and also marketing ones, I expand the phrase "Race to the Dan" to include all elements of the "Piedmont Campaign."

For this is military history too compelling to resist. Yes, the military historian may find her or himself absorbed in the strategies and tactics of partisan war, the false assumptions of England's "Southern Strategy," and the logistical challenges facing both sides. But for the casual reader, these discussions are, I suspect, mere ephemera. What first drew me to the Race to the Dan was its story, not the philosophical and practical applications of eighteenth-century military philosophy, and certainly not the overlap with the rivers of my conservation career. So I hope readers of this book will become captivated by that same compulsive narrative, even if they are forced to absorb my musings on broader contexts in the process.

I think it is fair to say the Race to the Dan is so little known today because it was a retreat. Indeed, Greene clearly understood the negative optics of his decision to abandon North Carolina, though he perhaps gave little consideration to how such optics would affect his twenty-first-century legacy. But it was strategic retreat—retreat designed to inflict a toll on his enemy while conserving his own military options further down the road. The type of retreat devised by a chess master, thinking moves ahead, designed to lure his opponent into a trap, while his opponents were confined to the present dimension—a novel, if not ingenious, brand of victory.

In terms of his mental conflict with Cornwallis, this metaphor of Greene the chess master is perhaps not 100 percent fair. Cornwallis did have his strategies, even if they were based on specious assumptions. But in chess, the player must never commit 100 percent to any one plan. Capable of these adjustments, Greene was always evaluating and reevaluating, attempting to influence his circumstances even as he was reacting to them. In contrast, Cornwallis was a gambler, "and a poor one because he could not take setbacks as part of the game," writes Henry Clinton's biographer, William B. Willcox, a sentiment he almost certainly shared with his subject. Here, I believe, Cornwallis's aristocratic disposition ultimately let him down. In his pursuit of Greene, he never stopped to consider the contingencies of Cowpens or the effect of his army's frustrations at Cowan's and Trading Ford. He expected to win, not because his strategies were superior but because he believed himself the superior player. And so he barged on, willing to risk all in a bet on his own instincts. But chess is not a gambler's game.[2]

And if Cornwallis had stopped and turned around at Cowan's or Trading Ford, or retrenched in South Carolina after Cowpens and never invaded North Carolina at all, we wouldn't have one of the American Revolution's most thrilling narratives. We might not even have the American South, at least not as we know it today. Briefly in this book, I ask the reader to consider what would've happened if the British had held onto the southern colonies of South Carolina and Georgia, leading perhaps to a vastly different American landscape.

Instead, Cornwallis continued to react to Greene, ceding his strategic and logistical advantages. The argument that the Race to the Dan was responsible for Cornwallis's move to Yorktown is a complicated one, requiring a context broader than that available to the casual American Revolution historian. I attempt it here, supported by historians more esteemed than myself, John Buchanan included, as well as Greene's subordinate officers Otho Holland Williams and Henry Lee, who defended the Race to the Dan's legacy in Greene's absence. After his masterful leadership in the southern campaigns, Greene died in 1786 at the age of just forty-three.

It was a tragically premature end to a remarkable American life. And it certainly diminished his historic legacy. One can only speculate on the role Nathanael Greene might have played in the foundation of America after the war. But we don't have to speculate on the remarkable legacy of Greene's wartime achievements. This leads me back to my confession. Yes, the Race to the Dan shares an overlap with the rivers of my conservation career. Yes, the Race to the Dan is real history suitable for the big screen, with dynamic characters and dramatic conflict. Yes, I believe its implication was the British surrender at Yorktown. But ultimately it is the study of Greene and his leadership that fascinates me, especially in contrast to Charles Cornwallis. We all need heroes, and through his resilience, his diligence, and his innovation, Greene has become one of mine. Cornwallis wasn't a lesser man, just a different one, as am I. Greene turned defeat into victory by committing himself to its cause wholeheartedly. His careful study of the Carolinas' rivers, the risks he entailed, and the camaraderie he shared with his "Southern Gentlemen" was a product of an extraordinary character. The Race to the Dan is its story.

PROLOGUE: ALEA IACTA EST

DID HE THINK OF CAESAR, the great conflagration reflecting in his eyes? No scholar was Charles, Lord Cornwallis. This one was a warrior, determined to join the British army from an early age. But as a teenager he had attended Eton, where the school's curriculum was based on Latin, and surely there he was as delighted by the phrase *alea iacta est* ("the die is cast") as any schoolboy before or since.

Did he think of his beloved wife, Jemima, dead now two years? Her death, attributed by friends to her husband's prolonged military absences, but perhaps due to hepatitis, devastated Cornwallis. His biographers call it the "greatest emotional experience in Charles' life."[1] Seeking solace in war, he abandoned a prolonged leave of absence in England during her illness and subsequent death to volunteer for a return to America, where now he found himself in command of this strange southern theater, a frontier of ruthless depredations and inhospitable wilds.

Or did he think of politics? For as the great fire burned, surely Cornwallis knew his actions would be heard of by his superiors, both General Henry Clinton, overall commander of the British forces in the American colonies, Cornwallis's immediate superior now ensconced comfortably in his New York City headquarters, and their mutual masters back in London: Lord Germain, the British secretary of state for the American colonies, responsible for conducting the American war, and British prime minister Lord North,[2] along with King George III himself.

Here, we must surmise, Cornwallis devoted at least some of his thoughts. For as his baggage burned at Ramsour's Mill on the shores of the Little Catawba River in west central North Carolina, just north of modern-day Lincolnton, North Carolina, surely he pondered his superiors' reactions. Though this movement into North Carolina was long planned and even longer contemplated, Cornwallis must have known that Clinton, at least, would disapprove of the circumstances under which it was now being executed.

Clinton's orders to Cornwallis upon his departure from New York in early June of that year were to safeguard Charleston and South Carolina as his primary responsibility. Clinton was aware Cornwallis planned to invade North Carolina that winter, writing of it in a correspondence to Cornwallis as recently as December 13, 1780,[3] but the British defeat at Cowpens on January 17, 1781, against a combined Continental and patriot militia army under command of Brigadier General Daniel Morgan had altered these strategic objectives. As Clinton would suggest in his post-war memoirs: "Under such circumstances as these . . . His Lordship might have thought himself justified in relinquishing his fruitless pursuit and returning to restore tranquility to South Carolina."[4]

But there was to be no relinquishing in Cornwallis, not here, not now, even if at some level he instinctively understood he was disregarding Clinton's preferences—he would not write to Clinton for three months after crossing into North Carolina, a period during which the entire landscape of the southern theater shifted against the British cause.[5]

Perhaps these were the things that crossed his mind, for they all played a role in the series of events that now found him standing in a remote area of the southern frontier, watching the great blaze. Perhaps his mind turned to darker corners, for in the disorientation of his bewildered pursuit, Cornwallis had acknowledged a despair and psychological isolation of which Caesar would certainly never admit. Cornwallis was a warrior, yes, but one capable of human flaw and emotion. Long accustomed to the routines and bureaucracies of the British army, the adversities he now faced stretched his psychological stamina to its limits.

What we can be certain Cornwallis thought of was his army, for he was as devoted to the soldiers as they were to him. Yet it was an army now severely limited in its mobility due to the disastrous defeat at Cowpens, where under the command of Cornwallis's young protégé, Lt. Colonel Banastre Tarleton, it had lost 110 dead, including ten officers, and 712 prisoners, almost all of Cornwallis's light troops, the most mobile part of his command. As he marched out of his South Carolina headquarters on January 19, determined to apprehend Morgan and cut him to shreds before he could reunite with the bulk of the Continental army under General Nathanael Greene, or isolate Greene's combined force from its safe havens in Virginia, almost all his remaining units were regiments of the line, accustomed to a traditional, European style of war and attended to by a slow and cumbersome baggage train, not to mention a large contingent of camp followers, including many women.

It was slow going, and pursuing Morgan two days in the wrong direction didn't help. Frustrated with the slow pace, Cornwallis ordered on January 21 that camp followers and some of the wagons be left behind in order to hasten the pursuit.[6] But when he arrived at Ramsour's Mill on January 25, only to find Morgan had safely escaped across the Catawba River, Cornwallis decided on drastic measures. So they could travel with minimal impediment, the army's baggage should be burned, he ordered, beginning with his own.

"Lord Cornwallis set the example, by burning all his Waggons, and destroying the greatest part of his Baggage, which was followed by every Officer of the Army without a single murmur," wrote Brigadier General Charles O'Hara, commanding Cornwallis's crack brigade of British guards.[7]

Explaining his actions to Lord Germain in a later letter, Cornwallis wrote, "As the loss of my light troops could only be remedied by the activity of the whole corps, I employed a halt . . . and in destroying superfluous baggage and all my waggons except those loaded with hospital stores, salt, and ammunition, and four reserved empty in readiness for sick and wounded. In this measure, though at the expense of a great deal of officers' baggage . . . I must, in justice to this army, say that there was the most general and cheerful acquiesence."[8]

And so, Latin scholar or not, the die was cast. Cornwallis was no Caesar. In history, he would go down as the loser of the American colonies, not their conqueror. Yet in destroying his army's baggage, beginning with his own, he reaffirmed his resolve with a dramatic, fiery flourish of which Caesar would approve. There would be no turning back for this army, not until Morgan and Greene were met in battle. Where his mind wandered as his baggage burned we can only wonder, where his army was headed there could be no doubt—forward, pursuing its prey across North Carolina at all costs.

For O'Hara, their destination was clear. "In this situation, without Baggage, necessaries, or Provisions of any sort for Officer or Soldier, in the most barren inhospitable unhealthy part of North America, opposed by the most savage, inveterate perfidious cruel Enemy, with zeal and with Bayonets only, it was resolv'd to follow Green's Army, to the end of the World."[9]

Part One

THE SOUTHERN THEATER

CHAPTER I

RIVERS AND ROADS

For a man obsessed with moving armies, Major General Nathanael Greene preferred traveling light. Perhaps after two and a half challenging years as the Continental army's quartermaster general—its head corporate officer in charge of transportation, supply, camps, and the movement of troops—it was the psychological freedom of unfettered movement he craved. As a young man, Greene frequently escaped the rigid order of his devout Quaker household with solitary idles, either to nearby bookstores or traveling the nighttime roads near his family homestead in Potowomut, Rhode Island, to a local "frolic," under the nose of his strict but loving father.[1] This trip south, finally free from the administrative burdens and political intrigues of the quartermaster general's office, may have felt much the same.

Greene's destination was the Southern Army, his new command, a ragtag collection of mostly Maryland and Delaware Continental soldiers joined by an ever-changing assortment of southern militia. This was the remnants of an army sent south in the spring of 1780 to help defend Charleston but arrived too late, then suffered under the inept leadership of General Horatio Gates at the Battle of Camden on August 16, 1780.

Departing Philadelphia on November 3, 1780, Greene's destination was Hillsboro, North Carolina, where this motley crew had retreated after Camden.[2] Greene traveled on horseback with only his fellow major general, Baron Friedrich von Steuben, and two aides. At key moments during the

Race to the Dan, we find Nathanael Greene alone or in limited company, an unusual situation for a man who was arguably the most strategically important American in the South.[3] But after six years as a general in the perennially overmatched Continental army—a period during which Greene and his fellow Continental officers often felt as if they were fighting their own government and public as much as they were the British army—Greene clearly craved solitude, taking it when available, no matter the circumstance.

For this journey, the solitude was more than literal. For the first time in the war, he would be commanding independent of his patron and mentor, George Washington. The two men had enjoyed a symbiotic relationship, conferring or corresponding closely on almost every major decision during the American Revolution, their accord so complete many accused Greene of having an undue influence on Washington.[4] Undue or not, the relationship was undeniably close; their parting must have been an emotional one, even for the taciturn Washington—after leaving Washington's headquarters at Totowa, New Jersey, on his journey south, Greene and Washington would not see each other for three years. Never again would they live, or think, so closely. Without either his mentor's counsel or protection, Greene's military career was headed toward uncharted waters.

On its way to North Carolina, the tiny group stopped in the capitals of Annapolis, Maryland, and Richmond, Virginia, where Greene implored the colonial governments there for troops and desperately needed supplies. "Any officials he [Greene] could not meet, he wrote to, often after riding horseback all day," note the editors of his papers.[5]

Of his meetings in Richmond with Governor Thomas Jefferson, Greene complained by letter to Washington, "Matters here are in the greatest state of confusion imaginable, and the business of government almost at a standstill for want of money and public credit. Our prospects with respect to supplies are very discouraging."[6]

These meetings reflect the stark economic realities facing not only Greene in the fall of 1780 but the entire Continental army. With the army's formation in 1775, the Continental Congress had attempted to take responsibility for its provision and recruitments, financed mostly through debt. This effort had always been a mixed success. And as the war progressed, the debt ballooned, leading to debilitating inflation. In response, Congress called on the individual states to shoulder an ever-increasing share of the military burden. But the states also struggled with a litany of fiscal and social problems—debt, a general distaste for levies and taxes, weak and decentralized governments, inefficient communications, and perhaps most significant of all, a politically divided populace—leaving them little to spare for the Continental soldiers. As the war effort ebbed and waned, so did its support, both among the state administrations and their people. Mostly this support came down to who felt threatened most.

Nowhere was this paradox more distinct than in the South, where far from the war's major campaigns in the Northeast, Congress saw little need for investing its scant resources during the latter half of the 1770s.[7] But this situation changed with the British capture of Savannah on December 29, 1778, and escalated with the British capture of Charleston, the South's most important port, in May 1780. Seduced by the persuasions of British Loyalists and their sympathizers in England, Britian's de facto prime minister, Frederick North, and his American secretary, George Germain, increasingly believed a British victory could still be achieved in the American South, where they were informed a strong but heretofore suppressed Loyalist contingent would turn out in force to support a British invasion. And if the British army could sweep north through the Carolinas into the strategically important Chesapeake region, the American resistance might falter.

Though this strategic shift was never based on realistic expectations, it caught unprepared the southern states and their meager Continental army occupation force. And the situation was exacerbated when Continental general Benjamin Lincoln surrendered Charleston with its 2,650 soldiers, essentially the whole of the Continental army's southern command.[8] To the rescue came Horatio Gates, the hero of the great American victory at Saratoga, as Lincoln's replacement. But Gates's defeat at Camden only made matters worse.

The American war system was broken, with its primary victim the Continental soldier. In his social history of the American Revolution, *A Revolutionary People at War*, author Charles Royster hypothesizes that this dysfunction led to a sense of psychological isolation and egotism among the Continental army and, especially, its officer corps. By the end of the 1770s, Royster argues, the revolutionary fervor that swept the colonies into war with England, what he labels the *rage militaire*, had faded among the general public. Most men eligible for military service preferred a short-term militia commitment, or no military commitment at all, to a long-term enlistment in the Continental army, leaving the army undermanned and forced to rely on the transient disposition of temporary troops.

Abandoned by most of their countrymen, mismanaged by their government, the officers of the Continental army increasingly considered themselves the only authentic examples of the American cause. After all, it was they who had endured long years of injury, sickness, starvation, deprivation, even death, in its service. And if the cause was lost, it was they who would be punished for its failure. "The [Continental] officers believed that they alone had maintained the *rage militaire* of 1775, which they associated with the true revolutionary spirit of virtuous effort," writes Royster. "Their separation from civilian society and their pride in the officer corps encouraged the first step in identifying the class of public-spirited men who could save independence."[9] Nathanael Greene expressed such a sentiment when he wrote to a fellow army officer in 1779: "We shall be happy to see you at Camp, where you will find the true military spirit, justice and generosity. The great body of the People you know are contracted, selfish and illiberal; and therefore not calculated to harmonize with a noble nature like yours."[10]

But Greene's frustrations with *rage militaire*'s decline didn't diminish his talents for *realpolitik*, and he had long ago mastered the art of incessant complaining. "A habit acquired during his quartermaster general days was now firmly rooted," observes historian M.F. Treacy, "From here on, whenever he was in need of anything, he asked for the whole of it from every possible source, believing that in this way he might get a grudging bit here and another scanty slice there . . . General Greene's own importunities embarrassed him not at all."[11]

Greene had tried to resist the quartermaster general appointment when it was thrust upon him in the spring of 1778, writing, "It was with the greatest difficulty that I could prevail on myself to engage in this business," and "Nobody ever heard of a quartermaster in history."[12] But he took the job at the insistence of Washington. In truth, he was gifted at it, blessed not only with a talent for administrative efficiency but also a cold-hearted ruthlessness he could call on when warranted. It was this talent he had displayed during the encampment at Valley Forge in the winter of 1778, when he had been placed in charge of foraging the vicinity. "You must forage the country naked," he had commanded his officers, and to Washington he acknowledged, "The inhabitants cry out and beset me from all quarters . . . but like Pharoh I harden my heart."[13]

Despite his talents for it, Greene was never satisfied as quartermaster general and longed for a return to combat, a lament he made frequently both to Washington and his contacts in Congress. Gates's disaster at Camden provided the opportunity he craved. After the debacle, Congress gave Washington the authority to appoint Gates's successor, and Washington awarded the job to his protégé, Greene.[14]

But even the man he still referred to as "Your Excellency" was not exempt from the ruthless efficiency of Greene's incessant solicitations. In response to one such request Greene penned as he journeyed south, Washington replied, "So fully sensible have I long been of the distressed situation not only of the Army in this quarter, but also at the Southward, and of all our great departments, from the embarrassed *state of our finances*, that it has been not only a constant subject of representation, in the strongest terms to Congress, and the States individually; but particularly so to the Minister of France in our last interview. And that a foreign loan was absolutely necessary to retrieve our affairs."[15]

In short, there was little Washington could do to help Greene without an infusion of French cash. But there was one dispensation Washington *was* able to make to Greene. As part of his new command, Greene solicited the services of Henry Lee, the talented Virginia cavalry officer who had distinguished himself several times during the course of the war. Washington granted Greene's request, sending Lee and his "legion" of mounted and light infantry south to join the Southern Army.[16] Though he would not arrive in the Carolinas until January 1781, pausing in Virginia to recruit and indulge his taste in fine horses, the famed "Light Horse Harry" would go on to provide invaluable service during Greene's southern campaign, which Lee would recount vividly in his later memoir.

And though Washington might have little he could send to the South, he shared with Greene an infatuation for its modes of transportation. In the southern frontier, moving supplies was as big an issue as procuring them, thanks to the region's primitive road system and innumerable rivers, creeks, and swamps. "I would recommend the building of a number of flat bottomed Boats of as large a construction as can be conveniently transported on Carriages. This I conceive might be of great utility, by furnishing the means to take advantage of the Enemy's situation in crossing those Rivers which would be otherwise impassable," Washington advised Greene.[17] Even the mostly ineffectual Jefferson shared an intellectual interest on the topic, soliciting both Washington and Greene for more information about the vessels' proposed design in hopes he could facilitate their construction, although Benedict Arnold's invasion of Virginia in December 1780 prevented him from taking any further action on the initiative.[18]

Rivers and roads preoccupied Greene's mind when he encountered Lieutenant Colonel Edward Carrington during his journey south. A Virginia artillery officer, Carrington had served in the North, most notably at Monmouth in June 1778, where his artillery ably defended a fierce attack from Britain's famous Black Watch Regiment.[19] In summer 1780, Carrington was assigned to the expeditionary force under General Johann de Kalb that arrived too late to relieve Charleston earlier that spring. When Gates arrived to relieve de Kalb at the Continental army camp at Deep River, North Carolina, on July 25, 1780, Carrington was one of the officers he found there. Preoccupied then with the same issues of supply and transport that now consumed Greene, Gates detached Carrington to Virginia to secure supplies and attend to their transportation southward.[20]

Thanks to this assignment, Carrington avoided capture or worse at Camden and had established a supply depot at Taylor's Ferry, on the main branch of the Roanoke River (in an area now submerged by the John H. Kerr Reservoir on the North Carolina/Virginia border). Writing to Gates from Taylor's Ferry on September 23, Carrington observed: "I have taken as good a view of the ground on the River hereabouts as I have been able, but the Country is so exceedingly thick Set with lofty Woods that a competent knowledge cannot be obtained without visiting every place. The Fording places, however, must at all events claim attention."[21] Carrington would spend much of the fall shuffling back and forth between Taylor's Ferry and Richmond, arranging supplies and transport to the Southern Army's headquarters in North Carolina.

Somewhere in Virginia, either in Richmond or on the road between Richmond and the Roanoke River, Carrington encountered Greene and traveled south with him to Hillsboro, North Carolina,[22] replacing in the tiny entourage Steuben, who was left behind in Richmond to command Continental army operations in Virginia.[23]

"On my arrival at Hillsborough I intend to have all the rivers examined in order to see if I cannot ease this heavy business by water transportation," Greene had informed Washington on November 19.[24] Now arrived there, it was to this task Greene assigned Carrington, ordering him to extend his survey of the Roanoke River fords upstream to include the Dan River, "as high as the upper Saura Town," an isolated mountain range in north central North Carolina in the vicinity of the Dan River near present-day Danbury, North Carolina.[25]

Greene was surprised to find the Continental army not at Hillsboro, as he believed, but moved to Charlotte by Gates, responding to a report from the North Carolina Board of War that food supplies there were more adequate.[26] Greene continued his journey to Charlotte, encountering General Edward Stevens along the way in Salisbury, North Carolina. Located just southwest of the Yadkin River's "Trading Ford," Salisbury was a funnel point for the Great Wagon Road, the main north-south settler highway from Pennsylvania into South Carolina and Georgia.[27]

Stevens had resigned his colonel commission in the Tenth Virginia Continental Regiment in 1778 but rejoined the Southern Army as a general of Virginia militia, fighting with Gates at Camden.[28] At Salisbury, Greene ordered Stevens to appoint one of his officers to survey the upper reaches of the Yadkin River. "Let the officer be very intelligible, and have a Charge to be particular in his observations," Greene commanded Stevens. "When the officer gets up to Hughes Creek [a tributary of the Yadkin], I wish him to take a Horse and ride across the Country from that place thro' the Town of Bethania to the upper Saura Town, and report the Distance and Condition of the Roads . . . I also wish the officer to make enquiry respecting the Transportation that may be had from the Yadkin to the Catawba River, and whether the Transportation cannot be performed with Batteaus [a shallow-draft, flat-bottomed boat] down that River."[29]

Greene finally arrived in Charlotte on December 2, 1780, relieving Horatio Gates of command. One of his first assignments was to Colonel Thaddeus Kosciuszko, ordered to make a "most minute enquiry" of the Catawba River and its tributaries and prepare a detailed report that would enable Greene to determine what uses of the river could be made "in the different Seasons of the Year."[30] Responsible for planning and building the defenses of West Point, Kosciuszko was a Pole whom Gates had named chief engineer of the Southern Army earlier that summer. Accompanying Kosciuszko on his Catawba River survey was Captain John Thomas, a militia officer in Thomas Sumter's South Carolina militia familiar with the Catawba River region.[31]

Either impressed by his discussions with Carrington during their journey south, or horrified by the condition of his new army, Greene moved quickly to name Carrington deputy quartermaster general, officially offering him the position in a letter dated December 4. "I have people now exploring the Yadkin and Catabaw Rivers, and have great Reason to hope the Plan of Transportation down those Rivers will succeed," his letter informed

Carrington. Still focused on the waterborne transportation system, Greene ordered Carrington to "consult with a good Shipwright" about "the Tools that will be necessary for Building about 100 Large Batteaus and to take measures for having them forwarded without Loss of Time."[32]

Greene's optimism for his water transportation plan was evident in a December 6 letter to Thomas Jefferson, written from his camp at Charlotte: "I have Parties now exploring the Rivers Dan, Yadkin and Catabaw and am not without Hopes of finding them navigable with Batteaus, which will enable us to transport from the Roanoke to this Place and even within 30 Miles of Charlestown with only 50 or 60 Miles L'd [land] Transportation."[33] Though this optimistic assessment would never materialize, the diligence with which Greene executed his survey of the Carolina river basins would prove fortuitous.

Writing to Greene on December 6, before receiving Greene's letter of December 4 offering him the position of deputy quartermaster general, Carrington gave the general an update on the Dan River survey, which he had assigned to his assistant, Captain John Smith. "I have got Capt. Smith off, on his expedition for exploring the Dan River . . . I have made enquiry as to the navigation of the River and am well assured we shall find transportation for a considerable way up very practicable." Despite his sanguine assessment, Carrington believed canoes, not batteaus, provided a more likely option for transport, at least in the shallower waters of the Dan. "With a view to being ready to take our measures, under every possible circumstance, I have instructed Capt. Smith to get a return of all good Canoes in the river . . . should we afterwards find Batteaux more advantageous, a Canoe split and widened, by letting in a plank through the middle, will make an excellent Batteaux."[34]

An officer of the Maryland line, Smith sent his report on the Dan River to Greene on December 25, 1780. It suggested Greene establish a commissary store at Dix's Ferry, located four miles south of the fall line, ninety miles by land to the Yadkin River, but also reported on other ferries and crossings farther north, before concluding with a list of canoes he found on the river.[35]

Greene never managed construction of the bateaux fleet he envisioned. Like many complex and long-term projects facing an underresourced organization, this water-transportation-system plan soon took a backseat to more immediate concerns, as Greene became intimately aware of the desperate situation facing his army. "The subsistence of this Army is so precarious and difficult to obtain either from real scarcity of supplies or for want of a more general and permanent arrangement that I am not a little alarmed for its existence," he complained to the North Carolina Board of War. "We are now fed with great difficulty by daily collections; and prospects grow more and more unpromising."[36]

Turning from his long-term transportation plans to his immediate needs for forage, Greene pressed William R. Davie into the role of commissary general. In the Continental army, the commissary officer was responsible for the procurement of food and clothing, while the quartermaster was responsible for procuring other necessary supplies and transport. Only twenty-four, though already distinguished by his service as a partisan commander, Davie had no interest in the job.

Davie is the type of man whose name one wanders past on university campuses, at state capitols, at county lines, in towns and roads and buildings across the state of North Carolina, a man whose deeds may be forgotten but whose influence is eternal. Born in England, Davie immigrated to the colonies as a child, settling with his family in 1763 in the Waxhaw settlement on the North Carolina/South Carolina border. With a prominent uncle as his patron, Davie graduated from Princeton with honors in 1776 and returned to study law in Salisbury, then the largest settlement in western North Carolina. Called to the American cause, Davie left his studies and formed a North Carolina militia cavalry troop in 1778, rising to the rank of major and eventually serving alongside Continental troops at Stono Ferry, South Carolina, on June 20, 1779, where he was seriously wounded in action.

Following a lengthy convalescence, he raised another body of militia cavalry and campaigned in the Waxhaws region following the surrender of Charleston, occasionally fighting in concert with South Carolina militia general Thomas Sumter. At Hanging Rock on August 6, 1780, Sumter proposed the Patriot militia ride their horses directly in front of the Loyalist positions, dismount, and then commence their attack. Davie "insisted on the necessity of leaving the horses . . . and marching to the attack on foot, urging the confusion always consequent of dismounting under a fire," but his objections were "over ruled."[37] Miraculously, Sumter's plan worked, giving the South Carolina Gamecock one of his greatest victories.

At Camden, Davie is credited with salvaging valuable supplies after the debacle, in contradiction to Gates's commands.[38] At the time of Greene's arrival in early December, Davie was "making arrangements to raise another body of Troops at the insistence of General [Daniel] Morgan, who was to be charged with a separate command to operate on the left of the Enemy, and fired with the prospect of serving under this celebrated commander was entirely absorbed with this favorite project."

Davie was a bold and skilled field officer, far from a typical commissariat, yet perhaps Greene saw something of himself in the young man. Davie certainly didn't see it in himself. Writing of himself in the third person in his memoir, Davie recalled, "The Colonel [Davie] having observed that . . . he knew nothing about *money* or *accounts* that he must therefore be unfit for such an appointment. . . . The General replied that as to *Money* and *accounts* the Colonel would be troubled with neither, that there was not a single dollar in the military chest nor any prospect of obtaining any, that he must accept the appointment, and supply the army in the same manner he had subsisted his own troops for the last six months." It was an argument Davie could not resist. "The Generals eloquence prevailed, and the Colonel accepted the appointment."[39]

Greene's disenchantment with his Charlotte location was growing quickly, detracting from his efforts to establish water transportation. On December 8, he ordered Kosciuszko into South Carolina to search out a new camp location in the environs of the Pee Dee River, putting to a halt his survey work on the Catawba River in North Carolina. Nevertheless, Kozciuszko's efforts would not be in vain. In just a few short weeks, when combat returned to the Catawba River vicinity, a North Carolina militia general would allegedly remark that "though General Greene had never seen the Catawba before, he appeared to know more about it than those who were raised on it."[40]

Carrington was ordered by Greene to "join the army the moment" he made the "necessary arrangements" to transport the supplies in Virginia south by land, not water, and that transportation on the Roanoke River, construction of bateaux, and other matters could be settled after Carrington arrived in camp.[41] The formal plan Carrington developed for waterborne transportation ultimately would have little utility for moving supplies, but in the tumultuous months to come, Greene's efforts to survey and explore the rivers and roads of the central Carolinas and southern Virginia would prove fruitful in securing a more precious cargo.[42]

CHAPTER 2

CORNWALLIS CONQUERS
THE SOUTH

O<small>N</small> A<small>UGUST</small> 16, 1780, Charles, Lord Cornwallis, lieutenant general of the British army, conquered the South. That day Cornwallis's army of approximately 2,200 men, comprised mostly of British regulars, including crack Loyalist, or provincial, units under seasoned commanders such as Banastre Tarleton and Francis, Lord Rawdon, thrashed and humiliated Continental General Horatio Gates's numerically superior "Grand Army of the Southern Department" at Camden, South Carolina.

"My Lord," Cornwallis addressed George Germain, British secretary of state for American colonies, responsible for conducting the American war, "It is with great pleasure I communicate to your Lordship an account of a compleat victory obtained on the 16th instant by His Majesty's troops under my command over the rebel southern army commanded by General Gates."

Learning of the Continental army's approach on August 9, Cornwallis had raced to Camden from his headquarters in Charleston, arriving there early in the morning on August 14, assuming command of British forces from the capable but still only twenty-five-year-old Rawdon. Believing Gates possessed upward of six thousand men, Cornwallis briefly considered retreat, but confident in the experience of his own army, and reluctant to leave behind at Camden over eight hundred sick, or to propose a retreat that might demoralize Loyalist support in the region, he ordered his out-manned army forward toward Gates's position at ten o'clock on the night of August 15 "to attack at day break." Unlike his commanding officers, Henry Clinton and Sir William Howe before him, Cornwallis embraced combat opportunities, only rarely passing them by.

Unknown to Cornwallis, Gates had ordered his larger but starving and considerably less organized, less disciplined army forward toward Camden that very same night, although contrary to many accounts, Gates's plan was to set up a position north of Camden to lure the British into an attack, not attack the town itself.[1] This was similar to the strategy Nathanael Greene would employ at the Battle of Hobkirk's Hill, also on the northern outskirts of Camden, seven months later. Nevertheless, by coincidence and Gates's bad timing, the two armies literally collided in the dark, and after some ini-tial skirmishing, they separated by about six hundred yards, forming their lines for the coming battle at dawn.

In the early morning haze, "the enemy, having persisted in their resolu-tion to fight, were form'd in two lines opposite and near to us." Cornwallis ordered Lt. Colonel Webster on the right side of his line to commence the attack, "which was done with great vigour, and in a few minutes the action was general along the whole front. . . . Our line continued to advance in good order and with the cool intrepidity of experienced soldiers, keeping up a constant fire or making use of bayonets as opportunities offered, and, after an obstinate resistance for three quarters of an hour, threw the enemy into total confusion and forced them to give way in all quarters."

Cornwallis had good reason to be pleased. "The loss of the enemy was very considerable," Cornwallis wrote Germain, reporting "between eight hundred and nine hundred were killed."[2] Although the actual number of American deaths was probably much fewer—best estimates put the total at approximately two hundred killed and five hundred wounded—the American army was in such disarray, no accurate total was ever counted. Among the American dead was Continental major general Johann de Kalb, known popularly in American history as the "Baron de Kalb," though he was born to Bavarian peasants, his nobility a fiction of his own making. Nevertheless, he was a competent and professional officer, his loss the bitter cherry atop Gates's disastrous defeat. For his part, Cornwallis lost 68 killed and 256 wounded.[3]

Even worse than the horrific carnage was the American army's total humiliation. Trained as an officer in the British army, Horatio Gates was the great "Hero of Saratoga," his victories in that campaign during the fall of 1777 positioning him as the most successful of the American generals to that point in the war, an admittedly limited competition, and, briefly, a rival to George Washington for commander in chief. But these efforts to usurp Washington, in which Gates had played a mostly passive role, had backfired. By the summer of 1780, he was on leave at his home in Traveller's Rest, Virginia, when his supporters in Congress once more resurrected his career, awarding him command over the Southern Army after the fall of Charleston.

Gates's conduct during his Camden campaign has vexed historians, as it surely befuddled his soldiers. He arrived at Kalb's camp on Deep River, near present-day Asheboro, North Carolina, on July 25, 1781, finding his new army mostly comprised of Continental regulars from Maryland and Delaware, along with three small companies of artillery, about 1,200 regulars in all, though half-starved and desperate for provisions. With Kalb were only eight cannons, for he had been forced to leave ten cannons behind on his route south for want of horses.[4]

"General Gates was received with respectful ceremony," noted Colonel Otho Holland Williams, a Maryland officer whose memoir recounts the Camden campaign and who will play an important role in our later narrative. "As if actuated by a spirit of great activity and enterprise, [Gates] ordered the troops to hold themselves in readiness *to march at a moment's warning* (Williams's italics)." The order astonished all who knew "the real situation of the troops. But all difficulties were removed by the general's assurances, that plentiful supplies of *rum* and *rations* were on the route, and would overtake them in a day or two—assurances that certainly were too fallacious, and that never were verified."[5]

Looking at the map, Gates decided to march toward Camden along the most direct route, through the Carolinas' notorious "Pine Barrens," a desolate, unpopulated region of sand, pine, and swamp covering areas of both North and South Carolina. Colonel Williams, serving as deputy adjutant general (or administrative officer), was nominated by Kalb to convince their new commander of this route's folly. Williams attempted to sway Gates toward a more westerly route, through Salisbury and Charlotte, a region friendly to the Patriot cause where the Continental army was more likely to find supplies and reinforcement, but Gates would not be deterred.

And so the exhausted, half-starved army set out through the inhospitable Pine Barrens, Gates pushing them on marches of eighteen miles a day, with little sustenance except the occasional field of green corn they ravished with predictable gastrointestinal results. Prior to Gates's arrival, Kalb had been awaiting a junction with a considerable body of North Carolina militia under General Richard Caswell, but as they marched, Gates received news that Caswell was ahead, near Lynches Creek, and feared attack by the advance British encampment there.[6]

Gates united with Caswell on August 7, adding 2,100 North Carolina militia to his ranks. On the thirteenth, arriving at Rugeley's Mill, twelve miles north of Camden, he was joined by seven hundred Virginia militia under General Edward Stevens, who would later oversee Greene's survey of the Yadkin River. But that same day, Gates dispatched four hundred troops, including two cannons and a hundred of his crack Maryland Continentals, to the command of South Carolina militia general Thomas Sumter, who proposed ambushing a British wagon train approaching Camden from the south. The troops dispatched to Sumter, especially the Marylanders, would've been useful in the battle to come.[7]

Believing his army now boasted seven thousand, Gates called his officers together on the night of August 15, informing them of the night march toward Camden. Otho Holland Williams immediately called on the regimental officers for instant returns. When the count came in at just 3,052 present and fit for duty, out of 4,100 rank and file in all, Gates replied, "these are enough for our purpose."[8]

Gates ordered his men to begin their march toward Camden at ten o'clock that night. Williams and the other American officers could not imagine "how it could be conceived that an army consisting of more than two-thirds militia which had never been once exercised in arms together, could form columns and perform manoeuvres in the night and in the face of the enemy."[9]

The folly continued in the morning, as the two armies finally positioned for battle. As was custom in the British army at that time, Cornwallis aligned his troops "right-handed," placing his best units on the right side of his line. A former British officer, Gates was well aware of this custom but placed on his left, facing the British right, the volunteer militia of North Carolina and Virginia, under Caswell and Stevens respectively. As the battle started, Cornwallis instinctively recognized the weakness of the American left, ordering elements of his right forward in a bayonet charge. Against

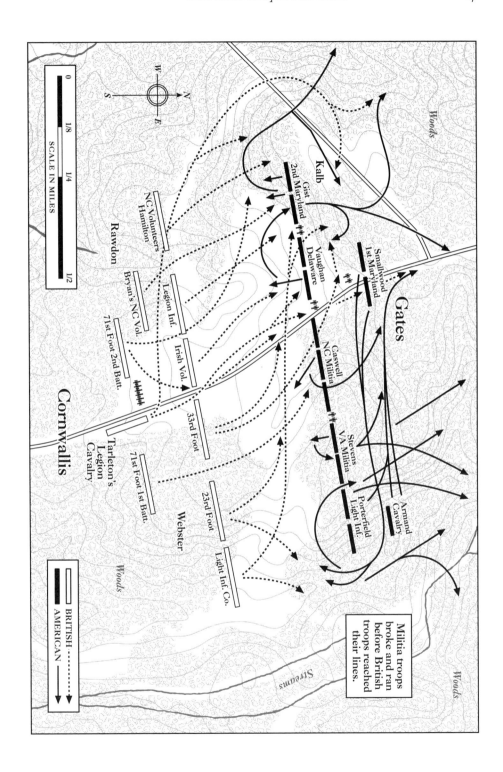

Militia troops broke and ran before British troops reached their lines.

the oncoming redcoats, the Patriot militia collapsed, retreating in waves of chaos and terror. Gates himself was "swept away" in the torrent, racing from the battlefield on his charger, the fastest horse in the army, until he arrived at Charlotte, sixty miles away. Unaware of the chaos to their left, and receiving no orders to retreat from their now-vanished general, the Maryland and Delaware Continentals on the American right continued to fight valiantly, until finally Kalb fell, said to be wounded eleven times, and his loyal Continentals retreated.[10]

In the aftermath of the battle, Gates's retreating supply train was captured by the Legion dragoons of Banastre Tarleton. Gates completed his humiliation by setting out for Hillsboro, North Carolina, the morning following the battle, arriving there on August 19. "General Gates perceived no effectual succour short of Hillsborough, where the general assembly were about to convene," notes Williams diplomatically. "Thither he repaired, with all possible expedition."[11] The approximately seven hundred Continental soldiers who found him there in the days and weeks to follow, mostly the Delaware and Maryland Continentals who would go on to form the backbone of Nathanael Greene's Southern Army, must have been exasperated to find the "Hero of Saratoga" waiting for them over two hundred miles away from the battlefield.

THE CONTINENTAL ARMY was decimated, their baggage and supplies captured, their general disgraced. The British army controlled Charleston, which had been surrendered to them in May 1780, and Savannah, the South's two most important ports. Their interior defenses stretched from Augusta, Georgia, across northern South Carolina to Georgetown on the coast. These defenses were anchored by strong positions at Camden and Ninety Six, an important trading post on the South Carolina frontier, located near present-day Greenwood, on what was then the main road to the Cherokee territories.

Camden was the jewel in the crown of British outposts, for it controlled the southern terminus of the Great Wagon Road, the main settler thoroughfare leading south from Pennsylvania. Control of the town, its roads, and its nearby crossing of the Wateree River effectively gave the British control of the central part of the state, as Gates had unhappily discovered. Though James Cook's 1773 "A map of the province of South Carolina" shows Camden as little more than a simple six by fifteen grid,[12] it was the closest thing to a "town" in the north central portion of the South Carolina colony. That it also touched the south-flowing Wateree River and was on one of the main trading routes to the port of Charleston made it an important crossroads in this increasingly populated region of the South Carolina backcountry.

Without orders for reassembling in the event of a defeat, the American forces scattered haphazardly across the countryside. "The North Carolina militia fled different ways," reported Williams, "as their hopes led, or their fears drove them. . . . Whatever these might have suffered from the disaffected, they probably were not worse off than those who returned the way they came, wherein they met many of their insidious friends, armed, and advancing to join the American Army." Learning of the disastrous defeat, these "friends" turned on their former allies, "capturing some, plundering others."[13] The capricious nature of backcountry allegiance, along with its sometimes-predatory disposition, could ravage Continental and redcoat alike.

Those that escaped the "insidious" barbarism of their alleged "friends" faced a miserable march north, first to Charlotte, which was deemed "defenceless," then to Salisbury. "A very lengthy line of march, occupied the road from Charlotte to Salisbury," reported Williams. "It consisted of the wretched remnants of the late southern army; a great number of distressed Whig families, and the whole tribe of Catawba Indians. . . . Those officers and men, who were recently wounded, and had resolution to undertake the fatigue were differently transported; some in waggons, some in litters, and some on horseback—their sufferings were indescribable. The distresses of the women and children, who fled from Charlotte and its neighbourhood. The nakedness of the Indians, and the number of their infants and aged persons, and the disorder of the whole line of march, conspired to render a scene too pictur[e]sque and complicated for description. A just representation would exhibit an image of compound wretchedness—care, anxiety, poverty, hurry, confusion, humiliation and dejection, would be characteristic traits in the mortifying picture."[14]

Such wretchedness confirms Camden's legacy. It has been described as "the most disastrous defeat ever inflicted on an American army,"[15] and the late nineteenth-century historian John Marshall wrote, "Never was a victory more complete, or a defeat more total."[16] Given such forthright assessments, Cornwallis had reason to gloat. To his subordinate, the Loyalist officer John Harris Cruger, now commanding the British outpost at Ninety

Six, Cornwallis reported of Camden, "in short, there never was a more complete victory."[17]

To be certain, the British still had "issues" in South Carolina. Thomas Sumter's raid on the British supply caravan, to which Gates had dispatched four hundred men and two cannons, was an initial success. Attacking on August 15, the day before the battle, Sumter took 40 British wagons, along with 150 prisoners.[18] That same day, a combined force of South Carolina, Georgia, and North Carolina militia attacked the Loyalist outpost of Musgrove's Mill, near present-day Laurens, South Carolina, in the western portion of the state, killing or wounding about 150 and taking 70 prisoners.[19] And on August 20, Colonel Francis Marion, in an effort that would add to his legendary status as "The Swamp Fox," rescued 160 Americans captured at Camden from their British and Tory guards. But after Sumter, Cornwallis dispatched Banastre Tarleton and his feared Legion. Tarleton surprised the Gamecock at his undefended camp on Fishing Creek on August 18, freeing Sumter's prisoners and retaking all of the British supply wagons. And hearing of Gates's utter defeat at Camden, the Patriots at Musgrove's Mill scattered to their respective homes, evacuating the region around Ninety Six.

CORNWALLIS HAD INDEED conquered the South, or at least the portion of it protected by his defensive line stretching from Augusta in the west to Georgetown on the coast. Florida had become a British colony in 1763, as part of the Treaty of Paris between England, France, and Spain that ended the "Seven Years War," also popularly known as "The French and Indian War." And thanks to the capture of Savannah in 1778, and establishment of the British outpost in Augusta, Georgia also was now under British control, despite pockets of Patriot resistance.

Perhaps it is the folly of the armchair strategist to consider "what ifs," but one need only look at the map of the South dated August 17, 1780, to imagine a radically different version of our nation's geography. The Treaty of Paris ceded all North American territory east of the Mississippi to England. What if instead of pushing their southern invasion north, the British army had focused instead on entrenching their southern defenses and eradicating Patriot resistance within this border? England now had dominion over a vast coastline extending from Charleston to Pensacola in an era when shipping and ports conveyed geopolitical control. Over time that control would have extended to the interiors of Alabama and Mississippi, creating a southern province comprised of what is now the American Deep South. With the Continental army in disarray, Cornwallis could have concentrated on solidifying his southern fortifications and supply lines, wiping out the insurgencies of Thomas Sumter, Francis Marion, and the Georgia partisan Elijah Clarke, then turning to face a resurgent yet still insufficient Continental army under Nathanael Greene from his superior defenses. After six long years of war, public sentiment in the American states was turning against more conflict. It's not hard to imagine that within the next year, maybe two, the British could have negotiated a peace that allowed them to retain this vast and resource-rich southern province.

Henry Clinton, for one, believed the outcome of the war hinged on this moment in time. "The victory of Camden and the entire dispersion of Sumter's corps two days after . . . had certainly greatly humbled the disaffected in South Carolina, and seemed to promise a restoration of tranquility to every part of that province," he posited in his post-war memoir. "And, indeed, there is every reason to believe this might have been the case could Lord Cornwallis have attended somewhat longer to that alone, and no unlucky check had intervened on our side to revive the spirits of the revolters and put them again in motion. But His Lordship was, of course, desirious of extending the consequences of his success as far as and as expeditiously as possible."[20]

This point—that Cornwallis should have stayed in South Carolina—would become the focal point of a long and bitter feud between Cornwallis and Clinton that ended only with Clinton's death in 1795. Clinton's case rested in part on his standing orders to Cornwallis upon his return to New York after the fall of Charleston. "For this end I requested his Lordship would constantly regard *the safety of Charleston and tranquility of South Carolina as the principal and indispensable objects of his attention.*"[21] According to Clinton, this directive absolved him of the calamities that would soon afflict Cornwallis's southern campaign.

At some level, however, Clinton probably realized his argument was insincere at best, disingenuous at worst, even if it gave him some political cover. What both Clinton and Cornwallis undoubtedly understood was that King George III and the British ministry had no interest in protracting the already interminable American war. The "Southern Strategy" was not an attempt at regional conquest but an effort to ignite Loyalist support in the South. With this groundswell of militia support, England could sweep north, recapturing the prize of Virginia, the region's most prosperous and strategically important colony, finally bringing George Washington to the decisive action that would decide the war.[22]

And if the "Southern Strategy" was one Clinton always sipped skeptically, Cornwallis drank deeply from its well. For one, his allegiances lay with Germain, not Clinton, and so his own career was vested in supporting Germain's strategies. For another, it suited his temperament. Cornwallis was a warrior, no political administrator of a captured province, at least not at this point in his career. He had long chafed under Clinton's cautiousness, and now that he was in command of his own theater, he yearned for the offensive.

Yet Cornwallis was also a man of curious contradictions, which could occasionally undermine his martial tendencies. An innate humanity conflicted with his aristocratic character and indoctrination in British army bureaucracy, leading to weaknesses Greene and his officers would exploit. This curious aristocrat was born on December 31, 1738, the eldest son of Charles, the first Earl Cornwallis. And though the family traced its aristocratic heritage back to the reign of Edward III in the 1300s, it never possessed a material wealth to accompany its noble lineage. Nevertheless, Cornwallis's birthright made him a peer of the realm—a select group of English nobles numbering just over two hundred—and guaranteed him a seat in Parliament.[23]

As a child, he received a typical aristocratic education, learning to ride and shoot at Culford, the family estate, and enrolling at Eton, a fashionable training ground for soldiers, statesmen, and men of letters. There, the curriculum was based on Latin, which "served as a way of maintaining class distinctions." Indeed, "the entire structure and policy of the school reminded the boys every day of social divisions," write Cornwallis's biographers.[24]

It was as a soldier that Cornwallis was called, excelling at sports and earning a description from his father as a "very military" young man. At Eton, Cornwallis suffered a hockey injury that disfigured his eye, forming a quizzical expression he bore throughout his life. His time at Eton was formative but brief, and by the age of eighteen, his family had purchased for him a commission in the 1st, or Grenadier, Guards. The acquisition of military commissions was a typical career path for young aristocrats and a convenient means of keeping the officer corps' aristocratic bent, since commoners could rarely afford the price. Untypical was a short attendance in

1757 at the military academy in Turin, considered one of the finest in Europe. There Cornwallis studied not only military tactics and strategy but also ballroom dancing, mathematics, and etiquette, attending the King of Sardinia's court.[25]

In 1758, his regiment was ordered to service in the Seven Years' War, but he was in Geneva, Switzerland, at the time and unable to join it. Instead he joined the staff of the Marquis of Granby, who would eventually become commanding general of the British forces in the European theater during the Seven Years' War. Overall, Cornwallis served three years on Granby's staff, rising through the ranks but missing the combat experience so crucial for a young officer. This changed after he was promoted to lieutenant colonel in May 1761; in the following year, he fought with distinction as a regimental combat commander, especially at Kirch Donkern and Grenestein. But in the summer of 1762 his father died and he returned to England to assume the title of Earl Cornwallis at the age of just twenty-three. That November he took his father's seat in the House of Lords.[26]

For the next decade, Cornwallis attended mostly to his estate, his family, and his increasingly important political roles. Although possessed of a "wry sense of humor and a great humanity," he never engaged in the "excessive drinking, reckless gambling, and continual round of parties which consumed so many of his compeers." His marriage in 1768 to the lovely and delicate Jemima Tullekin Jones was for love, not money, for her family was neither noble nor wealthy. Bearing two children, a son and a daughter, their union was a happy one and only confirmed him to his moderate habits.

These domestic virtues are probably what attracted him to King George III, whose affections for Cornwallis led to an increasingly impressive list of political appointments: from aide-de-camp to the king, to vice treasurer of Ireland, to privy councilor, to constable of the Tower of London. Both Charles and George III were "sober, dignified, temperate, and devoted family men," a rare breed in the royal court. Yet they were not always aligned politically. In 1765, Cornwallis voted to repeal the Stamp Act in opposition to the king. Charles was no firebrand; his politics were generally moderate, though as tensions with the American colonies increased, he was usually aligned with their grievances against George III's position.

Still, he was adroit enough to keep the king's favor, influencing both his military and political careers. In 1766, while serving as the king's aide-de-camp, he purchased the colonelcy of the 33rd Foot. In September 1775, he was promoted to major general and, on January 1, 1776, named lieutenant

general of the army in North America, traveling there with the 33rd Foot
to begin his service in the conflict.[27]

Contrary to popular myth, Cornwallis was never in overall command of
the British army during the American Revolution. First, he served under
General William Howe until Howe's resignation in 1778, then under Clinton until his surrender at Yorktown in 1781. Cornwallis was no innocent
in the origins of his troubled relationship with Clinton: shortly after the
Battle of White Plains in October 1776, Clinton had made a disparaging
remark about Howe in Cornwallis's presence. Cornwallis later repeated the
comment to Howe, who subsequently threw it in Clinton's face. Known
for a peevish, temperamental personality one biographer called "tortuous,"
Clinton neither forgave nor forgot Cornwallis's indiscretion. Indeed, the
incident reflects poorly on Cornwallis: "It was not treachery on Cornwallis's
part, but it was a dishonorable act by a normally honorable man," surmises
the historian John Buchanan.[28]

Of Cornwallis's occasional lapses in discretion and judgment we shall
soon read more, but he was certainly England's ablest combat commander
during the American Revolution, fighting bravely at the battles of Long
Island, Brandywine, and especially Monmouth, where he personally directed a fierce attack against Nathanael Greene's position on the American
right flank. Indeed, Cornwallis and Greene faced one another numerous
times on the battlefield in the year's leading up to the southern campaigns.
Only one campaign mars his otherwise stellar combat efforts during the
early years of the war: at Trenton, in January 1777, Cornwallis had Washington's army trapped against the Delaware River and its right flank exposed. However, instead of destroying Washington, he bivouacked his men
in the hills north of the village, waiting for more favorable conditions to
attack. The delay allowed Washington to escape Trenton and initiate a successful surprise attack on the British position at Princeton, boosting Patriot
morale throughout the otherwise gloomy winter.[29]

In many ways Cornwallis epitomized the eighteenth-century ideal of
the *homme de guerre*, or man of war, which the French lieutenant general
Comte de Tressan described as the soldier who would "distinguish between
the necessary evil and the unnecessary and . . . that pity should always have
easy access to his heart, and that nothing should ever banish from it justice,
disinterestedness, and the love of humanity." It is to this sense of humanity
his biographers prescribe his devotion to his troops. "The Earl's sense of
discipline, justice, and compassion made him, more than Howe or Clinton,

a part of the British army in America. He did not consider himself above it. If it prospered, he prospered, if it failed, he failed. He could never maintain that detachment from it that many of his fellows could." Not surprisingly, given the era, the noble spirit required of the *homme de guerre* was only thought possible in an aristocrat—the natural leader in times of war. To this aristocratic ethos of honor Cornwallis certainly prescribed, for it suited not only his leadership style but also cemented his privileged status in British society.[30]

But in an era of rapidly shifting military tactics and technology, this aristocratic outlook could also be a weakness. The British military was run by a massive, complex bureaucracy, which facilitated its global outreach through superior logistical and financial support but also bred conservatism, complacency, and political scapegoating. The patronage system of buying and selling officer commissions discouraged original and independent thought. "Army administration in England was a maze of conflicting jurisdiction, ambiguous offices and duties, and confused chain of command," write Franklin and Mary Wickwire, Cornwallis's most prominent biographers.[31] The British officer who dared to confront this bureaucracy not only threatened his military career but also his societal privilege. And talented soldiers who didn't have the means to buy an officer commission were simply out of luck.[32]

And so, Cornwallis was a paradox, representing both a new breed of military humanism and the very essence of British army conservatism. Though the southern theater was vastly different from the battlefields of Europe on which he'd been trained, Cornwallis remained devoted to conventional military tactics and strategy. "He was not strikingly original," his biographers admit,[33] though they credit him for progressive administrative reforms. And in critical ways, the innate humanity that endeared him to his troops was a weakness in the brutal American South, where nontraditional, partisan tactics characterized what was, in essence, a civil war.

It is possible that by the time Cornwallis conquered the South, his heart was no longer devoted to the British cause there, for he now felt betrayed both by army bureaucracy and fate. During the winter of 1777-78, while Cornwallis was visiting England on leave, Howe's resignation was accepted by the British ministry. Clinton was named the new commander in chief and Cornwallis his second-in-command, but the peevish Clinton suspected some conspiracy in the promotions, believing Cornwallis had tried to take advantage of his time in England to lobby for his own independent command. And with France entering the war that same winter, both men were unhappy with a change in British strategy, reassigning a portion of the British army to Florida and the West Indies to guard England's profitable sugar trade.

But with England's American occupation force diminished, offensive operations there were substantially reduced, if not eliminated, and Cornwallis offered his resignation to the British cabinet, complaining that he did not choose to operate in a theater where "no offensive operations can be undertaken."[34] The resignation was refused, and the following winter Cornwallis went to England again, this time on a mission from Clinton to use his rank and social influence to lobby the ministry for more troops.

But upon his arrival in London in December 1778, Cornwallis discovered his beloved Jemima had fallen seriously sick, her illness probably hepatitis. Though he made some efforts to lobby for more troops, his only discussion with Germain or King George was to once more resign his commission, a lapse Clinton would regard as yet another betrayal. This time, with Cornwallis obviously distressed over his wife's deteriorating condition, the resignation was accepted. Cornwallis hurried to his country home and remained by Jemima's side, devoted but increasingly distraught, until she died on February 16, 1779.

Cornwallis was devastated. "Everything he loved became repugnant to him. His young family, his beautiful country, his ancestral home—all served to remind him of his wife."[35] In the depths of his despair, he decided to recommit himself to service in America. To Clinton he wrote a long letter, disavowing any interest in supreme command. The king was happy to have back his favorite general, and at first, Clinton also seemed to welcome his talented subordinate, though the relationship dissolved almost as quickly as it had been resurrected. When Cornwallis returned to New York in July 1779 without the reinforcements Clinton had requested, Clinton considered it an affront and immediately submitted his own resignation. During the fall, while they awaited the ministry's response, the two generals coincided in a kind of limbo, the indecision providing ample opportunity for them to brood over one another's perceived slights. By the end of 1779, their troubled relationship was the subject of gossip and innuendo throughout New York, tongues wagging that Cornwallis had "no sincere regard for his chief."[36]

Under these circumstances, the southern campaign offered a reprieve for Cornwallis, Clinton, and the British war administration. For the British cabinet, it offered the opportunity to renew efforts to subdue the American Revolution in what they hoped would be a more favorable theater while enhancing protection of their strategic assets in the West Indies. Political pressure on Lord North and his cabinet was mounting. "Success in America became increasingly important not only as an end in itself but because failure might bring about the fall of the ministry," writes the historian John Pancake.[37] An expedition against Savannah in the winter of 1778-79 had been successful, a British assault capturing the town on December 29, 1778, and now the British controlled Florida and most of Georgia. Exiled Loyalists and their supporters in London assured the North cabinet an expedition to South Carolina would receive a similarly successful welcome.

Clinton had his doubts about such assurances, but at least a return to Charleston allowed him the opportunity to avenge one of his most humiliating defeats during the war—his unsuccessful attempt to seize the town with a combined naval and ground attack in June 1776. And though his memoir and correspondence suggest he never believed the "Southern Strategy" viable without the substantial infusion of troops he felt necessary, at least it gave him the opportunity to prove his point while still acquiescing to the demands of his political masters.

And for Cornwallis, the southern expedition gave him the opportunity to separate himself from Clinton. For although Clinton accompanied Cornwallis south and directed the land-based assault on Charleston himself, he had returned by sea to the more comfortable confines of New York City almost as soon as the city was defeated, departing Charleston harbor on June 5, leaving Cornwallis in command of the southern theater.

Cornwallis finally had the independence he craved. And his spectacular victory at Camden validated his reputation as the American campaign's ablest British officer. Cornwallis had conquered the South and decimated the American's Southern Army. What was left was only a sweep north into North Carolina and Virginia, where he would deliver to the American cause England's *coup de grace*.

CHAPTER 3

THAT RASCAL RUGELEY

———

Henry Rugeley was the type of man common in a political season. Ambitious, opportunistic, financially overextended, he was eager to avail himself to the new British administration in South Carolina. Today, thousands of such men and women descend on Washington, DC, in the transition between presidential administrations, seeking position and favors; Charleston in the summer of 1781 was much the same.

Following Charleston's capture, the British army needed merchants with business contacts in the South Carolina interior. Rugeley fit the bill—through the operation of the Charleston store he owned with his brother, Rowland, he had a commercial network that extended to the district around Camden. The brothers had invested some of their profits in real estate, and on one of these tracts north of Camden, Henry Rugeley built a small industrial village featuring a sawmill, gristmill, two bolting mills, a waterwheel, a tanyard, a store, and several slave dwellings, along with an "elegant" dwelling he named "Clermont."

Like many in the colonial era, the Rugeleys financed this empire mostly through debt, and when Rowland died in 1777, Henry became besieged by their creditors. Though he was apparently American born, and nothing in his background indicated a proclivity toward the Loyalist cause, Rugeley was happy to accept British patronage, perhaps seeing in it the opportunity to restore his stature, if not his fortune.[1]

Indeed, the very foundation of the British "Southern Strategy" was built on the assumption that the Rugeleys of the American South were only awaiting the opportunity to declare their devotion to the Crown. An attempt at a negotiated peace with the colonies in 1778, known as the Carlisle Commission, had failed when it became clear the Americans would settle for nothing less than full independence, and that was the price the king and his ministers would not pay.[2] Yet the cost of the American war continued to mushroom. Even while Henry Clinton clamored for more troops, recruitments in England were down, and already a considerable expense had been incurred on the twenty-five thousand German mercenaries sent to the colonies. Meanwhile, English sea power was diminished by her staggering debt, and its once-dominant navy now competed with France and Spain for control of the seas.

Now there was yet another war with France, and British interests stretched from India to Gibraltar to Ireland to Canada to defend, with the lucrative colonies in the West Indies deemed particularly vulnerable to any capitulation in America. West Indies' imports to England at this time are estimated at £4.5 million annually, more than double the value of mainland American imports.[3] England relied on this revenue to finance her mounting obligations, both at home and abroad; it could not be sacrificed to America's insolence.

Thanks to these pressures, though based on scant evidence, the ministry accepted reports there was a vast well of Loyalist sentiment in the southern colonies that would ignite if Great Britain would only send it her armies. North and Germain found themselves between a rock and a hard place: with Britain's resources diminished by interminable war, they were caught between their anti-war critics in Parliament and an intransigent king, the only way out total victory.[4] "In the final analysis, the scales were weighted by political pressure," in accepting the supposition that a strong Loyalist contingency only awaited British support in the South.[5] It was a fiction the British ministry needed to believe. And there was no shortage of supplicants whispering such fantasies in its ear. Joseph Galloway was a former member of the Continental Congress who had served as the principal Loyalist civil administrator in Philadelphia until its evacuation by the British in 1778. Galloway then traveled to England, becoming a fierce proponent for a more vigorous prosecution of the war, publishing several pamphlets insisting it could be won if England only supported her staunch American Loyalists. Upon their return from America, members of the Carlisle Com-

mission also spoke favorably of the dormant Loyalist opposition only awaiting more vigorous support. Meanwhile, a host of Loyalists wrote from the
colonies, including governors-in-exile William Campbell of South Carolina
and James Wright of Georgia, urging that if a southern expedition was undertaken, "the whole inhabitants of both Provinces would soon come in
and submit."[6]

This made the eager and connected Henry Rugeley precisely the kind
of man the British hoped to find in South Carolina, or he seemed to be.
And in addition to giving him commercial contracts, the British made him
officer of a Loyalist militia unit centered around Camden, despite lacking
any evidence of military prowess, first commissioning him major and then
colonel.[7] One can imagine "Colonel Rugeley" found his status and economic prospects much improved under British rule.

But British faith in their newly acquired "Mr. Rugeley" soured almost
as soon as it had been established. On July 27, 1780, just two months into
the British occupation of South Carolina, Rawdon delivered to Cornwallis
some disturbing intelligence.

A "rebel officer," traveling under a flag of truce, had stopped at Rugeley's
plantation shortly after delivering a message to Rawdon at Camden. "Having enquired for Rugeley, who was not at home, he very privately slipped a
note into the hand" of a woman he presumed to be Rugeley's wife, but she
was in fact a visitor named Sarah Harper, the wife of a prominent local
Loyalist. Realizing the woman was not Rugeley's wife, the rebel officer
quickly snatched the paper from Harper's hand, but not before she read
enough to report the letter was an "application" to Rugeley from John Rutledge, South Carolina's exiled Patriot governor, who had fled the colony
just before Charleston was captured.[8]

Was Rugeley to be trusted? Could the British trust anyone in the Carolina frontier? For assertions of the exiled governors and their London ad-
vocates about vast silent majorities of Loyalist inhabitants aside, the
countryside was soon awash in revolt and insurrection. On June 20, Loyalists and Patriots squared off in a bloody melee at Ramsour's Mill in North
Carolina, leaving almost three hundred killed and wounded from both
sides. On July 12, Loyalists and Patriots skirmished at Williamson's Plantation, Cedar Springs, and Stallion's Plantation in the South Carolina backcountry, and almost every subsequent day of that bloody July saw intense
fighting, some of it documented by history, much of it not, an insurrection
that culminated on August 1 when South Carolina militia general Thomas

Sumter, the famed South Carolina "Gamecock," killed or wounded 192 Loyalists in an attack on the British outpost at Hanging Rock north of Camden.[9]

True, there were devoted Loyalists in the region, men like Thomas Fletchall, a wealthy landowner, coroner, and magistrate who lived near the Fairforest settlement in modern-day Union County, South Carolina, and commanded a Tory militia unit of approximately two thousand men during the war. And also Robert Cunningham, from the nearby Little River District in modern-day Laurens County, South Carolina, who would go on to serve as a Loyalist brigadier general.[10] But these men were known to be staunch Loyalists since the earliest days of the war, and with reports like the one Rawdon sent about Rugeley filtering back to Cornwallis in Charleston, and the colony erupting in violence, the British general soon began to wonder if this new breed of Loyalist could truly be dependable, or if it existed at all.

As early as the end of June, just one month into his command of the South, with Clinton now returned to New York, Cornwallis believed an invasion into North Carolina would not only advance the Southern Strategy but also quell the growing resistance within South Carolina. "With the force at present under my command . . . I can leave South Carolina in security, and march about the beginning of September with a body of troops into the back part of North Carolina, with the greatest probability of reducing that province to its duty," he wrote to Clinton on June 30, 1780. "I am of opinion that . . . it would prove an effectual barrier for South Carolina and Georgia, and could be kept, with the assistance of our friends there."[11]

By August 6, Cornwallis was feeling less certain about the security of South Carolina but still committed to his plans for a northward invasion. "It may be doubted by some whether the invasion of North Carolina may be a prudent measure, but I am convinced it is a necessary one that, if we do not attack that province, we must give up South Carolina and Georgia and retire within the walls of Charleston," he wrote to Clinton.[12]

And despite Clinton's post-war assertions that "the safety of Charleston and tranquility of South Carolina" should be "the principal and indispensable objects" of Cornwallis's attention, his orders to Cornwallis were schizophrenic at best, at least half of them pertaining to plans for operations in the Chesapeake Bay area.[13] And Cornwallis had kept Clinton well apprised of his plans for the North Carolina invasion throughout the course of the summer.

Our armchair strategist might then wonder why Cornwallis didn't take advantage of the momentum he'd gained at Camden, sweeping into North Carolina after his decisive victory there, obliterating the remnants of the Continental army and, with it, remaining Patriot sentiment in the American South. If his original plan was to begin his North Carolina offensive in September, he would never have better momentum than after destroying Gates on August 16. Cornwallis's talented subordinate, Banastre Tarleton, who would also go on to become a Cornwallis critic after the war, would agree with this theory. "The immediate advance of the King's troops into North Carolina would undoubtedly, at this critical period, have been productive of various and important advantages," he wrote in his memoir.[14]

Yet Cornwallis's instincts told him he didn't yet have the manpower to press forward into North Carolina. Following the invasion of Charleston, British rank and file in South Carolina consisted of approximately 8,300 men—six British, one Hessian, and six Loyalist regiments.[15] Added to that were thousands more in Loyalist volunteer militia. But much of that army was required to defend Charleston and the other British outposts. Of the 2,100 soldiers he fought with at Camden, Cornwallis lost 324 killed or wounded, a casualty rate of approximately 15 percent. And that didn't include the eight hundred sick at Camden he reported to Germain.[16]

The innate conservatism of British military doctrine was kicking in, warning him that overwhelming force was more important than strategic momentum, and here it served him poorly. As August bled into September, his letters to Clinton contain both lengthy laments about the sickly condition of his own army and continual requests for his superior to commence a planned expedition to the Chesapeake, believing such an expedition paramount to the success of his own push north. Also, there was "the absolute necessity of adding some force to the Carolinas" to support his invasion plans.[17]

The truth was the British army simply wasn't built for swift and unplanned pursuit, as we shall soon see. True, Tarleton's British Legion was a ruthless, mobile, and efficient light brigade, led by a talented officer, but Cornwallis had few other light units at his disposal. The rest of his army moved cumbersomely, dependent on wagons, baggage, and camp followers. His correspondence suggests he recognized the opportunity lost in not immediately pursuing Gates into North Carolina but argued vehemently there was little else he could do given the strategic conditions and the state of his army.

Nor did he display much interest in brutally suppressing the burgeoning Patriot resistance growing within South Carolina. "Cornwallis possessed a soldier's conception of honor and straight dealing," his biographers assert. "He never quite understood that to quell revolutionaries—men fired with dedication to an ideal above themselves—he had to be as ruthless as they: that he had to use terror, oppression, confiscation, and brutality on a grand scale."[18] Though he made harsh proclamations in the aftermath of Camden, ordering the property of Patriot sympathizers, "either in the service, or acting under the authority of the rebel congress . . . wicked and dangerous traitors," to be sequestered, and anyone attempting to hinder such sequestration arrested, in reality he did little to enforce these threats.[19]

In his humanistic outlook, his disposition against ruthless suppression, Cornwallis may have represented the values of the *homme de guerre*, but it was a value system in flux. Younger officers like Tarleton and Rawdon recognized the brutality necessary to suppress the American rebellion and became frustrated with Cornwallis for his refusal to enact it. Earlier in the war, Rawdon had proposed that the British army "should (when we get further into the country) give free liberty to the soldiers to ravage at will, that these infatuated wretches should feel what a calamity war is." And in his post-war memoir, Tarleton criticized Cornwallis for his "lenity and generosity," which "did not experience in America the merited returns of gratitude and affection." These opinions "reflect a deep tension in the British army over the conduct of the war, with many officers endorsing a hard-line war and expressing frustration over the restraints imposed on them," writes historian Armstrong Starkey.[20]

Which isn't to say he completely ignored the rebellion. In early September, he ordered Major James Wemyss east into the Pee Dee River region with a detachment of approximately three hundred mounted soldiers to quell resistance there. Wemyss succeeded in burning fifty Rebel homes and plantations but had little luck forming a Loyalist militia. Meanwhile, Cornwallis authorized Major Patrick Ferguson and his Loyalist militia of approximately 650 to advance into North Carolina's Tryon County (present-day Rutherford, Burke, and McDowell Counties) to secure the left flank of his planned invasion.[21]

But mostly he spent late August and early September securing his supply lines and provisioning his army for the fall push into North Carolina. And while Cornwallis gathered his supplies, the Patriots regrouped. Patrick Ferguson's incursion into the North Carolina mountains, coupled with his audacious proclamation that if the rebels "did not desist from their opposition to the British Arms" he would "hang their leaders and lay their country waste with fire and sword,"[22] angered the men of the Watauga settlements in what is now western North Carolina, southwestern Virginia, and eastern Tennessee. After Camden, the young and talented North Carolina militia officer Colonel William R. Davie, who would go on to reluctantly serve as Greene's adjutant general, regrouped his militia brigade of dragoons and light infantry in the Charlotte vicinity. And in late September, a veteran officer arrived in the Hillsboro camp of Gates's decimated Continental army to take command of its light troops. That officer was Daniel Morgan.

Morgan had a reputation as a talented officer, known for maintaining the delicate balance between discipline and bonhomie with his troops. Born in 1735 or 1736 in either New Jersey or Pennsylvania—we don't know—to Welsh immigrants, Morgan left home at the age of seventeen, exploring Virginia, working as a miller and teamster, and learning the manners and customs of the frontier. He was imposing in physical appearance, well over six feet, stout and muscular but athletic. Though his temper could flare, Morgan's benevolence and good humor, along with a keen instinct for human nature, drew men to him. By the time of the French and Indian War, he had established his own teamster business and, in 1755, joined British general Edward Braddock's expedition against the French as a "waggoner," traveling with Braddock to fight in what is now the vicinity of Pittsburgh, Pennsylvania. It was during this service that he struck an English officer and received a punishment of five hundred lashes. Later in life he would joke the English drummer miscounted, and he owed the British one "stripe." By 1762 the six-foot, two-hundred-pound Morgan had left British service and settled near Winchester, Virginia, prospering as a farmer.

In 1775 he was commissioned captain of a Virginia rifle company and assimilated into the Continental army during the siege of Boston. As Christopher Ward noted, "his courage, daring, and resourcefulness in military affairs, added to his other characteristics, made him a great leader of men in the war upon which he was now entering."[23] When Benedict Arnold was wounded during the assault on Quebec, December 31, 1775, Morgan took command but was taken prisoner during the battle and not exchanged until the fall of 1776. Later that same fall he was commissioned a colonel and spent the winter recruiting a new regiment in Virginia, before joining Washington in New Jersey in April 1777. During that spring Daniel Morgan, and other Continental officers like him, mastered the tenets of partisan war.

If the 1700s was an age of Enlightenment—characterized by intellectual criticism of established religious, political, and philosophical dogma—the study of warfare was not immune to these intellectual explorations. Already we have read of the Comte de Tressan's concept of *homme de guerre,* and to this conception we can add new theories toward partisan tactics, or *petite guerre,* literally "little war." Espoused by military thinkers such as the Polish officer Herman Maurice de Saxe (also known as the "Comte de Saxe") and Hungarian Louis Michele de Jeney (his French nom de plume),[24] partisan warfare theories focused on "light," or mobile, units acting semi-independently on the outskirts of conventional warfare in patrols, raids, outposts, and disrupting enemy communications. "These were instinctive tactics of ambush and surprise, based on local knowledge and aimed at the opponent's weakest point," writes historian Albert Louis Zambone.[25]

Petite guerre's theorists recognized, however, that its success relied on officers whose "bravery, professionalism, and humanity would inspire obedience . . . Partisan warfare required a level of independence and self-reliance not seen in line battalions. Issues of recruitment, leadership, and training of these men coincided with a belief that soldiers should be looked upon as human beings rather than mindless instruments of war."[26]

Their forces weakened in spring 1777 by the disastrous defeat at Brooklyn and New York the previous fall, forage and provisions scant, and the British position too entrenched for conventional tactics, Continental officers such as George Washington and Nathanael Greene employed the tactics of *petite guerre* not as a philosophical exercise but out of tactical necessity, deploying bands of partisan units in a wide arc around the British positions on the Raritan River. Indeed, historians consider New Jersey *petite guerre*'s test kitchen, at least as far as the Continental army is concerned, "the only officer training school the Continental army could afford."[27]

And though the Continental army lacked manpower and resources, it was blessed with talented officers like Daniel Morgan, formed by native experience and blessed with natural charisma, a far cry from England's system of acquired officer commissions available mostly to the aristocracy. Deployed to the area around Morristown, New Jersey, in April 1777 with his newly recruited Virginia troops, Morgan learned partisan war on the job, conducting skirmish, ambush, and psychological manipulation, charming the local population if possible but threatening them when not, all the while instructing his young officers in these same skills.[28]

Important for the Continental army's partisan warfare tactics was the rifle. The British army relied on the smoothbore musket. Though not tremendously accurate, the musket could be mass produced and loaded quickly using a standard caliber ammunition. Most importantly, it was an effective conveyance for the bayonet, the British army's weapon of choice. Standard British battlefield tactics called for waves of musket fire to clear advance pickets and create psychological panic before the bayonet charge descended on a terrified opponent. Many American officers preferred the musket for the same reasons. Most custom-made rifle barrels could not accommodate a bayonet, and rifles took longer to load, jeopardizing the soldiers who fired them.

But the more accurate and deadly rifle, with its grooved barrel, was the preferred weapon of the American frontier, both as an armament and hunting instrument. Given the Continental army's perpetually depleted state, and its reliance on volunteer militia support, it's not surprising many of its soldiers used rifles, which they brought with them to war. And in partisan warfare, the accuracy and range of the rifle provided tactical advantages. Recognizing these advantages, and seeking to exploit them more fully, Washington formed a new unit titled the "Provisional Rifle Corps" in June 1777, detaching to it the most talented riflemen from Pennsylvania, Virginia, Maryland, and New Jersey regiments. And in command of this new unit, while retaining command of his own Virginia regiment, Washington placed Daniel Morgan.

The Provisional Rifle Corps first saw major action in the Saratoga campaign of Fall 1777, where Washington had detached Morgan to support the Northern Army of Horatio Gates. There Morgan used his new corps masterfully, both in partisan skirmishing and battlefield combat. At the Battle of Bemis Heights on October 7, the bayonet charges of the Continental infantry formed a protective screen for Morgan's riflemen, allowing them to pour deadly fire from their slow-loading rifles into the British right flank. According to tradition, an accurate shot by a Morgan rifleman named Tim Murphy killed British general Simon Fraser, effectively ending British resistance in the battle.[29]

Though Horatio Gates emerged as the "Hero of Saratoga," the first great American victory of the war, many attribute the triumph to his talented officers, including Benedict Arnold and Daniel Morgan. After

Saratoga, Morgan refused to join Gates's intrigues against Washington and returned to the main body of the Continental army, campaigning in New Jersey under the command of Nathanael Greene in November and December 1777 before wintering at Valley Forge. In 1779 he resigned from the army in a dispute over a promotion, though he claimed bad health, and returned to his farm near Winchester, but in June 1780, Congress ordered him to report to Gates once more in the South. A promotion did not accompany the orders, and Morgan delayed, but he relented after the disaster at Camden, taking command of Gates's light troops on October 2, just a few days after arriving in the southern camp. On October 13, Congress granted him the commission of brigadier general he had long sought.[30]

BY EARLY SEPTEMBER, Cornwallis had assembled his baggage train and finally was prepared for his North Carolina invasion. On the morning of September 8, he departed Camden in two divisions. The principal one under his command consisted of four British infantry regiments, the Volunteers of Ireland (a Loyalist regiment recruited and trained in the Northeast), four cannon, a detachment of horse, and a regiment of North Carolina Loyalists under Colonel Morgan Bryan. This force marched up the east side of the Wateree River toward the Waxhaws settlement south of Charlotte. A division of the British Legion cavalry and infantry, along with an additional detachment of light infantry and a small fieldpiece, marched up the west side of the Wateree under Banastre Tarleton.

But almost as soon as he got started, Cornwallis faltered again, now delayed by illness. Tarleton was stricken with malaria, as was much of the British army. Cornwallis stopped at the Waxhaws, the settlement on the North Carolina border where just four months earlier Tarleton had slaughtered Colonel Abraham Buford's Virginia Continentals. Buford was overtaken by Tarleton as he retreated from Charleston on May 29, 1781. After a brisk battle, the Continentals attempted to surrender, but Tarleton's soldiers refused their requests for "quarters." According to American accounts, British soldiers plunged bayonets into any Patriot showing signs of life. "Tarleton's Quarters" soon became a rallying cry for the American resistance, while Banastre Tarleton gained a reputation for infamy that would precede him through the centuries.[31] Thanks to this notoriety, the reception received by the British army at the Waxhaws the following September was hardly a warm one.

Meanwhile, during the course of the summer, the British had put their concerns over Henry Rugeley's loyalties aside, promoting him to colonel of the Camden militia. In a letter to Clinton dated August 6, Cornwallis described Rugeley as a "very active and spirited man,"[32] and sometime during the summer, perhaps in the lead-up to the Battle of Camden, Rugeley had converted a log barn on his Camden property into a blockhouse, fortifying it with an entrenchment and line of abatis (branches or cut tree trunks, ends sharpened and laid in a row, pointing outward) rendering it "impregnable to small arms."[33] British correspondence suggests Rugeley's militia performed admirably in supporting Cornwallis's advance toward Charlotte, attending to forage, prisoners, and security in the Waxhaws vicinity during Cornwallis's encampment there.[34]

British security was no match for William R. Davie and his Patriot horsemen, however. On the morning of September 21, Davie initiated a successful sneak attack on the British Legion, now under command of George Hanger during Tarleton's illness, at their camp at Wahab's Plantation. "The British left fifteen or 20 dead on the field and had about forty wounded," Davie recounted in his memoir. "They were surprised, pushed off their reflection, & made no resistance."[35]

Cornwallis encountered Davie again on September 26, as the British army attempted to occupy Charlotte. Davie posted twenty of his 150 men "under the Court-house where they were covered breast-high by a stone wall, and two other companies were advanced about eighty yards and posted behind some houses and gardens on each side of the street."[36] From their defensive position, Davie's brigade repulsed two attacks from the British army vanguard, delaying Cornwallis's capture of the town, before retreating in good order in front of a third.

After this action, Davie and his men joined with North Carolina militia under General William Davidson to harass and ambush British foraging parties and couriers, effectively controlling the countryside around Charlotte. "No British commander could obtain any information in that position, which would facilitate his designs, or guide his future conduct," complained Banastre Tarleton, and after Ferguson's defeat at King's Mountain, Cornwallis had had enough of Davie and his partisans. "Let's get out of here; this place is a damned hornet's nest," Cornwallis allegedly said as he prepared to depart Charlotte.[37]

Meanwhile, the militia of the Watauga settlements had organized into an army known to history as the "Overmountain Men" and were bearing down on Patrick Ferguson, who was retreating toward Charlotte. By now Cornwallis had contracted his own serious bout of malaria. Evidence suggests he ignored Ferguson's requests for reinforcement, just as it suggests he was never much of a Ferguson fan. True, Ferguson's appointment as inspector of militia was made by Clinton, the Scottish major's patron. And true, Ferguson was always a bit of an oddball in the rigidly conformist British army. But it is also true Cornwallis could've done more to help Ferguson, who set up his defenses on King's Mountain, awaiting reinforcements that never came. That is where an army of nine hundred men, mounted elements of the Overmountain Men joined by other North and South Carolina militia, routed his Loyalist force of 1,100 on October 7, 1780. Almost every man under Ferguson's command was either killed (157), wounded (163), or captured (698), while the Patriots lost only twenty-eight killed and sixty-eight wounded.[38]

King's Mountain was a disaster for Cornwallis's invasion plans, if not the British cause in North America. "The destruction of Ferguson and his corps marked the period and the extent of the first expedition into North Carolina," writes Tarleton. "The weakness of his [Cornwallis's] army, the extent and poverty of North Carolina, the want of knowledge of his enemies designs, and the total ruin of his militia, presented a gloomy prospect at the commencement of the campaign."[39]

Rumor swept the British army that the Overmountain Men were marching next for Ninety Six and Camden, their numbers inflated by thousands. The rumors weren't true. In fact, immediately after the battle, the Overmountain Men retreated north with their prisoners toward their mountain homes. But what *was* true is that the victory galvanized South Carolina's Patriot sentiment, drawing new recruits to the militia of Thomas Sumter, Francis Marion, and others. The disaster at King's Mountain, Henry Clinton believed, "so encouraged that spirit of rebellion in both the Carolinas that it never could be afterward humbled."[40]

And for opportunists like Henry Rugeley, and others who had embraced the Loyalist cause in the summer of 1780, it may have been a sign they had picked the wrong side. Certainly, Rugeley would have been concerned to learn that, in the aftermath of King's Mountain, Cornwallis planned a retreat from Charlotte to the small settlement of Winnsboro. Located strategically between Camden and Ninety Six, the Winnsboro camp nevertheless put Rugeley's fortified mill in a newly vulnerable position forward of the British line.

On October 14, the retreat from Charlotte to Winnsboro began, com-
mencing for fifteen days on muddy roads in heavy, incessant rain. It was a
miserable march. There was no food and the men, lacking tents, spent their
nights in the open on wet ground. Cornwallis was still so sick with fever
he travelled in the back of a wagon.[41] If Cornwallis had conquered the
South in August 1780, by October that conquest was melting with the rain
in front of his malaria-stained eyes. Perhaps the cause was undue cautiousness, a failure to seize momentum in the aftermath of Camden. Perhaps it
was the lord's innate humanity, a reluctance to administer the type of terror
necessary to subdue a conquered people. Whatever the cause, the tide of
war had shifted, and Henry Rugeley's loyalties shifted with it.

And so Rugeley must have received news of the Continental army's advance toward Charlotte in October 1780 with both dread and concern.
First Morgan arrived with what remained of Gates's "light troops"—three
companies of Maryland and Delaware infantry, sixty Virginia riflemen,
some other Virginia militia, and seventy cavalrymen under command of
William Washington, a cousin of George Washington. Joined by North
Carolina militia under General William Davidson, this advance force set
up camp in late October at a place called New Providence twelve miles
south of Charlotte. And on November 11, Gates and the remainder of the
Continental army, about seven hundred men, also arrived in Charlotte.[42]

Morgan was eager to begin campaigning with his "Flying Army," a
highly mobile combination of light infantry, riflemen, and cavalry that de
Saxe, de Jeney, and other Enlightenment writers would call a "legion." According to historian Armstrong Starkey, a legion "was a flexible, self-con-
tained force of infantry, cavalry, and light artillery capable of sustaining
itself in both offensive and defensive action."[43] Though Morgan notably
didn't have any artillery, in every other manner his force fit this bill, including a plethora of talented and experienced officers, among them the afore-
mentioned Washington, along with John Eager Howard of Maryland and
Francis Triplett of Virginia, who had fought with Morgan in the French
and Indian War.

Indeed, British correspondence suggests Rugeley was now far from the
spirited and active officer he had been just a few short months before. At
the end of October, British officer George Turnbull wrote to Rawdon, noting that the "greatest part of Rugeley's" regiment was dispersed, and the
"Colonel himself I don't know where."[44] From November 4 through 9,
Morgan marched toward Camden to "reconnoiter the enemies lines and

procure forage, marching as far as the Hanging Rock,"[45] but on November 17, Rawdon reported to Cornwallis that "To my great disappointment . . . Rugeley knows nothing" about the advance of the Continental troops, clearly suggesting it was a report he found difficult to believe.[46]

But just as clearly, Morgan knew about Rugeley and put our intrepid opportunist's fortified mill dead in his sites. "Morgan felt a strong desire to uproot this nest of Tories," writes his biographer, James Graham.[47] So did he send spies to recruit Rugeley to the Patriot cause? There is nothing in the historical record to suggest it, though South Carolina governor John Rutledge, the alleged orchestrator of the first attempt to turn Rugeley's allegiance, was now also in Gates's Charlotte camp.

According to the journal of William Seymour, Morgan marched with his "Horse and Infantry" for Rugeley's Mill on November 28, coming to the fort on December 1[48] but deeming it "too hazardous" to "approach it with his infantry."[49] Instead he sent forward his cavalry under Washington to reconnoiter the site. Washington "humorously ordered his men to paint the trunk of an old pine tree, in the manner of a field piece," recalled Otho Holland Williams, which Washington placed in sight of Rugeley's fort. "At the same time, dismounting some of his men to appear as infantry, and displaying his cavalry to the best advantage, he sent a corporal of dragoons to summon . . . an *immediate* surrender." Intimidated by the fake gun, and the corporal's stern demands, "Colonel Rugeley did not hesitate to comply immediately; and the whole garrison marched out prisoners of war."[50]

Washington's *ruse de guerre*, known as a "Quaker gun," delighted the Continental troops, as it has delighted readers of American history ever since. Rugeley, however, was humiliated, and the British infuriated. Hearing of Morgan's approach, Rawdon had ordered Rugeley to retreat toward Camden. "I own I tremble for Rugeley and most heartily wish that he had retired as you desired him," admitted Cornwallis to Rawdon in a letter dated December 2.[51] But as news of Rugeley's disgraceful surrender filtered back to camp, such apprehensions turned to contempt. "Rugeley . . . had full time to retire in case he did not mean to defend himself. *I am confident he has betrayed his men* (italics original)," fumed Rawdon. "I have thought it likely to happen and have always had my precautions."[52]

And despite his previous assertions that Rugeley was an "active and spirited man," Cornwallis now asserted he doubted Rugeley's loyalties all along. "Your account of Rugeley vexed me altho' it did not surprise me," he admitted to Rawdon.[53] And to Lieutenant Colonel Nisbet Balfour in

Charleston, Cornwallis wrote, "You will have heard of that rascal Rugeley. I think from the circumstance of his not retiring, when directed to do so by Rawdon, and promising to defend himself to the last extremity and afterwards surrendering to a detachment of cavalry only without firing a shot is a plain proof that he must be a traitor."[54]

The Rugeley affair helped convince Cornwallis that the "friends" promised by Germain, Galloway, and others were not to be trusted. If the Southern Strategy was to work, it would not be due to Loyalist support, which had proven capricious and ineffectual, but rather the skill, daring, and loyalty of his beloved British soldiers. Only his officers and soldiers could be counted on in the treacherous landscape that was the American South, and only with the final annihilation of the decimated Continental army, and the subjugation of first North Carolina, then Virginia, could it truly be conquered.

CHAPTER 4

THE SOUTHERN GENTLEMEN

Nᴇᴡs ᴏꜰ Rᴜɢᴇʟᴇʏ's sᴜʀʀᴇɴᴅᴇʀ reached the Southern Army's camp in Charlotte on December 2, just hours after General Nathanael Greene arrived there to take command from the disgraced Horatio Gates. "Soldiers, like sailors, have always a little superstition about them," wrote Otho Holland Williams, who witnessed the day's events. "Although neither General Gates nor General Greene, could be considered as having any agency in this successful little affair [the capture of Rugeley's Mill], it was regarded by some, and even mentioned, as a presage of the good fortune which the army would derive from the genius of the latter."[1]

Perhaps as eager to welcome their new general as they were to celebrate Rugeley's ignominious surrender, the men fired a *feu de joie* in celebration, news of which reached the disgruntled Cornwallis back at his camp in Winnsboro.[2] A *feu de joie* is a celebratory rifle salute of soldiers firing their rifles into the air in rapid succession, the effect a cascading wall of sound. "The happy union of triumph and mirth, diffused through the camp by this fortunate though ludicrous occurrence, gave the first day of vivacity to the army that it had enjoyed since the late defeat [at Camden]."[3]

If Greene's reputation as a talented general preceded him, for he was known to many in the Southern Army camp, including Williams, who had served with him notably in the 1778 Monmouth campaign, he was not distinguished by his appearance. He sported a stout physique and walked with a limp, perhaps the result of an accident at his family's forge in Rhode Island. At times, he suffered from asthma. "In person he was rather corpulent, and above the common size," recalled Henry Lee. "His complexion was fair and florid; his countenance serene and mild. . . . His health was delicate, but preserved by temperance and exercise." Neither Lee nor anyone else would ever call him dashing or, like Washington, physically impressive.

Yet clearly there was something charismatic about the man, a prodigious, relentless intellect that could comprehend complex problems and then instinctively chart their solutions in his mind. And if this understanding is the quality of everyday brilliance, then Greene possessed that even rarer genius—the ability to lead others toward their resolution. "A wide sphere of intellectual resources enabled him to inspire confidence, to rekindle courage, to decide hesitation, and infuse the spirit of exalted patriotism in the citizens of the State," Lee continued. "By his own example he showed the incalculable value of obedience, of patience, of vigilance, and temperance. Dispensing justice, with an even hand, to the citizen and soldier; benign in heart, and happy in manners, he acquired the durable attachment and esteem of all. He collected around his person able and respectable officers and selected, for the several departments, those who were best qualified to fill them. His operations were then commenced with a boldness of design, well calculated to raise the drooping hopes of his country, and to excite the respect of his enemy."[4]

Another Greene biographer, his grandson George Washington Greene, described eyes that "seem to be lambent with combined light, partly from within and partly from without, as of a soul alternately questioning itself and the world that surrounds it,"[5] and perhaps this also was a key to his charisma, for Nathanael Greene's critical mind could just as easily turn on itself as the exterior world, always assessing and reassessing his own suppositions as he processed new information.

As a general and military administrator, he came by these traits honestly, learning them through rough and violent experience, although one must allot at least some credit to his innate intelligence and religious upbringing. For a time in American history, it was popular to contrast Greene's Quaker heritage, and that religion's pacifist principles, with his later status as a "warrior." Popular biographies of Greene have sported titles such as *The Fighting Quaker* and *Quaker Commander,* among others that make reference to this dichotomy.

It's true Greene grew up in a Quaker household. His father, Nathanael Greene, Sr., was the spiritual leader of a Quaker congregation near the Greene home in Potowumut, a part of Warwick, Rhode Island, though separated from it by Greenwich Bay.[6] Here Greene was born on July 27, 1742, and grew up in a large and loving family, sharing the Potowumut home with his father, stepmother (for his own mother had died in 1753, when Greene was only eleven years old), and seven brothers, of which Nathanael was the fourth born.

Though Greene Sr. *was* a devoutly spiritual man, he was also an industrious Yankee merchant through and through. Either alone or with family partners, he owned a store, sawmill, flour mill, gristmill, forge, anchor works, wharf, and warehouses, along with shipping and real estate interests. The editors of Nathanael Greene's papers chart his father's business success by noting he was the second-highest taxpayer in Warwick, Rhode Island, in 1763. From an early age, his sons worked hard at the family businesses, gaining valuable experience in management and administration. "When Nathanael Greene became quartermaster general of the Continental army, his experience as a merchant served him well."[7]

A regular theme among Greene's biographers is his father's repudiation of formal education. "His own limited education, the fanaticism of the times, and something of the peculiar opinions of his sect, had impressed him with an opinion, that the Bible was the only book worthy of the study of an intellectual being," writes an early Greene biographer of Nathanael Sr. "I lament the want of a liberal Education," Greene would write himself as a young man. "My Father was a man [of] great Piety, had an excellent understanding; and was govern'd in his conduct of Humanity and kind Benevolence. But his mind was over shadow'd with prejudice against Literary Accomplishments." Yet the Greene boys needed to read, so they could study the Bible, and cipher, so they could attend to accounts, and so they received rudimentary instruction from an itinerant instructor.[8]

And it would be a mistake to equate Greene's lack of educational training with the lack of an intellectual life. Part of this life included Quaker meetings, when the society gathered in local homes. Here the Greene boys were brought into "closer contact with thoughtful men and women in their most thoughtful mood. It was part of the Quaker's moral and social training."[9] Politics was a popular topic at the Greene family table, and even as a young boy, Greene's work and social life, his family obligations, took him among the realms of commerce, religion, politics, and law in New England society.

In this curious intellectual tradition Greene was raised, with formal education repudiated, but human nature relentlessly analyzed and discussed. But Greene thirsted for more, and on one of his idylls, he met a young collegian named Ezra Stiles, who would go on to become the president of Yale College. "Nathanael Greene returned from that day's walk another boy . . . The day of unquestioning faith was passed. Henceforth, to believe, he must first understand."[10] Stiles ignited in Greene a relentless thirst for knowledge, and from that day forward, Greene read every book and article he could find, begging his father for more formal academic training. Eventually, remarkably, Greene Sr. relented, hiring a local schoolmaster to tutor his son in Latin and mathematics.[11]

Through books Greene cultivated his own education. An early influence was John Locke's *Essay Concerning Human Understanding*, whose "most abstruse discussions" Greene mastered. In its emphasis on empiricism, the theory that all knowledge can be derived from sense experience, Locke's *Essay* initiated a new intellectual model of radical equality, the idea that all human beings are born with equal capacity for knowledge and understanding.[12] Surely this concept appealed to Greene, who lamented the "want of a liberal education" even as he awakened to the "lambent" intellect recognized so clearly in him by others. To the world he may have appeared the uneducated son of a Yankee merchant; inside his mind was on fire.

Soon Greene was studying other Enlightenment philosophers, including David Hume, along with mathematics, classics of Greek and Latin, English literature, and grammar. But it was to politics, soldiery, and the Patriot cause Greene was drawn, especially after his father died in 1770. By then he was twenty-eight and still single. His attendance at Quaker meetings waned, and on July 5, 1773, he was suspended from the Quaker fellowship in East Greenwich, Rhode Island, perhaps for participating in a military exercise.[13] Greene's political fervor was solidified when the British navy seized the *Fortune*, a trading vessel owned by the Greene family. Though the vessel probably was engaged in smuggling, as the British charged, Greene's family filed a lawsuit against the British officer responsible for the seizure, a political provocation for the time. By now Greene was frequently traveling to Boston, where tensions between royal authorities and local Patriots were enflamed, seeking texts both political and military, as well as the company of prominent Patriots such as Henry Knox, a local bookseller and Patriot sympathizer who would go on to become a Continental officer, and later, President George Washington's secretary of war.[14]

To the influence of Knox we can probably attribute Greene's growing interest in military texts. From references in his letters, we know Greene studied Enlightenment military thinkers such as Saxe, with his emphasis on mobile legions and *petite guerre*, along with Frederick the Great's *Instructions to His Generals*.[15] Greene's intellectual pursuits stand him in stark contrast to Cornwallis. Born to status and nobility, Cornwallis's heritage marked him a part of the status quo Enlightenment thinkers such as Locke strove to repudiate. Surely, such intellectual repudiation appealed to Nathanael Greene, born of common stock and denied the formal education, he believed, necessary to validate his unusual intellect. If Cornwallis was endowed with status by birth, Greene could seek it through his own empirical quest for understanding. His books took him on that journey. It would be a mistake to claim Greene was a devotee of Saxe or Frederick the Great, that he consciously and systematically applied their principles to his military tactics. Nothing in his letters indicates such a methodical approach. But his study of these texts suggests a military leader unbound by the conventions governing Cornwallis and the British army. In combat and strategy, Greene used his own reason and assessment, filtered through his considerable experience and coupled with an intellectual understanding of tactics both conventional and not, to adapt to situational contingencies. In the conflict to come, Cornwallis and his British army would possess superiority in troops, weaponry, naval support, and logistics, but Greene was his superior in an intellectual creativity that could equal the field of play.

In 1774, when he was thirty-one years old, Greene's pursuits turned to love when he married Catharine Littlefield, the cousin of his friend and former Rhode Island governor Samuel Ward. Twelve years Greene's junior, "Caty" was a vivacious and quixotic bride. Much has been written about this complex and sometimes troubled marriage. During its time, rumors swirled about Caty's alleged infidelity, though they were never proved. Caty Greene would become an important character in Greene's biography during the early part of the American Revolution, when she often accompanied Greene to his winter quarters, and again after its conclusion, but alas not during the Race to the Dan, and so we leave her here to tempt further exploration for the burgeoning Greene enthusiast.

War clouds quickly interrupted Greene's romantic interlude with Caty. As tensions between Patriot and British continued to mount in New England, Greene participated in the formation of a Rhode Island militia unit called the Kentish Guards. When the unit elected officers in October 1774, Greene was passed over due to his limp. "I was informd the Gentlemen of East Greenwich said that I was a blemish to the company," Greene wrote to James Varnum. "I confess it is my misfortune to limp a little . . . I feel more mortification than resentment, but I think it would have manifested a more generous temper to have given me their Oppinions in private than to make proclamation of it in publick."[16] Humiliated, Greene continued to drill with the unit as a mere private.

If there are suggestions of an inferiority complex in Greene's later military career, a propensity to take offense too quickly when his competence or service was questioned, perhaps we see elements of its origin here, the classic inhibitions of the physically inferior. Its roots may also lie in insecurities about his education or lack thereof. But Greene's stint as buck private lasted only six months. On May 8, 1775, shortly after the clash between the redcoats and minutemen in Lexington and Concord that April, Greene was appointed brigadier general of Rhode Island's newly organized "Army of Observation." And when the Continental Congress established the Continental army a month later, on June 14, 1775, Greene's Rhode Island rank transferred to it, making him its youngest and most junior brigadier general.[17]

This remarkable promotion remains one of the great mysteries of Greene's career. No historian has deduced, precisely, the circumstances of it, though his family's political connections and Greene's talent for cultivating important patrons undoubtedly played a role. Now one of eight brigadier generals in the Continental army (in addition to four major generals, a quartermaster general, adjutant general, paymaster general, commissary general, and George Washington, the commander in chief), Greene underwent a literal trial by fire, employing as a rookie general the military tactics he had studied intellectually for years.

At first, he failed. At New York in 1776, his refusal to evacuate Fort Washington led to its surrender on November 14, along with fifty-three dead and the capture of 2,800 American men and officers.[18] A week later Greene was forced to evacuate Fort Lee, guarding the Hudson River, in the face of a British assault.

But these early failures solidified his relationship with George Washington, who in some measure shared in their blame and would become his mentor, the man Greene relentlessly referred to as "His Excellency." Now promoted to major general, Greene led well during the American successes at Princeton and Trenton in January 1777, and again during the retreats at Brandywine and Germantown later that year. When Washington needed a talented administrator to take the position of quartermaster general in 1778, he knew just the right man for the job. And though Greene would famously remark, "Nobody ever heard of a quarter master in history," he reluctantly accepted the appointment.[19]

As quartermaster general, Greene's job focused on supply, logistics, and transport. Though his administrative talents served him exceptionally well in this role, his tenure was not without controversy. As was common for the time, Greene negotiated a commission on all items purchased for the Continental army under his administration. Over the two years he was in the job, this amounted to a substantial sum, but as the Continental army's supply budget exploded under his administration, members of the Continental Congress began to question his expenses, some even accusing Greene of inflating them to profit personally. It was an affront Greene was ill equipped to bear. On three separate occasions Greene angrily offered his resignation from the appointment; the last time, in July 1780, many in Congress found his resignation letter so offensively hostile they wanted to rescind his major general's commission as well. But each time Greene's pride and insecurities led him into conflict with his political masters, Washington's patronage saved his neck. In summer 1780, his resignation as quartermaster general finally was accepted. And it's worth noting that almost all of the commission he earned on the job was lost in a series of bad business investments.[20]

After Continental general Benjamin Lincoln surrendered at Charleston, Washington wanted Greene to take his place as commander of the Southern Department, but Congress wanted Gates, the "Hero of Saratoga," and picked him instead. But Gates's disaster at Camden proved Congress was ill equipped to appoint commanders in the South. With the job open again, this time Congress was more than happy to defer the decision to Washington. He chose Greene.

Greene received news of his appointment on October 15, 1780. "I beg your excellency to be persuaded that I am fully sensible of the honour you do me, and will endeavour to manifest my gratitude by conduct that will not disgrace the appointment." It was a humble response from a man who had shown little humility during his unhappy stint as quartermaster general. Yet Greene was no Pollyanna about the job's challenges. "I foresee the command will be accompanied with innumerable embarrassments; but the gen-

erous support I expect from the partiality of the southern gentlemen . . .
shall afford me some consolation in contemplating these difficulties."[21]

THE SOUTHERN GENTLEMEN upon whose "generous support" Greene intended to rely undoubtedly included politicians like Thomas Jefferson, the
governor of Virginia, whom Greene would solicit for troops, food, and
ammunition for his army. At heart, Greene was a pragmatist. Though he
recognized the capricious nature of these politicians, and the equally ir-
resolute public they purported to serve, he understood they could not be
ignored. If he was to be constantly disappointed in the South's political
support, his incessant solicitations to its elected leaders provided political
cover. Apprised and consulted on his strategy, implored for their support,
these politicians could not claim ignorance or chagrin if things went
wrong. Though the Continental army officer Greene was by now inured
to the shortcomings of America's political system, he was nevertheless a
master of it.

The politicians, the local militia, the public support—these were all necessary components of a military campaign in the American Revolution.
But their support was unreliable, their allegiance arbitrary. For Greene, it
was his fellow Continental officers, and their soldiers, to whom he would
truly devote his faith, for it was they who had endured and shared long sacrifice in what he deemed a noble quest for the American cause. It was they
with whom Greene had formed a fraternity of honor and dignity through
six long years of war, and it was only they upon whose "generous support"
Greene would truly depend in the most difficult of circumstances to come.

To his adept, if somewhat reluctant, logistics officers, Lt. Colonel Edward Carrington and William R. Davie, we have already been introduced.
And also to his most talented field officer, Daniel Morgan. But Morgan
was a relatively recent addition to the tiny army Greene inherited from
Gates, which consisted primarily of Continental soldiers from Maryland,
Delaware, and Virginia. The Maryland and Delaware troops were the remnants of those who had marched south with Kalb in April 1780. But what
this army lacked in quantity, it made up for in quality. Two of these regiments—the 1st Maryland and the Delaware Regiment, its strength now
reduced to only about a hundred men—had fought in every major engagement of the American Revolution from Long Island to Monmouth Courthouse and now on to Camden and the southern campaign that lay ahead.[22]

The veteran Maryland regiments were distinguished by their colonels, John Eager Howard and Otho Holland Williams. Both would play critical roles during the Race to the Dan. From Williams, we have already heard. His "Narrative of the Southern Campaign of 1780" remains a vital source on the Battle of Camden and Gates's administration of the Southern Army. Sadly for historians, his narrative ends with the transfer of command to Greene, though his role in history was far from finished.

Born in 1749, Williams's early career was as a county clerk in Frederick and Baltimore, Maryland. In June 1775, he joined the Frederick City rifle corps, which was assimilated into the Continental army during the siege of Boston. Promoted to major, he was taken prisoner during the defense of Fort Washington in November 1776 and earned a promotion to colonel while still a prisoner of war. Finally exchanged in 1778, he led the 6th Maryland Continental Regiment during the Monmouth campaign later that year and marched south with Kalb in April 1780.

Though orphaned at an early age, Williams was from a prominent Maryland family and better educated than most of his compatriots, though popular with them, with a physical appearance that was tall and "elegantly formed."[23] Recognizing his talents and appeal, Gates made him assistant adjutant general, charged with the near impossible task of making sure orders were properly transmitted down the line and other personnel responsibilities in the ragtag Southern Army.[24] Greene would retain him in this role, though his duties would soon exceed far beyond the administrative.

Lieutenant Colonel John Eager Howard also was well educated, the son of a Maryland planter. Volunteering in 1776, he was commissioned a major of the 4th Maryland Continental Regiment in February 1777 and fought with distinction at White Plains, Germantown, Monmouth, and Camden. Notes Henry Lee: "Trained to infantry service, he was invariably employed in that line, and was always to be found where the battle raged, pressing into close action to wrestle with fixed bayonet. Placid in temper and reserved in deportment, he never lessened his martial fame by arrogance or ostentation, nor clouded it with garrulity or self-conceit."[25]

Battle hardened and experienced in most of the American Revolution's major campaigns, the Delaware Regiment had been decimated at the Battle of Camden, losing ten officers. In October, Gates reorganized the regiment into two ninety-six-man companies under the overall command of Howard. Commanding one of the remaining Delaware companies was Captain Robert Kirkwood. Educated at Newark Academy, Kirkwood was a Delaware farmer of English descent. When the Delaware Regiment was formed in January 1776, he was commissioned a lieutenant, fighting at Long Island, Trenton, and Princeton, then commissioned a captain a year later.[26]

Kirkwood also traveled south with Kalb in 1780 and would go on to fight in all the major battles of the southern campaign, including Cowpens, Guilford Courthouse, Hobkirk's Hill, and Eutaw Springs. Writing of Greene's Delaware troops, biographer William Johnson notes, "This little corps . . . was the admiration of the army, and their leader Kirkwood was the American Diomed," referencing the Greek hero Diomedes, who fought more battles than any other Greek soldier during the Trojan War. "Like the Marylanders they [the Delaware Regiment] had been enlisted for the war, and like veterans of that brigade, were not excelled by any troops in America, perhaps in the world."[27]

Despite his outstanding service, Kirkwood remained a captain throughout the war. "As the line of Delaware consisted of but one regiment, and that regiment reduced to a captain's command, Kirkwood never could be promoted in regular routine—a very glaring defect in the organization of the army," explains Henry Lee.[28] Nevertheless, he was highly regarded in the Continental camp.

Not yet arrived at Greene's camp, but on his way, was one of our primary correspondents, the inestimable Henry Lee. He was born into a prominent Virginia family that dated its ancestry back to the earliest days of the English monarchy and lived a young life of privilege, becoming an outstanding horseman and attending Princeton College (then the College of New Jersey). He was preparing to study law in England when the American Revolution erupted. Commissioned a captain in the Virginia cavalry when he was just twenty years old, Lee's company joined the 1st Continental Dragoons in 1776, where he soon became an intimate of George Washington. They would become lifelong friends; it was Lee who wrote of Washington, "First in war, first in peace, first in the hearts of his countrymen," for the founding father's funeral oration.

Lee distinguished himself in service with Washington, displaying a mastery of the partisan fighting that would later distinguish his service in the southern campaign. His skillful horsemanship earned him the nickname "Light Horse Harry." Promoted to major in 1778 and given his first command, Lee's reputation soared with his surprise attack on the British garrison at Paulus Hook, New Jersey, in August 1779. Though a relatively minor victory, it boosted American morale and earned him one of only eight gold medals awarded by the Continental Congress during the war.

He was promoted to lieutenant colonel on November 30, 1780, and given command of his "Legion," the three cavalry companies already under his command plus three infantry companies. The Legion's original strength was one hundred cavalry and 180 infantry. Lee outfitted his cavalry in short green jackets, similar to the jackets worn by Banastre Tarleton's British Legion, and insisted on the finest quality horses for his men.

As we have read, Greene made a special request to Washington for Lee's services as part of his appointment to the Southern Department, and Lee would become Greene's most trusted officer, acting with unusual autonomy, often in conjunction with the South Carolina partisans of Francis Marion, the famed "Swamp Fox." In 1812, Lee published his memoir titled *Memoirs of the War in the Southern Department of the United States*, as an attempt to get out of debt. Though not a financial success, it has endured as a lively and essential account of the American Revolution, especially the southern campaign, and will be referenced many times in this work.[29]

The other Virginia cavalry officer who would play a prominent role in Greene's southern campaign was William Washington, a distant cousin of the commander in chief. A seminary student prior to the war, William Washington was commissioned a captain in the 3rd Virginia Continentals in February 1776 and was wounded twice during the New York and New Jersey campaigns. In 1777 he was commissioned a major in a new regiment of dragoons, eventually rising to the rank of lieutenant colonel.

Late in 1779 or early in 1780, Washington was ordered south to support General Benjamin Lincoln at Charleston. There, Washington attempted to keep the British from completing their encirclement of the city, encountering Banastre Tarleton's Legion in action at Monck's Corner and Lenud's Ferry, both sound defeats for the Continental forces. At Lenud's, Washington escaped only by swimming the river, a desperate escape during which a number of Continental soldiers drowned.[30]

"He possessed a stout frame, being six feet in height, broad strong, and corpulent," recounted Lee, who knew him well. "In temper he was good-humored; in disposition amiable; in heart upright, generous, and friendly; in manners lively, innocent, and agreeable. . . . Bold, collected, and persevering, he preferred the heat of action to the collection and sifting of intelligence . . . and was better fitted for the field of battle than for the drudgery of camp and the watchfulness of preparation."[31]

After escaping to eastern North Carolina during the siege of Charleston's final stages, Washington "applied to General Gates for the aid of his name and authority to expedite restoration and equipment" of his regiment. But this "salutary and proper request was . . . injudiciously disregarded" by Gates,[32] who bewilderingly saw little use for cavalry in his upcoming assault on Camden. Nevertheless, Washington restored his regiment and rejoined Gates after Camden, where he was assigned to the light corps commanded by General Daniel Morgan, in whose service Greene would find him.

Other senior Continental officers at camp in Charlotte when Greene arrived were William Smallwood and Isaac Huger. Born in 1732, Smallwood was, like Williams and Howard, from yet another prominent Maryland family. Commissioned colonel of a Maryland regiment in 1776, Smallwood would go on to fight at the Battle of Long Island and the Battle of White Plains later that year. Wounded at White Plains, he was subsequently promoted to brigadier general. In April 1780, he, too, marched south with Kalb in the detachment that never reached Charleston and was later taken over by Gates. At the Battle of Camden, Smallwood was separated from his brigade by the flood of retreating militia, and although his service there was undistinguished, his seniority gained him that September a promotion to major general. As such, he was disgruntled when Gates was relieved and Greene given command, a status he believed rightfully belonged to him. This discontent was well known when Greene arrived at the Continental camp; the issue was resolved when Greene returned him to Maryland to raise troops and supplies.[33]

Isaac Huger (pronounced "You-gee") was one of five brothers from a South Carolina family of French Huguenot planters. Raised on the family's Santee River plantation, all five received liberal educations and played prominent roles in South Carolina politics and military affairs. Isaac was born in 1743 and in 1775 commissioned lieutenant colonel in the 1st South Carolina Regiment, which was assimilated into the Continental army after serving in the defense of Charleston in 1776. (It is from the symbol worn on the hats of the 1st and 2nd South Carolina Regiments that the state derives its famous reverse crescent, a symbol of "liberty.") Promoted to brigadier general in 1779, he was wounded at Stono Ferry that June but led Georgia and South Carolina militia in the unsuccessful attack on Savannah that October.

Again in command of Georgia and South Carolina militia in April 1780, Huger was with William Washington fighting against Banastre Tarleton at the Battle of Monck's Corner on April 14. Tarleton's victory completed the encirclement of the city, allowing the British to initiate their siege. At Monck's Corner, "Huger and his colonels had committed errors grievous enough to warrant a court martial," according to historian John Buchanan, but because he fled to the swamps after the defeat, he became the highest-ranking officer from the Carolinas or Georgia to avoid capture when Charleston was surrendered on May 12. Like William Washington, Huger made his way to Gates's Continental camp after Charleston, where he would've been introduced to Greene on December 2.[34]

William Seymour, Thomas Anderson, and William Beatty were junior Continental officers who left written accounts of their service in the southern campaign. Seymour was a sergeant major in the Delaware Regiment. His *Journal of the Southern Edition, 1780-1783*, is an invaluable resource for southern campaign historians. Delaware lieutenant Thomas Anderson also left a detailed account of the Battle of Cowpens. Captain William Beatty of Maryland joined the Continental army in 1776 and served almost continuously until his death at Hobkirk's Hill in April 1781.[35]

These were far from the only talented and brave American soldiers who took part in the Race to the Dan. To others, like militia officers Samuel Hammond, Andrew Pickens, and William Graham, or young militia soldiers like Thomas Young and James Collins, we shall soon be introduced. But it was this corps of dedicated Continental officers—Morgan, Carrington, Williams, Howard, Davie, Lee, Kirkwood, Washington, and Huger— upon whom Greene would rely foremost in the campaign to come. "By the end of the war, Continental soldiers began to regard themselves as a distinct class within American society, one forged by military professionalism and a common sense of patriotism and sacrifice," writes historian Armstrong Starkey.[36] And though Starkey isn't referring specifically to these "southern gentlemen" Greene found awaiting him at camp in Charlotte, they had already proved themselves part of the honorable fraternity of soldiers Greene regarded so highly.

Despite the quality of his officer corps, the situation Greene encountered at camp near Charlotte was dire. On his first night, he toured the camp to discover no more than three days' supply of provisions were on hand, and ammunition was dangerously low. "Nothing can be more wretched and distressing than the condition of the troops, starving with cold and hunger, without tents and camp equipage," Greene complained in a letter to George Washington. "Those of the Virginia line are literally naked, and a great part totally unfit for any kind of duty, and must remain so until clothing can be had from the Northward."[37]

To his wife, Caty, he wrote similarly, "I arrived here on the 2nd of this month and have been in search of the Army I am to command; but without much success; having found nothing but a few half-starved Soldiers who are remarkable for nothing but poverty and distress." But in this unofficial correspondence he ends hopefully: "But I am in hopes matters will mend. I am in good health and good spirits; and am unhappy for nothing except the separation from you and the rest of my friends."[38]

Some of this cheer must be attributed to the *ruse de guerre* that fooled Rugeley. And Greene worked hard to cultivate a similar spirit of comradeship, particularly among his officers, even as he labored exhaustively to instill discipline and order. During those first weeks, Greene spent his days diligently attending to camp business, discipline, and administration. At night he worked on his correspondence, "written by his own hand and distributed to his aides," until midnight, then read and reflected deeply into the midnight hours. But dinner was for his officers, who received regular, rotated invitations to the general's table. Greene's biographer William Johnson creates a vivid portrait of these mealtime conversations: "At the social board the restraints of parade no longer existed. . . . On these occasions the sentiments of the young were enlisted and the diffident encouraged to adventure in conversation. . . . Modesty never was permitted at his table to repine at the superior attention commanded by the gay and the forward, and no guest left it dissatisfied either with himself or his entertainer."[39]

Though brief and not entirely successful at eliminating petty jealousies and rivalries, these efforts at *esprit de corps* would prove fruitful in the months to come. To Caty he would write, "To inspire a noble emulation, far above yielding to the low suggestions of selfishness in his officers, is of incalculable importance to him who stands responsible for the conduct of an army."[40] Little would he realize how prescient those words would become over the course of the next three months.

Part Two

COWPENS

CHAPTER 5

FLYING ARMY

In his officers, Greene was among the experienced fraternity with which he had endured six years of war, that band of brothers who were, to one another, beyond selfishness in their quest for an American cause. This was his family, not unlike the rambunctious band of New England intellectuals with whom he was raised, and like his father, Nathanael Sr., Greene ruled over it with both discipline and empathy. But as contented as Nathanael Greene was with his officer corps, he was discontented with his army.

By the return dated December 8, 1780, Greene had on hand 821 Continental infantry, 90 cavalry, 60 artillerymen, and 128 Continentals on extra service. Including his volunteer militia, the Southern Army consisted of 2,307, although over five hundred of those were "on command" and not in camp.[1] Not only was this force's number woefully inadequate to face Cornwallis's British occupation force and their stoutly defended garrisons, it was also in dreadful condition—starving, threadbare, and lacking discipline. During his first night in camp at Charlotte, Greene surveyed the surrounding countryside with Colonel Thomas Polk, chief of Gates's commissariat. By the "following morning, he [Greene] better understood" the supply issues facing his army than "Gates had done in the whole period of his command," Polk would later recall.[2]

His assessment was a brutal one. "I find the Troops under his [Gates] Command in a most wretched Condition, destitute of every thing necessary either for the Comfort or Convenience of Soldiers," he complained to Thomas Jefferson. "It is impossible that Men can render any Service, if they are ever so well disposed whilst they are starving with Cold and Hunger. Your Troops may litterally be said to be naked, and I shall be obliged to send a considerable Number of them away into some secure place and warm Quarters until they can be furnished with Cloathing."[3]

Due to the shortages, soldiers were leaving camp without permission to search for food, an intolerable breakdown in discipline. "The troops had not only lost their discipline; but they were so addicted to plundering that they were a terror to the Country," Greene complained to his friend Alexander Hamilton.[4] One of Greene's first acts was arresting a deserter as he returned to camp, trying him quickly, and hanging him in front of the whole army, with intended effect. "It is new lords new laws," Greene's men were said to utter around their campfires.[5]

While he ordered the soldiers drilled relentlessly, Greene immediately began reorganizing his staff department, offering Carrington, still occupied on the Dan River, the position of deputy quartermaster general just one day after assuming command. Little more than a week later, after Polk resigned, he convinced the reluctant William Davie to take the post of commissary general. (Recall that in the Continental army, quartermasters supplied equipment and uniforms, along with transportation; the commissary officer supplied food and other subsistence supplies.) He also initiated his survey of the Catawba River during these first few days,[6] as he had done for the Yadkin just a few days prior to his arrival in Charlotte.[7]

But he soon determined the countryside around Charlotte was too depleted to adequately support his starving troops. Dismayed by the dismal conditions in Charlotte, he sought a "camp of repose" where he could rebuild his army.[8] On December 8, he ordered Kosciuszko to abandon his exploration of the Catawba River region and instead focus on the Pee Dee River in South Carolina, east of Camden, and "search for a good position for the army. You will report the make of the Country . . . the number of Mills and the water transportation that may be had up and down the River."[9]

When he received Kosciuszko's favorable report of South Carolina's Cheraws area, on the Pee Dee River just south of the North Carolina state line, Greene decided to split his army. The decision was a monumental one, as we shall see, spinning a thread deeply woven into the fabric of our nation's history. Subsequently, it has fascinated historians for centuries, who use it to illustrate Greene's unconventional brilliance, even describing it "as the most audacious and ingenious piece of military strategy of the war."[10]

Genius it may have been, though its genesis was a complicated one, far from original inspiration. True, Greene had proposed use of a "Flying Army" in the South as early as November 2. Writing that day to Samuel Huntington, president of the Continental Congress, Greene proposed: "As it must be some time before the southern Army can be collected and equipped in sufficient force . . . it will be my first endeavor to form a flying army to consist of Infantry and horse. It appears to me that Cavalry and Partizan Corps are best adapted to the make of the Country and the state of the war in that quarter, both for heading and encouraging the Militia as well as protecting the persons and property of the inhabitants."[11]

In its time, the use of detachments was controversial, for it defied the military convention against splitting an inferior army in the face of a superior foe. To this point, Frederick the Great, perhaps the greatest military thinker of the eighteenth century, wrote: "If you are less than half as strong as the enemy . . . do not detach any unit from your troops because you will be beaten in detail. Act only with your entire army."[12]

That was a lesson George Washington learned painfully in August 1776, when he detached portions of his force from Manhattan to defend Long Island, contributing to his disastrous defeat in New York. In fall 1780, Patrick Ferguson's Loyalist division was detached to western North Carolina to guard the left flank of Cornwallis's planned invasion; its destruction at King's Mountain ruined Cornwallis's plans for a fall invasion of North Carolina.[13]

In contrast, take the case of Horatio Gates, who ignored the offer of William Washington to raise cavalry, dispatched perhaps the greatest partisan fighter of them all, Francis Marion, from his camp, deeming the famed Swamp Fox's appearance "so burlesque . . . the general himself was glad of the opportunity" for getting rid of him,[14] and ordered his entire army on a brutal march south to Camden, where he immediately slammed it into Cornwallis's superiorly trained and outfitted British army, with disastrous results. Say what you want about Gates, at least he played by the established rules of war.

True, times were changing, and both armies were adopting use of the mobile "legions"—combined forces of light infantry and mounted dragoons—endorsed by military theorists like Saxe and Jeney. In the South, the British army had used Banastre Tarleton's "Legion" with deadly effect at Monck's Corner, Lenud's Ferry, and the Waxhaws, and with more mixed results in detachments against South Carolina militia leaders Thomas Sumter and Francis Marion. The "Queen's Rangers," originally commanded by Colonel Robert Rogers and later by Lt. Col. John Graves Simcoe was also a "legionary" corps, consisting of both mounted and infantry soldiers, used primarily in the northeastern theater earlier in the war.[15] However, both of these were "Provincial," or Loyalist, units, raised in America. The native British of the army's rank and file were mostly retained in their conventional infantry and cavalry roles. Though the use of detachments was evolving, it was always a strategy to be considered cautiously, especially in the British army, as in the case of Patrick Ferguson.

But far from the armies of Washington and Clinton, the stalemate and entrenched positions of the northeast, the southern landscape demanded a novel brand of war, one which Greene both learned from his allies and seemed to understand instinctually. Sumter, Marion, and Davie were prime examples of how lightly armed, highly mobile detachments could be used effectively in the South's confusing, seemingly impenetrable landscape. Marion, in particular, was the master of partisan tactics, ambushing when a superior force was at its most vulnerable, then disappearing into the swamps of eastern South Carolina. And we have already seen how Davie used his mounted militia with expertise at Charlotte, engaging the whole of Cornwallis's expeditionary force in a wildly successful delaying action.

In fact, the division of the Continental army into a "Flying" legion had already been proposed by North Carolina militia general William Davidson, even before Greene arrived to take command. Davidson had suggested the idea in a "Council of War" held by Gates in Charlotte on November 25, and again to the North Carolina Board of War in a letter dated November 27. "My scheme is to send Genl. Morgan to the Westward with his light Troops & Rifle men, 1000 volunteer Militia which I can raise in 20 days & the Refugees from South Carolina and Georgia . . . and proceed immediately to 96 and possess ourselves of the western part of South Carolina."[16] Sumter apparently made a similar proposal to Greene when the two met on December 8.[17] Even our much-maligned anti-hero, Horatio Gates, employed the idea to some extent, detaching Morgan and Washington into a light force to reconnoiter the Camden vicinity, leading to their success at Rugeley's Mill.

But Greene, and also Morgan, deserve credit for refining the idea into one that completely disrupted the British strategy, with monumental consequences. According to historian William Gordon, who was in correspondence with Greene after the war, Greene believed, "the newness of his troops, the nature of the country, filled with woods and swamps, and thinly inhabited, the toryism of numbers, and the want of magazines, led the general to conclude on a partizan war."[18] And from wherever the idea originated, or to whomever it should be authentically attributed, its final design was of Greene's singular inspiration, its novelty the great distance Greene ordered between the two Continental corps and also the complexity of its psychological objectives.

In his official orders from Greene, written December 16, Morgan was commanded to the "West side of the Catawba River" with a force of Maryland and Delaware infantry under command of John Eager Howard and Robert Kirkwood, Virginia riflemen under captains Triplett and Tate, and William Washington's dragoons. "The object of this detachment is to give protection to that part of the country and spirit up the people, to annoy the enemy in that quarter; collect the provisions and forage out of the way of the enemy." Meanwhile, Greene would move with the regular troops to the Cheraws.

These orders separated Morgan's Flying Army of approximately six hundred from Greene's force of 1,110 by well over a hundred miles, roughly the same distance Ferguson had been separated from Cornwallis when he learned of the Overmountain Men's pursuit. But Ferguson's Loyalist division was only a small fraction of the overall British command, one whose usefulness Cornwallis always viewed skeptically. Morgan's Flying Army was one-third of Greene's command, led by his most capable officer and consisting of his most valuable troops. Its destruction could mean the loss of the South.

Recognizing the jeopardy created by this distance, Greene ordered "caution and avoiding surprizes by every precaution." Still, Morgan had permission to use "this force and such others as may join you . . . either offensively or defensively as your prudence and discretion may direct, acting with caution and avoiding surprizes by every possible precaution," but "should the enemy move in force towards the Pedee . . . you will move in such direction as to enable you to join me if necessary, or fall upon the flank or into the rear of the enemy as occasion may require. . . . Confiding in your abilities and activity, I intrust you with this command, being persuaded you will do every thing in your power to distress the enemy and afford protection to the Country."[19]

As suggested by Gordon, Morgan's mission was partisan war, his objectives not military targets but broad and loosely defined psychological operations—propaganda, disruption, intelligence. In calling for an attack on Ninety Six, Davidson and Sumter's plans lacked dimension. True, a successful attack on Ninety Six would give the Americans control of western South Carolina, but an unsuccessful one could ruin any chance at victory in the South. Greene's orders reflect a more nuanced, complex strategy, suggesting the influence of the Enlightenment thinkers but based on his own empirical understanding. He was playing chess, positioning the board for an endgame he could not yet foresee. And Morgan was his knight, a dangerous target for a hasty queen.

And true to the writings of Saxe and Jeney, if not influenced by them, Greene's most important asset was not the number of his troops, nor the power of his armaments (for Morgan marched without cannon), but the quality of his officers. The partisan officer should "possess a talent for sudden and appropriate improvisation," writes Saxe. "He should be able to penetrate the minds of other men, while remaining impenetrable himself. He should be endowed with the capacity of being prepared for everything, with activity accompanied by judgement, with skill to make a proper decision on all occasion, and with exactness of discernment."[20]

Adds Jeney: "He should be blessed with an Imagination fruitful in Projects, Stratagems, and Resources. A penetrating Mind, capable of combining instantly, every Circumstance of an Action."[21] In Howard, Kirkwood, and Washington, Morgan's Flying Army had experienced officers that embodied many of these qualities. In Morgan, it had a textbook example.

Greene would admit it was a plan born partly out of desperation, taking him farther away from Cornwallis's position at Winnsboro, providing an open door for the British to march into North Carolina. In his instructions to Morgan to keep the Whigs of the western districts roused, he understood the retrograde movement could be viewed as a retreat. But he believed his army, in its current state, could not oppose Cornwallis without food, clothing, and time to improve the "discipline and spirit of my men," let alone launch offensive operations.

He needed time and believed Morgan's detachment could provide it. He also understood the great distance between his and Morgan's force placed Cornwallis in a strategic quandary of his own. If Cornwallis moved west to engage Morgan, he left open his eastern flank. If he moved east toward Greene, he imperiled his western outposts. As Greene later explained,

"It [the split] makes the most of my inferior force, for it compels my adversary to divide his, and holds him in doubt as to his own line of conduct. He cannot leave Morgan behind him to come at me, or his posts of Ninety Six and Augusta would be exposed. And he cannot chase Morgan far, or prosecute his views upon Virginia, while I am here with the whole open country before me. I am as near to Charleston, as he is."[22]

It rained for eleven straight days in middle December 1780, but on December 20, Greene finally led his force out of Charlotte. They marched seventy-five miles in six days across the sodden Carolina countryside until reaching camp on the Pee Dee River across from Cheraw, South Carolina. With him were 650 Continental infantry and approximately 450 militia.[23] Meanwhile, Morgan moved west from Charlotte a day later, on December 21, with a light infantry of 320 Delaware and Maryland Continentals under command of Major John Eager Howard, with Captain Robert Kirkwood notably commanding the Delaware company, and approximately two hundred Virginia riflemen under captains Triplett and Tate. Important to note is that these riflemen were former Continentals who had re-enlisted on a temporary, militia basis. Though this practice frustrated Greene and other Continental generals, who would've preferred the more bonding term of a regular Continental enlistment, it meant the Virginia militia with Morgan were actually combat veterans, not green, untrained recruits. And armed with their long rifles, they embodied Morgan's favorite tool of war. Traveling separately on a more southerly route than Morgan's infantry and riflemen was Lt. Colonel William Washington's regiment of approximately eighty Continental mounted dragoons.[24]

Greene would find his camp at the Cheraws a satisfactory "repose, improving the discipline and spirits of my men, and the opportunity for looking about me." Though forage and provision were still scarce, he was able to employ the neighboring militia in their collection, giving him opportunity to impress upon his troops "those habits of acting and thinking, to instruct it in that camp economy, and inspire it with that martial spirit, which were necessary to prepare it for the active scenes now confidently anticipated." As always, he devoted the late evening hours to his correspondence, his tent light on long after midnight, though meals were still a time for enjoying officer camaraderie.[25]

It was at the Cheraws on January 8, 1780, where Greene was finally joined by Lt. Col. Henry Lee and his legion—180 light infantry and a hundred mounted dragoons. Though modest in number, the addition was significant for Greene's tiny army. Formed only at the end of November 1780, upon Lee's promotion to lieutenant colonel and his assignment to the Southern Army, Lee had handpicked his officers and men from other army units, selecting officers with "reference only to their talents . . . and the men by a proportionable selection from the troops of each state enlisted for three years of the war."[26] A horse snob, Lee had ensured his men were mounted on the finest horseflesh he could find, part of the reason for their delayed arrival. This handpicked and superbly mounted unit would prove invaluable to Greene in the actions to come.

With strategy ever on his mind, Greene did not permit Lee and his crack troops long to tarry in the Continental camp. On January 9, Greene ordered Lee to join his legion with the partisan fighters of Francis Marion for an operation against the British outpost at Georgetown, an important harbor on the Carolina coast. Greene hoped a successful attack there would rouse the militia of the coastal region, leaving them "more at liberty" to join operations against the British and their supporters.[27]

While Greene drilled and established the routines of camp life, Morgan headed west, "it being very difficult marching in crossing deep swamps and very steep hills which rendered our marching difficult," for five days, fifty-eight miles, recalled the Delaware sergeant William Seymour.[28] The region they were traveling into was known as the "Ninety Six District"—the western part of colonial South Carolina, roughly encompassing the modern-day counties of Abbeville, McCormick, Edgefield, Saluda, Cherokee, Greenwood, Laurens, Union, and Spartanburg. At that time, the far northwestern corner of the South Carolina upstate—Greenville, Pickens, Anderson, and Oconee Counties—was still considered Cherokee territory. And within the regional Ninety Six District were smaller subdistricts such as the Spartan District in modern-day Spartanburg County, the Little River District centered in modern-day Laurens County, and the Long Canes District in the basin traversing the Savannah River. The Ninety Six District was administered from its namesake town, an important Cherokee trading post during the Colonial era the British had incorporated into their system of garrisoned outposts in summer 1780. Ninety Six's unusual name was derived from a prominent early survey, denoting its distance in miles from the lower Cherokee towns.

The loyalties of individual backcountry settlements often depended on the political leanings of its leaders. During the American Revolution, many of the Little River District's Loyalists were led by Robert Cunningham.

Jailed by the provincial government for his Loyalist sentiments early in the war, Cunningham returned to Little River District following his release, where his local prominence was so great, he was elected to South Carolina's pro-Patriot Provincial senate in 1778, defeating his Patriot rival James Williams. During the election, tensions ran high. At a campaign appearance, Williams attacked Cunningham, with Williams's wife participating in the fisticuffs.[29]

Despite the British army presence, the Ninety Six District had been awash in brutal civil war since the summer of 1780, with prominent local leaders like Cunningham and Williams taking leadership roles in either Loyalist or Whig militia units. It was in the Ninety Six district where Patriot militia had routed Loyalist militia at Musgrove's Mill on August 19, 1780, and the region's civil war had hardly settled since. Of this barbarism, one Patriot wrote the Whig residents of Ninety Six District were "like sheep among wolves," their Tory neighbors "set to Rob us taking all our living, horses, Cows, Sheep, Clothing . . . in fine Everything that sooted them. Until we were Stript Naked."[30] But according to Loyalist accounts, the Whigs often were wolf-like themselves: following the war, in April 1782, Loyalists of the Ninety Six and Camden districts filed a petition with the British House of Lords listing the names of three hundred men "massacred in this province" by Patriot marauders. And the actual number of murdered was fully "thrice that number," the petition claimed.[31]

On December 25, 1780, Morgan set up camp within the Ninety Six District at a crossing on the Pacolet River known as Grindal Shoals, not far from modern-day Spartanburg, South Carolina. Located along a main road that continued to Ninety Six, the property belonged to a well-known local Loyalist named Alexander Chesney and had only been secured the day before by the Patriot Little River militia. The location would've been well-known to local Patriot militia, who Morgan hoped would rally to him there. Morgan set up camp and immediately set about plundering Chesney's property.[32] Though such plunder may have been necessary to feed his hungry troops, it also intimidated the local Tory populace, the practice of terror and intimidation not limited to militia regiments.

That same night South Carolina militia colonel Andrew Pickens arrived in Morgan's camp with a hundred men from South Carolina and Georgia. The addition of Pickens was a coup for Morgan. Born in 1739 in Pennsylvania, Pickens had migrated to South Carolina with his family as a boy, eventually settling in the Long Cane Creek area in southwestern South

Carolina, not far from Ninety Six. There he met and married Rebecca Calhoun, an aunt of the famous South Carolina politician John C. Calhoun,
establishing himself as a farmer, justice of the peace, and militia captain in
the Long Canes settlement.

On November 19, 1775, Pickens fought in the Battle of Ninety Six, the
first military engagement of the American Revolution in the Carolinas. He
was one of about five hundred Patriots who defended an improvised stockade against about nineteen hundred Loyalists in a two-day gunfight that
ended in stalemate. Campaigning in the Augusta, Georgia, area following
the British capture of Savannah in late 1778, Pickens displayed his tactical
skills at the Battle of Kettle Creek on February 14, 1779, where he stalked
and surprised a superior Tory force.

After the British capture of Charleston in May 1780, Pickens accepted
British parole. With his Long Canes settlement located in between the
now strongly reinforced British outposts at Ninety Six and Augusta, further
resistance appeared useless. A devout Presbyterian who took his oaths seriously, he stuck to his word during the campaigns of fall 1780, despite the
efforts of many to lobby him back to the Patriot side. But after his plantation was plundered by a Tory raid in late fall 1780, Pickens considered the
terms of his parole violated, freeing him once more to join the Patriot
cause.[33] Both Morgan and Greene would find his services invaluable.

William Washington's eighty mounted dragoons had now also arrived
in the Ninety Six District and almost immediately found themselves em-
broiled in the region's civil war. Reporting to Greene on Sunday, December
24, from the property of Robert McClary, probably just south of the Enoree
River on the main road from Grindal Shoals to Ninety Six, which also
passed by a place called Hammond's Store,[34] Washington described Tory
marauding in the region: "The Distress of the Women and Children
stripp'd of every thing by plundering Villains cries aloud for redress."[35]

Morgan undoubtedly received several such pleas for "redress" as Patriot
militia units streamed into his camp during the last days of 1780; perhaps
Greene's instructions to "spirit up the people" were much on his mind when
he received word of a Tory raiding party operating about twenty miles from
his Grindal Shoals camp. The news may have come from William Washington himself.[36] "On the 27th (of December) I received Intelligence that
a Body of Georgian Tories About 250 in Number had advanced as far as
the Fair Forest and were insulting and Plundering The good people in that
Neighbourhood," Morgan later recounted to Greene.

On December 29, Morgan "dispatched Lieutenant Colonel Washington with his own Regiment and two hundred Militia Horse, who had joined me, to Attack them."[37] Learning of Washington's pursuit, the Tories retreated about twenty miles, south by southeast toward Ninety Six, to Hammond's Store near the modern-day town of Clinton in Laurens County. There, Washington's force came upon them.[38]

Primary accounts suggest what followed was a slaughter on scale with both the Waxhaws and the aftermath of King's Mountain, where accounts suggest the Overmountain Men attacked defenseless Loyalist soldiers as they were attempting to surrender. With Washington at Hammond's Store was a young South Carolina Patriot named Thomas Young, who left an account of the action in his Revolutionary War memoir: "When we came in sight, we perceived that the tories had formed in line on the brow of the hill opposite us. We had a long hill to descend and another to rise. Col. Washington and his dragoons gave a shout, drew swords, and charged down a hill like madmen. The tories fled in every direction without firing a gun. We took a great many prisoners and killed a few."[39]

The dead seem to have been quite more than "a few." Writing a day after the event, Morgan reported: "150 were killed and wounded & About 40 Taken Prisoners. What makes this success more Valuable it was Attained without the Loss of a man."[40] For perspective, 113 Continentals and Patriots were killed at the Waxhaws, compared to five British deaths; at King's Mountain, approximately 160 Loyalist militia were killed, with twenty-eight Americans killed.[41]

These numbers suggest the engagement at Hammond's Store was more slaughter than battle. Though his memory may have been fuzzy on the extent of the butchery, Young remembered one incident that characterizes it. "In Washington's corps there was a boy of fourteen or fifteen, a mere lad, who in crossing Tiger River was ducked by a blunder of his horse. The men laughed and jeered at him very much, at which he got very mad, and swore that boy or no boy, he would kill a man that day or die. He accomplished the former. I remember very well being highly amused at the little fellow charging round a crib after a tory, cutting and slashing away with his puny arm, til he brought him down."[42]

Following the attack, the retreating Tories fled along the Ninety Six road toward a Loyalist stockade called Williams Fort, located on the Little River in what is now Laurens County[43] approximately seven miles south of Hammond's Store.[44] The stockade had been established earlier that fall by

Patrick Ferguson on property seized from Patriot militia leader James Williams, the same James Williams who had wrestled with Robert Cunningham during the 1778 senate election. Williams was now dead from wounds received at King's Mountain, and the commander of the fort on his confiscated property was none other than his archrival, Robert Cunningham, whom Cornwallis had appointed brigadier general of the district's Loyalist militia on November 22, 1780.[45] With Cunningham at this time were approximately two hundred men of the Loyalist Little River militia.[46]

After the action at Hammond's Store, Washington ordered South Carolina militia under the command of Joseph Hayes, James Williams's replacement as commander of the Patriot Little River militia, along with a small detachment of approximately ten dragoons under Cornet James Simon, to pursue the retreating Loyalists.[47] According to one account, upon arriving at Williams Fort, Simon granted Cunningham and his men thirty minutes to consider terms of surrender. While Simon waited, Cunningham and most of the men deserted the stockade.[48] However, British accounts submitted to Cornwallis reported Cunningham and the majority of his militia abandoned the fort for Ninety Six on the night of December 30, leaving it for Hayes and Simon to capture the following morning; five Loyalists were killed and between twenty and thirty were captured in the ensuing action.[49] Hayes and Simon burned or demolished Williams Fort, then rejoined Washington.[50] Growing worried about the advanced position of Washington's detachment, Morgan ordered them to return to camp at Grindal Shoals.[51]

Greene apparently found nothing unusual about the casualty reports from Hammond's Store, expressing only satisfaction in his correspondence with Morgan: "Nothing could have afforded more pleasure than the successful attack of Lt. Col. Washington, upon the Tories. I hope it will be attended with a happy influence upon both Whig & tory, to the reclaiming of one, and encouragement of the other."[52] As Greene's southern campaign progressed, he would become despondent, at times morose, about the atrocities plaguing both sides of the Revolutionary cause; after Hammond's Store, he suggests naively it might sway opinion to the Patriots.

Though today we are perhaps more sensitive to such equivocations, nineteenth-century historians found little in the massacre to suggest moral ambiguity, instead preferring to cast the action at Hammond's Store as just deserts for Tory depredations. "It was a flight and not a conflict that ensued," admits William Johnson, writing in the 1820s. "Such were the bloody sacrifices at that time offered up at the shrine of civil discord! Posterity will never conceive an adequate idea of the dreadful state of society then prevailing in that unhappy country. Yet let not unmerited censure fall on the officers who commanded."[53]

Writing six decades later, historian David Shenck adds: "It was a bloody retribution that so early overtook these marauders. These men, cowardly and vindictive, had come to plunder and oppress their neighbors, supposing that there was no resistance to encounter, and they fell victims of justice before an outraged foe. . . . Such fiends deserved every vengeance that justice could inflict."[54]

And if the casualty figures from Hammond's Store hint at war crimes, William Washington's historic legacy remains untarnished by it, largely due to his heroics at Cowpens just nineteen days later. Washington's letter to Greene from December 24, where he expresses a yearning for "redress," indicates his state of mind, yet historian Lee F. McGee notes many of Washington's Continental dragoons were relatively raw recruits, serving with him less than a year, the Patriot militia fighting alongside them notoriously undisciplined.[55] Given the partisan tensions and bloodshed enflaming the region, any officer may have struggled to restrain his troops under similar circumstance, such arguments suggest. Yet the Waxhaws was a similar melee, and Banastre Tarleton's historic legacy is undeniably tarnished by it. Such are the fortunes of war.

CHAPTER 6

PERFECT INTENTIONS

"GREENE MARCHED ON Wednesday last toward the Cheraws . . . and that on Thursday and Friday last Morgan and Washington passed the Catawba," Cornwallis reported to Rawdon on December 26, relaying the news of a Loyalist spy. Cornwallis didn't believe the news, he told Rawdon, "but still the report is worth some attention."[1]

Even after confirming the reports, Cornwallis did "not think it possible for him [Greene] to strike any blow that would materially affect my movements,"[2] for Major General Alexander Leslie had arrived in Charleston with 2,500 British troops on December 14. Originally sent south by Clinton to disrupt Patriot bases and supply lines in the Chesapeake region, Leslie was ordered to Charleston to reinforce Cornwallis after the Loyalist defeat at King's Mountain. At Charleston, he left one thousand troops to help garrison the town, and he was now marching toward Cornwallis's camp at Winnsboro with his remaining 1,500 men, including 750 from the Brigade of Guards, one of England's best fighting units.[3] Also referenced as the "British Guards" in some texts, they were specially selected for the American conflict from three existing British Guard regiments—the First Foot Guards, the Coldstream Guards, and the Third Foot Guards—based on a demanding physical standard and exemplary service record.[4] According to Tarleton's memoir, Cornwallis believed any offensive operations contemplated by Greene in the east would soon be disregarded by news of Leslie's arrival.[5] "I do not think it necessary to make any alteration in my plan," Cornwallis wrote Rawdon on December 28.[6]

Greene was not aware of Leslie's arrival when he made the decision to split his army, learning of it only on December 24 in a letter from Francis Marion.[7] Though he had been tracking Leslie's movements through his correspondents prior to their Charleston arrival, he believed the British force bound for the Cape Fear region around Wilmington.[8] However, the development mattered little to Greene's plan, for his objectives were not offensive. Writing of Leslie's arrival, Greene complained to General Robert Howe: "What the enemy may attempt I know not, but it is certain, we have it not in our Power to attempt any Thing at all, or at least nothing but some little Partizan Strokes."[9]

Tarleton reported that while Cornwallis awaited Leslie's reinforcements, he "employed various measures, in order to acquire daily intelligence of the enemy, and to obtain a competent knowledge of the nature of the country in his front. . . . This information was peculiarly necessary for a general who was about to invade a province not remarkable for its fertility, and which has no navigable rivers to convey supplies to the interior parts of the country."[10]

Such measures seem obvious, given the strategic significance Cornwallis placed on his invasion plans. And hadn't Greene attempted something similar in the river surveys he'd ordered that same December? But there's little in Cornwallis's correspondence to suggest he devoted to these efforts the same careful attention Greene devoted to his. For the most part, Cornwallis appeared to rely on Tory reports, their scope not stretching far beyond his immediate environs near Winnsboro and northern South Carolina. In light of the mistakes to come, Tarleton's claims that Cornwallis sought "competent knowledge" in his "front," seem dubious, but perhaps only in comparison to Greene's more exhaustive efforts.

Yet even with Morgan now on his western flank, Cornwallis was determined to pursue his original North Carolina invasion plans: Tarleton would march up the Broad River to guard the western flank while Cornwallis would "move up the middle road" from Winnsboro, and "Leslie going at the same time up the road by the Wateree."[11] But Ninety Six was much on his mind, thanks as much to Pickens's defection as Morgan's detachment, and quickly he decided some action against Morgan must be undertaken.[12] In the South, Cornwallis had come to rely on one man for this type of operation. And so, on December 27, a note was delivered to Banastre Tarleton: "If it would not be inconvenient to you, his Lordship would like to see you tomorrow."[13]

Of Banastre Tarleton's brutal efficiency in the southern campaign, much has already been reported. In command of his British Legion, he had performed brilliantly, if ruthlessly, in the Charleston campaign, scoring important victories at Monck's Corner on April 14 and Lenud's Ferry on May 6. And at the Waxhaws on May 29, he not only annihilated the Continental army's resolve, permitting scores of defenseless or prostrate Continental soldiers to be slaughtered in the battle's aftermath, but also earned the contempt of the entire region, who would come to know him as "Bloody Ban," or more familiarly, "Banny."

Tarleton was born to a wealthy and prominent family in Liverpool, England, where his father served as mayor. He was educated at the University of Liverpool and Oxford, then briefly studied law in London, where he earned the reputation of a rake, gambling away an inherited fortune and devoting more time to the city's social circles than he spent at school. Clearly no scholar, he entered the army in April 1775 at the age of twenty-one, when his family purchased for him a cornet's commission in the King's Dragoon Guards. Shortly thereafter he volunteered for service in America and was sent to the Cape Fear region in May 1776 to support Clinton's first, unsuccessful attack on Charleston that June.

A talented horseman, Tarleton was one of four officers and twenty-five soldiers who captured Continental major general Charles Lee at White's Tavern in Basking, New Jersey, on December 13, 1776. Though a famous portrait of Tarleton painted by Sir Joshua Reynolds in 1782 depicts him as a dashing and handsome cavalry officer, with red hair and notably prominent legs wrapped in tight riding breeches, he was apparently rather stocky in appearance, with a prominent nose and a naturally arrogant demeanor. His biographers describe him as having a powerful frame and coarse features. Yet Tarleton's aristocratic background and natural aggression served him well in the British army. Considered by his superiors to be "full of enterprise and spirit, and anxious of every opportunity of distinguishing himself," he was promoted to captain in January 1778, skipping the rank of lieutenant, then given a brevet, or field, commission to lieutenant colonel of the British Legion later that August. "He had gone from cornet to lieutenant colonel in four years," notes historian John Buchanan, "and he was not quite twenty-four years old."[14]

The British Legion had been formed in 1778, originally recruited from Loyalists from New York and Philadelphia on the "American Establishment." This meant they were a "Provincial" unit, not entitled to regular British army pay and retirement.[15] As already described, a "legion" was a mobile unit imitating the classic formation of the Roman army and made popular in the eighteenth century by the writings of Saxe, among others, who advocated their use in mobile operations such as scouting, ambush, disrupting supply lines, and flanking maneuvers. A typical legion was formed in two rough halves: light cavalry (or "dragoons") and light infantry. Though the term "light" is used generically, essentially these were troops trained and outfitted to operate with more mobility than their "conventional" army counterparts. By the time of the American Revolution, each British regiment included a "light" company. But the primary role of British "light infantry" was to act as skirmishers, protecting the regular infantry's flanks during combat; the light troops of the legion typically operated in more mobile and independent operations.[16]

In the Charleston campaign, Tarleton's Legion occasionally operated in conjunction with a troop of the 17th Light Dragoons, a regular British army mounted unit. Known for their distinctive green cavalry jackets, similar to the ones worn by Henry Lee's Continental Legion, Tarleton's Legion was not immune to the snobbery and conventions of the British army; it is said the dragoons of the 17th refused to wear the green jackets because they held the "irregulars in some contempt."[17]

Perhaps this contempt was deserved, for even before the Waxhaws, Tarleton's Legion garnered a reputation for brutality found distasteful by some in the regular army. In one infamous incident, Legion dragoons stormed the Monck's Corner plantation of Sir John Colleton, a prominent Tory. Inside the house was Lady Colleton and several other women, whom the dragoons "attempted to ravish." Though they apparently escaped with their virtue intact, the women were "most barbously treated" by the Legion soldiers, some slashed with swords. British major Patrick Ferguson, fighting in conjunction with Tarleton at this time, was so incensed he wanted the offenders put "to instant death," though they were only arrested and sent to Charleston for punishment.[18]

For some historians, the incident showcases the disciplinary breakdowns Tarleton too often tolerated. In Tarleton's defense, terror was part of the Legion's job, inevitably requiring some measure of collateral damage. "Cavalry acts chiefly upon the nerves," Cornwallis wrote during the summer of 1780, "and if it loses its terror, it loses its greatest force."[19]

In battle during the southern campaigns, Tarleton was known for swift and decisive attack, taking advantage of his Legion's mobility with sword and bayonet charges that typically overwhelmed his terrorized opponents. Indeed, Tarleton relied on the instantaneous assault so often, he became well known for it among his opponents, though at first there seemed little anyone could do to stop it. But it was in the aftermath of battle where his discipline sometimes faltered, as at the Waxhaws and Colleton's. Comprised of Loyalists, Legion soldiers were more prone than their conventional army counterparts to the vicious political animosity afflicting both Tory and Rebel during the American Revolution, resulting in the looting, barbarism, and terror that characterized the war in the South.[20] And as the campaign progressed, and new Legion recruits were added from the South to replace those from the North lost to death, injury, or desertion, these loyalties faltered. Historians Lawrence E. Babits and Joshua B. Howard report of the 123 men who enlisted in the British Legion from August to October 1780, more than one hundred were former American soldiers captured at Camden, primarily Continentals from the Maryland and Delaware regiments. "Faced with a choice between a slow death on a prison hulk or service with a British unit that would feed, clothe, and pay them," most of these Continentals, "chose the latter option."[21] Though these new recruits helped fill Tarleton's ranks, their allegiances were suspect.

Tarleton had stumbled at times during the southern campaign, most notably at Blackstock's Farm on November 20, 1780. There his combined force of 520 was defeated by up to one thousand Patriot militia under Thomas Sumter, fighting from a hilltop position behind the defenses of the farm outbuildings and a stout wooden fence. In typical fashion, Tarleton ordered his cavalry forward in a hurried frontal attack, without sufficiently reconnoitering Sumter's position or waiting for his infantry and artillery, which had been left behind during the day's long pursuit. The results were disastrous. In fierce fighting that lasted approximately two hours, Tarleton lost ninety-two killed and seventy-six wounded. Rebel casualties were estimated at three dead and four wounded.[22]

But even at Blackstocks, the good luck that marked his southern campaign clung to Tarleton, for when the rebels vanished in the night following the battle, he took the field, allowing him to claim some measure of victory from the defeat. Cornwallis seemed to enjoy a special affinity for his two most talented young officers, Tarleton and Rawdon, and even though his letters to Rawdon convey more personal sentiment, his trust in Tarleton's capabilities remained strident, despite the misstep at Blackstocks. "You must use your discretion and live as well as you can . . . always endeavouring to strike some blow if an opening should offer, and taking up all that have been violent against us to change for our friends," Cornwallis had instructed Tarleton back in November,[23] and it was with this same trust in his most successful officer that Cornwallis now summoned Tarleton to Winnsboro.

We have no record of precisely what was discussed between Cornwallis and Tarleton at that December 28 meeting, though undoubtedly it included strategy for the coming invasion of North Carolina. Presumably they discussed the disposition of troops, for at this time Tarleton was in command of his 450-man Legion, along with a battalion of the British 71st infantry, the 71st light infantry, and an artillery company with two field pieces which included the 16th Regiment's light infantry, in all a little over eight hundred men.[24] Noteworthy is the composition of the 71st. Originally raised in Scotland in 1775 by general Simon Fraser, the 71st was a veteran regiment known as the "Highlanders" that fought in kilts of the "Black Watch" pattern.

But as of that date, there appeared to be no urgency to the matter of Morgan, as Leslie was not yet in position to commence the winter campaign and Cornwallis did not believe the garrison at Ninety Six threatened. According to Tarleton's biographer, Tarleton's mission at this time was to provide security to the Ninety Six District and prevent any "punishment that Morgan and the militia might inflict upon the Loyalists."[25]

That changed on January 1, when Cornwallis received news of Hammond's Store and the fall of Williams Fort. A Tory spy named David George reported to Cornwallis he was "well inform'd" that Morgan and Washington intended to "march as fast as they can for Ninety Six" with artillery and up to three thousand men.[26] The report was wildly inaccurate. Morgan was still at Grindal Shoals, had no cannon, and had ordered Washington and his men to return there.[27] Yet the slaughter at Hammond's Store was yielding a disruptive effect, leading to panic and wild rumor among the Loyalists of the region, upon whom Cornwallis relied for intelligence. And with the (false) reports that Morgan was headed to Ninety Six with cannon, Cornwallis decided he must reinforce the outpost there.

At this time, Tarleton was camped at Brierly's Ferry on the Broad River, roughly halfway between Winnsboro and Ninety Six, and about forty miles south of Morgan's position on the Pacolet. On January 1, a messenger arrived there with orders from Cornwallis for Tarleton to cross the Broad River and defend Ninety Six against Morgan's reported attack.[28] The next day, Cornwallis wrote to Tarleton: "If Morgan . . . is anywhere within your reach, I should wish you to push him to the utmost. . . . Ninety Six is of so much consequence that no time is to be lost."[29]

Now on the move, Tarleton soon determined Morgan was still on the Pacolet, posing no immediate threat to Ninety Six. Yet his blood was up. Tarleton halted at Brooke's River Plantation, just twenty miles north of Brierly's, to provision his men and forage his horses. Here he proposed a scheme to Cornwallis: "When I advance, I must either destroy Morgan's corps, or push it before me over Broad River, toward King's Mountain." Meanwhile, Tarleton suggested Cornwallis move north with the main army, putting Morgan in a trap between the two British divisions. "The advance of the army should commence (when his lordship orders his corps to move) onward's for King's Mountain," Tarleton wrote.[30] Cornwallis replied the next day, January 5. "You have exactly done what I wished you to do and understand my intentions perfectly."[31]

Historians have long obsessed over Greene's decision to split his army. Cornwallis's decision to do the same prior to Cowpens receives scant attention, perhaps because the maxim against it pertains only to an inferior force. In the early winter of 1781, Cornwallis's force was superior in almost every way. With the arrival of Leslie's 1,500 reinforcements, Cornwallis now had in his command a trained and seasoned army of approximately 3,800 regulars for his North Carolina invasion, not including the 9,500 more occupying Charleston and a string of outposts across the Carolina frontier. Greene's Continental army, not including his untrained and notoriously unreliable militia, now consisted roughly of 1,200 men, the vast majority poorly clothed and shod. With Morgan were approximately six hundred of those regulars.[32]

Cornwallis's army was better trained, better equipped, and better armed. Arguably, they were better disciplined. But they were burdened with custom, and perhaps over acclimated to the more civilized confines of Europe and the American Northeast. They traveled heavily, with accoutrements, and enjoyed their creature comforts, particularly when preparing for a long campaign, such as the one Cornwallis envisioned for North Carolina. Like Greene's trust in Morgan, Cornwallis trusted Tarleton implicitly, perhaps too much. Granted, he had little reason to think otherwise, despite the setback at Blackstocks. Tarleton was no Morgan, as we shall soon see, though Cornwallis placed the fate of his army in Tarleton's hands.

And with Greene over a hundred miles away, Cornwallis had Morgan in a trap of Greene's own making. He need only act decisively to set the snare. At Tarleton's request, he reinforced Tarleton with cavalry from the 17th Light Dragoons and 167 infantry of the 7th Royal Fusiliers, so named because it was originally formed as a *fusilier* regiment, or ordnance regiment, to escort artillery. And then he waited. In his letter to Tarleton on January 5, Cornwallis proposed they commence their joint operation against Morgan in two days, on January 7, but Tarleton was delayed until January 11 while he awaited his baggage and reinforcements from the 7th Fusiliers, bringing his total force to approximately 1,100 men.[33] But this was no normal 1,100 men. Indicative of the great trust he placed in Tarleton, Cornwallis had sent him the cream of his invasion force, in particular the "light" companies of the 17th, 16th, and 71st, along with the regular infantry of the 71st "Highlanders." Though the 7th Fusiliers were recent recruits, the rest were seasoned, veteran troops, including the entirety of Cornwallis's "light" troops, his regular soldiers trained and equipped for more mobile fighting in support of the regular infantry.

Leslie and his 1,500 men, along with wagons and baggage to support the North Carolina invasion, were now at Camden, where they had been deliberately halted in an effort to "conceal from the American general the road which the British army meant to take" into North Carolina.[34] Sometime prior to January 6, Cornwallis abandoned his plan to march into North Carolina in three columns, perhaps because he had sent so many of his own troops to reinforce Tarleton. That day he ordered Leslie to march from Camden and follow him to the Broad River region for a proposed rendezvous at Bullock Creek, near present-day Fort Mill.[35]

But the incessant rains that had plagued both Continental and British through December continued into January. Though Cornwallis finally broke camp at Winnsboro on January 8, he halted at a place called McAlister's Plantation on January 9, informing Rawdon, "I think it prudent to remain here a day or two longer, otherwise by the corps on my flanks being so far behind, I should be in danger of losing my communication. I have not heard from Tarleton this day, nor am I sure whether he has passed the Enoree."[36]

With three columns moving separately through rotten weather and rough terrain, Cornwallis's communication system faltered. On January 12, still at McAlister's, he wrote to Leslie, "The Broad River exceedingly high,

I have not heard from Tarleton. . . . I believe he is as much embarrassed by the waters as you are." On the same day, he informed Rawdon, "the rains have impeded operations on all sides."[37]

But earlier that morning, Tarleton learned the location of Morgan's camp at Grindal Shoals. Dashing off a report of his findings to Cornwallis, he was on the move just a few hours later. Though the Tyger and Enoree Rivers were too swollen to ford on foot, Tarleton built rafts for his infantry, crossing both rivers in the next two days.[38] On January 14, Cornwallis responded to Tarleton's report about Morgan's camp, indicating he would resume his own march the next day,[39] but by January 17, he and his army had traveled only forty miles north of Winnsboro to Turkey Creek, where he awaited a junction with Leslie at the farm of William Hillhouse.[40] It was at Hillhouse's farm on Turkey Creek where Cornwallis would receive news of the Battle of Cowpens.

According to Tarleton's memoir, he sent word to Cornwallis on the fourteenth that he was preparing to pass the Pacolet to commence his pursuit of Morgan "and requested his lordship to proceed up the eastern bank [of the Broad] without delay."[41] In a letter to Tarleton dated January 16, Cornwallis says he has not heard from Tarleton since the report of January 12,[42] making Tarleton's latter recollection about a correspondence on the fourteenth questionable. Clinton, in his own memoir, seemed to believe Tarleton's side of the story: "As Lieutenant Colonel Tarleton had not received any letter or order from Lord Cornwallis since that of the 14th, and was from thence persuaded His Lordship was in a situation to cooperate as had been preconcerted, he did not hesitate to move . . . against the enemy."[43]

Whether due to miscommunication between Tarleton or Cornwallis, or false assumption on either side, Cornwallis was not in position to cut off Morgan's retreat. Blame it on Cornwallis or blame it on Tarleton. Blame it on the weather or blame it on the whole damn eighteenth century, its lousy roads and antiquated communications. Whatever the reason, the perfect intentions Tarleton and Cornwallis shared earlier in January were no longer in accord. Finally across the Enoree and Tyger Rivers, with a superior fighting force and only the Pacolet remaining between him and his prey, Tarleton the hunter would not be delayed.

CRIME OF WAR HAMMOND'S STORE may have been, but it helped Morgan achieve Greene's strategic objective to "spirit up the people,"[44] in Morgan's opinion a bit too well. General William Davidson arrived at Morgan's camp with 120 North Carolina militia from Mecklenburg County and soon departed to collect another five hundred (thus missing the Battle of Cowpens).[45] Major Joseph McDowell arrived with another 190 North Carolina riflemen from Burke County.[46] Four brigades of South Carolina militia were formed under Andrew Pickens and camped in the Fair Forest community near present-day Union, South Carolina, not far from Grindal Shoals.[47]

The problem was that Morgan had few means of feeding this expanding force. Like other regions of the Carolinas encountered by the Continental army, the Pacolet River region was now depleted of provisions. "The Militia are increasing fast, so that we Cannot be Supplied in this Nieghbourhood more than two or three Days at farthest," Morgan complained to Greene. Magnifying the problem was the Patriot militia's practice of traveling on horseback, meaning Morgan not only had to provide feed for his Continental horses but for the militia mounts as well. In response, he proposed an expedition west into Georgia. "To me it appears an Adviseable Scheme," Morgan wrote to Greene on December 31, 1780, less than a week after arriving on the Pacolet. "I have consulted with Genl Davidson and Col. Pickens whether we could secure a safe Retreate should we be pushed by a superior Force. They tell me it can be easily Effeted by passing up the Savannah."[48]

While he awaited Greene's reply to this proposal to move into Georgia, Morgan directed his commissary officer Captain C.K. Chitty to call on militia colonel William Hill to seek assistance in the establishment of "magazines of forage and provisions." The militia leader from what was called the "New Acquisition District" in South Carolina's Catawba River Valley, located south of modern-day Charlotte around the South Carolina city of Fort Mill, Hill was a close subordinate of South Carolina brigadier general Thomas Sumter, who was recently incapacitated from a serious wound received at the Battle of Blackstocks on November 20, 1780, though still actively directing militia during his recuperation. Greene's orders of December 16 had given Morgan command of all the South Carolina militia in the vicinity, including the "militia lately under the command of Brig'r Genl Sumter."[49] But Greene and Sumter appeared to have different opinions on this matter. Hill refused Chitty's request, assuring him that General Sumter had directed him to obey no orders from Morgan, unless they came through Sumter himself.[50]

The matter became a minor diplomatic dustup, with Greene demanding an explanation from Sumter, and Sumter attempting to disregard it as only a misunderstanding. Yet the incident would portend more serious conflicts to come between Greene and Sumter. Their feud would continue to grow in consequence when Greene returned to South Carolina following the Battle of Guilford Courthouse and would end only when Sumter resigned his commission to join the South Carolina legislature in the closing stages of the southern campaign.[51] And it is worth noting that of the South Carolina militia that fought so valiantly at the forthcoming Battle of Cowpens, none consisted of units from South Carolina's Catawba River region, the area considered most loyal to Sumter.

While Morgan awaited Greene's response to his plan to move into Georgia and fretted over provisions, the incessant rain plaguing Cornwallis also settled on Morgan's Pacolet River camp, exacerbating the rheumatism or sciatica that had tormented him the last several years. Already the aching in his joints and bones was making it uncomfortable for Morgan to ride a horse, and from experience, he knew the discomfort would only become worse the longer he stayed in the field.[52]

Greene would soon respond, opposing Morgan's plan. "Should you go into Georgia and the enemy push this way your whole force will be useless," he responded sensibly in a letter written January 8.[53] But after his letter of January 4, Morgan did not write to Greene again until January 15. The writer M.F. Treacy explains this curious lapse by suggesting Morgan's January 15 letter was written over a period of time and interruptions.[54] Indeed, the letter does ramble over various incidents and themes—more background on the incident at Hammond's Store, the squabble with William Hill over the instructions of Thomas Sumter, complaints about forage and the inadequacy of his force. In this light, the letter provides insight on Morgan's disposition in the days leading up to the Battle of Cowpens. The Old Waggoner seems disgruntled here, tired and grumpy. Clearly he has become frustrated with the ambiguities of Greene's strategy; the bouts of sciatica or rheumatism were becoming ever more intolerable in the gloomy, wet weather. Yet this litany of complaints ends with blockbuster news: "Colonel Tarleton has crossed the Tyger at Musgrove's Mill. . . . It is more than probable we are his object."[55]

Charles, Lord Cornwallis, left, from later in his career. Considered England's most able field commander during the American Revolution, Cornwallis was beloved by his troops but subject to bouts of despondency and carelessness that limited his strategic vision and execution. (*New York Public Library*) Son of a Quaker merchant, **Nathanael Greene,** right, learned warfare from the books he read as a young man, and later, as an inexperienced general in the makeshift Continental army. His prodigious, relentless intellect made him a superior strategist but often guided him toward caution, not daring, on the battlefield. (*Yale University Art Gallery*)

Horatio Gates, left. The Hero of Saratoga's disastrous defeat at the Battle of Camden on August 16, 1780, ruined his military reputation but permitted George Washington to appoint Nathanael Greene as commander of the Continental army's Southern Department. (*National Portrait Gallery*) Brigadier General **Charles O'Hara,** right, commanded the British Guards, a crack brigade of specially selected troops. "With all these Storms gathering round Us some desperate Vigerous measure however desperate was to be adopted," he would write of Cornwallis's decision to pursue Greene across North Carolina. (*New York Public Library*)

Daniel Morgan, left. Born of humble circumstances, Morgan's stunning victory at Cowpens earned him a Congressional gold medal and a revered place in American history. "The defeat of his majesty's troops at the Cowpens formed a very principal link in the chain of circumstances which led to the independence of America," observed one British historian. (*Independence National Historical Park*) Just twenty-six years old at Cowpens, **Banastre Tarleton,** right, was one of Cornwallis's most trusted officers, but by 1780 his preference for the straight-ahead charge was well-known to the Americans. (*New York Public Library*)

William Washington, left, was a distant cousin of George Washington who proved himself an able cavalry officer under the command of Morgan and Greene. "Bold, collected, and persevering, he preferred the heat of action to the collection and sifting of intelligence," observed Henry Lee. (*National Park Service*) Alongside Morgan, **Henry Lee,** right, was Greene's most talented officer. Though today perhaps best remembered as the father of Robert E. Lee, Lee's memoir of the American Revolution provides a valuable and lively account of the Race to the Dan. (*Independence National Historical Park*)

"The Battle of Cowpens" by Frederick Kemmelmeyer, c. 1809. "The Troops I have had the Honor to command have been so fortunate as to obtain a compleat victory," Morgan reported proudly to Nathanael Greene of the battle's outcome. (*Yale University Art Gallery*)

Andrew Pickens, left, was a highly regarded militia commander whose arrival at Morgan's camp on Grindal Shoals roused the American cause. For his heroics at Cowpens, Pickens received a sword from the Continental Congress, the highest official honor awarded to a militia officer during the American Revolution. (*New York Public Library*) **John Eager Howard**, right, was a Maryland officer whose cool performance under fire turned the tide at Cowpens. A line from Maryland's state song, "Maryland, My Maryland," honors his heroics there, and later he would serve as the state's governor. (*National Park Service*)

Another Maryland officer, **Otho Holland Williams**, left, replaced Daniel Morgan in command of the "Flying Army" during the Race to the Dan, permitting Greene and the bulk of the Southern Army to escape across the river. (*New York Public Library*) Wounded in action a few weeks before Cowpens, South Carolina militia general **Thomas Sumter**, right, would feud with Daniel Morgan over status and command in western South Carolina. After the Race to the Dan, he would become one of Nathanael Greene's most important allies in the effort to liberate South Carolina. (*Columbia Museum of Art, South Carolina*)

CHAPTER 7

BANNY IS COMING

A s Daniel Morgan worried over supplies and contemplated a move west in the weeks before Cowpens, a father brought his nine-year-old son into the Continental camp at Grindal Shoals. The boy had a story for the general, the man said, and he wanted Morgan to hear it from the child himself.

Morgan offered the lad a gold guinea for his tale, but the boy refused. "I drove the old bull and some potatoes down to the British camp, and daddy told me not to forget anything I heard," the boy said. He told Morgan he was near the tent of General Cornwallis when Tarleton arrived. "The colonel was ordered to take a thousand men and follow you up and fight you wherever you could be found, and they know where you are now." Morgan thanked the child for the news, urging him to accept the gold piece, but still the boy refused. Instead he asked to serve as a drummer in Morgan's army.[1]

Apocryphal perhaps, but the story illustrates the nature of backcountry espionage during the American Revolution, where even a nine-year-old boy could be a spy. In his memoir of the campaign, William Seymour wrote, "On the 27th [of December] the General received intelligence that Colonel Tarleton was advancing in order to surprise us."[2] This corresponds with the meeting between Cornwallis and Tarleton on December 28 (assuming Seymour mistook the date by a day). Morgan made no mention of this intelligence in his letter to Greene of January 4, though even Greene had learned of the British plan by January 15, writing in a letter Morgan would not receive until after Cowpens, "Co. Tarlton is said to be on his way to pay you a visit. I doubt not but he will have a decent reception and proper dismission."[3]

With intelligence networks superior to Cornwallis's, Morgan likely received several accounts of British movements throughout his stay at Grindal Shoals; quality of intelligence was the issue, not quantity. But sometime around January 14, Morgan received definitive news Tarleton was headed his way. He broke camp at Grindal Shoals that day and marched approximately ten miles north, camping that night at a place called "Burr's Mill." It is from Burr's Mill that he sent his letter of January 15, the long, grumpy diatribe about provision and irascible militia that ends with the news, "Colonel Tarleton has crossed the Tyger at Musgrove's Mill. . . . It is more than probable we are his object."[4]

And even though news of Tarleton's approach could not have come as a surprise, it forced Morgan into deliberations for which there was no clear answer. He knew he didn't want to stand and fight Tarleton on the Pacolet. "A successful defense of the fords of the Pacolet would be attended by no other result, than to give Cornwallis time to gain his rear," writes Morgan biographer James Graham.[5] With Cornwallis approaching from the east, he would have to retreat north. But to do that he needed to get his army across the Broad in advance of both British forces, no simple task with the notoriously hard-charging Tarleton in his rear and winter rains swelling every river and creek in his path.

As he headed toward the Broad, Morgan's initial objective probably was Cherokee Ford, a popular Broad River crossing just east of modern-day Gaffney, South Carolina. But given the recent rains, fording there was no guarantee, and he feared being pinned by Tarleton against a flooded river. His pace was encumbered by his wagons, and he was not yet joined by all the militia units he had dispersed throughout the surrounding countryside to feed and forage. In particular, he awaited the arrival of the trusted Andrew Pickens, who had departed camp earlier in the month to recruit more troops and was en route back with 150 militia soldiers. And instinctively, Morgan understood if he crossed the Broad, the militia he had with him would consider it a retreat, scattering and returning to their homes, eliminating any opportunity to fight.

He needed a well-known meeting place on the west side of the Broad to collect his militia and scout the river for crossings. By luck, there was one nearby: Cowpens. At the time it was known as "Hannah's Cowpens" after its owner, just one of many "cow pens," or open meadows that dotted the colonial countryside, where drovers gathered their stock before taking them to market. Hannah's Cowpens was located at an intersection on the Green River Road, which led north to the Broad River, and was known throughout the region.[6] It was here the Overmountain Men had joined with the South Carolina militia on the night before the battle at King's Mountain in October 1780, just four short months ago, and it was here where Daniel Morgan would call in his militia.[7]

On the night of January 15, with Morgan camped at Burr's Mill, Tarleton reached the Pacolet, only to find its crossings still guarded by Morgan's pickets. Believing the guards indicated Morgan was still in camp at Grindal Shoals, Tarleton ordered his men north, toward a crossing near Wofford's Ironworks, outside modern-day Spartanburg. Patriot pickets followed Tarleton up the east side of the river, but Tarleton double backed on them during the night, crossing the unguarded Pacolet early in the morning of January 16, only to find Morgan's Grindal Shoals camp deserted.[8]

Upon learning Tarleton had now crossed the Pacolet, Morgan quickly broke camp at Burr's Mill that same morning, January 15, his fires still burning. He marched all day, approximately twelve miles,[9] arriving at Cowpens early in the evening. Opposing scouts were monitoring the progress of both armies all day; as his men settled in, Morgan received news Tarleton now occupied his camp at Burr's Mill, where they were enjoying the breakfasts the Continentals had left cooking in their fires.[10] Time was running out; by the next day, Tarleton would be upon him. Morgan paused now to survey the landscape and consider his contingencies. One historian even has Morgan, his body wracked with sciatic pain, climbing a tree to look over the Cowpens plain from above.[11]

Whether or not he observed it from treetop, Morgan's survey of Cowpens revealed a gently rolling field. Approximately five hundred yards long, and equally as wide, the meadow was dotted with trees and covered with coarse wild grass. Much has been written about the topography of Cowpens, and indeed, the field did rise and fall, though probably not much more than forty-five feet, its vertical profile today. About fifteen feet wide, the Green River Road traversed the high ground south-to-north through the plain. On both the east and west side were small ravines, where water rolled off the plain to create wetland areas covered in thick cane. As the road emerged from the forest to the south, it rose prominently about twenty feet to a rise overlooking the western ravine, then followed a more gradual rise along the high ground to a ridge about three hundred yards north of the treeline. Behind this ridge, the road dipped again into a swale, then rose gradually to another ridge about eighty yards north of the first. Behind this second ridge was more open wood and the Broad River six miles in his rear.[12]

Morgan realized that as Tarleton, following him on the Green River Road, emerged from the forest to the south into the open meadow, he would be looking upward toward the rising ground. Morgan understood instinctively he could use this topography to his advantage. For he knew his foe. Many of the militia in his camp had fought Tarleton at the nearby Blackstock's Farm on November 20, 1780. From them he would've heard of Tarleton's impulsive, hard-charging style, if not from his Maryland and Delaware Continentals, who had faced him at Camden. Tarleton's tactics seem "to have borne a stronger affinity to the ferocity of the bloodhound than to the bravery of the bulldog," wrote Graham, "and to have been more thoroughly aroused by the flight of the enemy than by his opposition."[13]

But Morgan's mind was still not set on battle, though word spread through the countryside a fight was coming. Militia soldiers like Thomas Young welcomed the news. "We arrived at the field of the Cowpens about sun-down, and were told that there we should meet the enemy. The news was received with great joy by the army. We were very anxious for battle, and many a hearty curse had been vented against Gen. Morgan during that day's March, for retreating, as we thought, to avoid a fight."[14]

Maryland colonel John Eager Howard recalled, "I well remember that parties were coming in most of the night, and calling on Morgan for ammunition, and to know the state of affairs. They were all in good spirits, related circumstances of Tarleton's cruelty, and expressed the strongest desire to check his progress." But according to Howard, it was the arrival of the stalwart Pickens that finally convinced Morgan to stand and fight.[15] And sometime during the night, Morgan received news Cornwallis was still at Turkey Creek, awaiting the arrival of Leslie, meaning any junction between the two divisions was still at least a day or two away, and strengthening his resolve to face Tarleton.[16]

His decision made, Morgan began to lay out his legendary battle plan. As far as three miles in advance of Cowpens, Morgan would place pickets, or "videttes," their job to skirmish with the British vanguard and provide advance notice of Tarleton's approach. These skirmishers consisted of both

Georgia militia and a platoon of Continental dragoons. On his first line, atop the rise closest to the southern woods, Morgan would place militia sharpshooters. Next would come his main militia line, under the command of Andrew Pickens. This line he would place at the main ridge, or "Militia Ridge," about 150 yards north of his skirmishers.[17]

At the crest of the second rise, or "Morgan Hill," Morgan would place his line of Continentals. This line would be commanded by John Eager Howard, the experienced Maryland lieutenant colonel, its core the experienced Maryland and Delaware infantry, including Captain Robert Kirkwood's company. In reserve, behind the main line, Morgan would position his cavalry under the command of William Washington.[18]

In placing his irregular troops at the front of his formation, Morgan's disposition broke military orthodoxy, which demanded the strongest troops be placed in front. His officers protested as much. "The profession of arms does not often attract innovative minds," noted John Buchanan. "This untutored son of the frontier [Morgan] was the only general in the American Revolution, on either side, to produce a significant original tactical thought."[19]

And Morgan knew his troops. The battle plan allowed his militia to fire at the approaching British from a relatively safe distance with their accurate rifles but didn't require them to stand and face a deadly bayonet charge. It also took advantage of the mixed rifle/musket formations he had employed at Saratoga. Once the fighting reached his main line, his regular Continental infantry in the center of the line could meet the British bayonet charge, while his riflemen would pour in fire from the flanks.

As the officers dispensed field assignments to the troops, Morgan visited their campfires all through the night, joking with the young men and rehashing his old anecdote about owing the British a lick, challenging militia from one state to outdo the others, perhaps even displaying the scars from his long-ago whipping to the rapt crowd.[20] The sciatica that had tormented him through the day disappeared in the bonhomie of the night and the adrenaline of a coming fight.

Thomas Young remembered it well: "It was upon this occasion I was more perfectly convinced of the Gen.'s qualifications to command militia, than I had ever before been. He went among the volunteers, helped them fix their swords, joked with them about their sweet-hearts, told them to keep in good spirits, and the day would be ours. And long after I laid down, he was going about among the soldiers encouraging them, and telling them that the old wagoner would crack his whip over Ben (Tarleton) in the morning, as sure as they lived. 'Just hold your heads, boys, three fires,' he would say, 'and you are free, and then when you return to your homes, how the old folks will bless you, and the girls kiss you, for your gallant conduct!' I don't believe he slept a wink that night!"[21]

While he joshed with the men, he prepared for battle. Expresses were sent to militia that had not yet joined his camp. As the militia came in, they were organized into smaller companies within their own battalions to enhance control during the chaos to come.[22] Meanwhile, patrolling parties were sent in "different directions on the flanks and in the front, to watch the movements of the enemy, and guard against stratagem or surprise."[23] He ordered cattle slaughtered and made sure his men were well fed. To his militia commanders he ordered that each of their men receive "twenty-four rounds of balls prepared and ready for use, before they retired."[24] Historian Lawrence Babits believes even this disposition of ammunition contained strategic foresight: "By stipulating the number of bullets a man carried, Morgan knew how long a unit could keep firing and when it should be ordered to the rear. . . . Men could be withdrawn while still possessing ammunition for self-defense and psychological security, reducing chances of a rout."[25]

Concerned about Tarleton's superiority in cavalry, he asked for militia volunteers to serve as dragoons during the battle. About forty-five men immediately volunteered, including Thomas Young. "We drew swords that night, and were informed we had authority to press any horse not belonging to a dragoon or an officer, into our service for the day," he recalled.[26] Here, also, is evidence of Morgan's innovation, though born out of necessity: rarely in the southern campaigns did Continental officers employ mounted militia in formal battle.[27] As the night wore on, he ordered his supply wagons to move five miles to the rear, almost to the Broad River, in case of retreat.

While Morgan bantered with his men and prepared them for battle, Tarleton continued his pursuit. At Burr's Mill, his soldiers dined on the half-cooked breakfasts the Patriots had left behind.[28] The night was filled with the comings and goings of spies and patrols. Early in the night "a party of determined loyalists made an American colonel prisoner, who had casually left the line of march, and conducted him to the British camp." Tarleton interrogated the American, who told him Morgan had almost two thousand men. This may have been a deliberate ruse, the American a Morgan spy. Nevertheless, the intelligence inspired Tarleton to strike quickly on the morrow, "to impede the junction of reinforcements, said to be approaching, and likewise to prevent his [Morgan's] passing the Broad River." At midnight, Tarleton received reports on the approach of a "corps of mountaineers." Ever since King's Mountain, the British had been paranoid about the return of the Overmountain Men, the fierce militia from the mountain settlements of western North Carolina, eastern Tennessee, and southwestern Virginia that had destroyed Ferguson. The news "proved the exigency of moving to watch the enemy closely, in order to take advantage of any favourable opportunity that might offer."[29]

Though his men had been marching hard for days, Tarleton ordered the British camp broken and their march commenced at 3 a.m. With their baggage left behind at Burr's Mill, Tarleton's soldiers traveled through the night, the ground "being broken and much intersected by creeks and ravines."[30] Just before dawn, an advance guard of British cavalry encountered Morgan's advance scouts. Tarleton ordered his dragoons to move forward and "harass the rear of the enemy. The march had not continued long in this manner, before the commanding officer in front reported that the American troops were halted and forming." In his memoir, Tarleton recounted conversations with his Tory guides about the ground Morgan occupied and the country in his rear: "They said the woods were open and free from swamps; that the part of the Broad River . . . was about six miles distant from the enemy's left flank."[31]

In short, a field ideal to Tarleton, or so it seemed. In his own memoir, Tarleton's fellow cavalry officer Henry Lee would belabor this point: "The ground about the Cowpens is covered with open wood, admitting the operation of cavalry with facility. . . . His [Morgan's] flanks had no resting-place, but were exposed to be readily turned; and Broad River ran parallel to his rear, forbidding the hope of a safe retreat in the event of disaster."[32] Thanks to the scholarship of Babits, we know these flanks were not as open as they seemed, for they were guarded somewhat by the marshes at the edges of the ravines, but the point remains that Tarleton's superiority in cavalry gave him a decided advantage on the open field.

Morgan knew his hunter was approaching. He ordered the infantry horses secured well to the rear of the field of battle, saddled and bridled in case of immediate need, but closely guarded to prevent misappropriation by the skittish and terrified. He had the camp woken early, in time to prepare a breakfast. In the early morning light, the stentorian voice that had been such a source of spirit and bonhomie the night before echoed out over the Cowpens plain, "Boys get up, Bannie is coming!"[33]

As the weak, winter sun rose over the Cowpens plain, with the sound of picket fire echoing through the forest, Morgan made his final dispositions, placing the militia that had come in during the night and reminding each line of their orders. Though he had spent many hours the night before walking from fire to fire, explaining the battle formation, surely he still called out to his troops with reminders and alterations, even as the men were cleaning up their breakfast and preparing for war.

At the start of the battle, his forward skirmish line consisted of approximately 150 militia sharpshooters armed with rifles. North Carolina militia were under the command of Major Joseph McDowell, while the Georgia troops were commanded by Major John Cunningham. Joining them on Cunningham's left were South Carolina state troops under Major Samuel Hammond. These troops were likely not deployed in a formal line but organized in loose clumps surrounding their officers, using the scattered trees and terrain for cover.[34]

About 150 yards away, on "Militia Ridge," was the main militia line under the overall command of Andrew Pickens, consisting mostly of local South Carolina Regiments, including the Spartan and Fair Forest (or Second Spartan) regiments from modern-day Spartanburg County, along with troops from the Little River Regiment of modern-day Laurens County.[35]

At Militia Ridge, Morgan used a "reverse slope" defense, placing his men on the northern downslope beyond the crest of the ridge. This achieved several tactical advantages. First, as the British advanced up the slope from the south, the militia position was concealed behind the crest of the ridge. Also, by this point in the war, the Continental officers had recognized a British tendency to overshoot with their inaccurate, smoothbore muskets; Morgan's strategy forced the British to shoot downhill at his militia, accentuating this bad habit. In contrast, the approaching British would be silhouetted at the top of the ridge, enhancing their target profile for his sharpshooting militia. Finally, the boggy ground on the east and west side of the downslope would provide some cover for the militia flanks.[36]

Another 150 yards north, at the top of the second rise, or "Morgan Hill," was John Edgar Howard's light infantry of Maryland and Delaware Continentals anchoring the center. On their left were Virginia riflemen under the command of Major Francis Triplett joined by some North Carolina

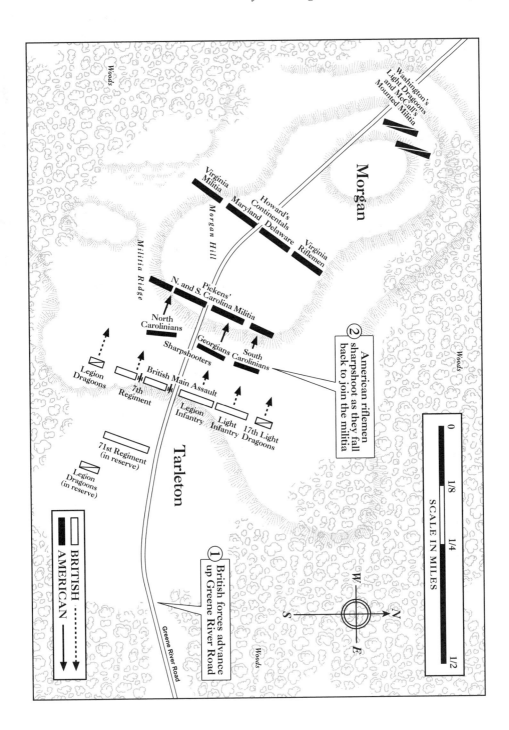

militia. On the right were Virginia militia under the command of Captain Edmund Tate, joined by some of the Georgia militia. These Virginians under Triplett and Tate were militia, not Continental regulars, but they had served in Morgan's "Flying Army" since October 1780. And recall these were the men who had already served in the Continental army but had reenlisted only on a militia basis; in short, they were trained and experienced soldiers, familiar with Continental army drill and tactics.[37] In all, this main line was composed of approximately six hundred men spread across two hundred yards.[38]

In the swale behind "Morgan Hill," positioned so they could not be seen from the uphill approach of Tarleton, were the mounted troops under Lt. Col. William Washington, consisting of about eighty Continental dragoons, the forty-five militia volunteers, and fifty South Carolina state dragoons under Major James McCall. The mounted troops were to serve as reserve but were also posted to guard the horses, preventing skittish militia from attempting to flee the field of battle.[39]

Estimates on the total number of Morgan's troops vary. In his report on the battle to Nathanael Greene, Morgan reported his strength during the battle at eight hundred men, "two thirds of which were militia."[40] The historian Christopher Ward counted Morgan's strength at 1,040.[41] In his memoir of the war, Banastre Tarleton reported Morgan had just over 1,900 men under his command, a number widely believed exaggerated to justify his defeat.[42] However, Babits's scholarship estimates Morgan's force at somewhere between 1,600 and 2,400 men. Though some of Morgan's miscalculation may have been due to the shifting nature of the force under his command, with militia units arriving throughout the preceding night, Babits believes Morgan probably intentionally underestimated the number of militia to deliberately portray the victory as a Continental one over regular British troops, not necessarily a militia one.[43]

Morgan continued to ride up and down the lines, exhorting and encouraging his troops even as they arranged themselves for battle. To his militia sharpshooters from Georgia and the Carolinas on the skirmish line, he commanded them to use the available cover, firing upon the enemy only when they were within "good shooting distance," then retire as the enemy advanced, loading and firing as they returned to the main militia line. "Let me see which are most entitled to the credit of brave men, the boys of Carolina or those of Georgia," he teased, using their natural rivalry as motivation.

Now riding to the main militia line, Morgan ordered them to hold their fire until the enemy was within fifty yards. At that distance, they were ordered to give two well-directed rounds, then retreat in good order to a position in the rear of the Continental line on the left side. Ever the backcountry psychologist, Morgan now used every trick in his book to calm their frayed nerves: "He complimented them upon the spirit which they had so frequently displayed . . . and expressed his fervent hopes that upon this occasion they would add to the reputation they already enjoyed. . . . He asked but an ordinary display of manhood on their part to render victory certain; frankly declaring, that flight would but insure their destruction. . . . For himself, he said, he had not a doubt of the result, if they performed their simple duty."

To his main line of Continentals he ordered to fire low and deliberate. He reminded them not to be alarmed at the planned retreat of the militia and to stand firm. If forced to retire, he ordered them to rally on the hill to their rear, where they would be supported by the cavalry reserve and the militia, which would be reformed in their rear.[44] To Washington's mounted troops, he commanded they assist in rallying the militia as they retreated, protecting them from the pursuing British if necessary. His arrangements now completed, Morgan ordered the men to "ease their joints," resting without breaking their ranks, while he confidently assumed his post at the rear of the main line, awaiting the approach of the enemy.[45]

Just before 7 a.m. the British army finally emerged from the southern tree line onto the Cowpens plain. Thanks to the efficiency of the British army, we have a much clearer idea of the composition of Tarleton's troops. His own British Legion was comprised of 450: 250 light infantry and two hundred mounted dragoons. Added to that were 167 regular infantry from the 7th Fusiliers and 249 from the 71st Highlanders. Additional light infantry consisted of sixty-nine men from the 71st "Light" Company and forty-one from the 16th. Also with Tarleton were an additional fifty dragoons from the 17th Light Dragoons and a small detachment of the Royal Artillery, manning the two field pieces, the three-pounders called "Grasshoppers." In all, with allowances for officers, sergeants, and drummers, his troops totaled 1,150 men.[46] Some accounts include a detachment of Tory militia fighting with Tarleton, but in Tarleton's memoir, he only mentions them as guides, and unreliable ones at that.

Tarleton's memoir describes the moments his army first marched onto the Cowpens. "Lieutenant-Colonel Tarleton having attained a position, which he certainly might deem advantageous, on account of the vulnerable situation of the enemy . . . did not hesitate to undertake those measures which the instructions of his commanding officer imposed, and his own judgment, under the present appearances, equally recommended."

The days of pursuit, the long night, and the thrill of finding his prey vulnerably arrayed on an open field enticed the "hard-charging" Tarleton into attack. Without pausing to consult his two experienced infantry commanders, Major Archibald McArthur of the 71st and Major Timothy Newmarsh of the 7th Fusiliers, Tarleton instantly ordered forward his Legion infantry to a center position. On their right, he placed his light infantry, about 110 men. The two field pieces on their "grasshopper" legs were placed midway on the left and right, "and, under the fire of a three-pounder, this part of the British troops was instructed to advance within three hundred yards of the enemy."[47]

But according to Tarlteon's memoir, he ordered the advance to halt while he ordered up the 7th Fusiliers. Recall, these were regular infantry but new recruits, about to experience their first battle. On each flank, he placed fifty dragoons "to protect their own, and threaten the flanks of the enemy." In reserve, he placed the remainder of the 71st and two hundred dragoons from the British Legion."[48]

With drums beating and fifes shrilling, British artillery starting to pound, Tarleton ordered forward his infantry. "The Disposition of Battle being thus formed . . . their whole Line moved on with the greatest Impetuosity shouting as they advanced,"[49] recalled Thomas Young, who was dazzled by the British pageantry. "About sunrise, the British line advanced at a sort of trot, with a loud halloo. It was the most beautiful line I ever saw. When they shouted, I heard Morgan say, 'They give us the British halloo, boys, give them the Indian halloo, by G—,' and he galloped along the lines, cheering the men, and telling them not to fire until we could see the whites of their eyes."[50]

James Collins was another young militia soldier, posted in the line under command of Andrew Pickens. "About sunrise on the 17th January, 1781, the enemy came in full view," he recalled. "The sight, to me at least, seemed somewhat imposing; they halted for a short time, and then advanced rapidly, as if certain of victory."[51]

CHAPTER 8

VICTORY COMPLEAT

To young, teenage militia soldiers like Thomas Young and James Collins, the British infantry advance onto the Cowpens plain was spectacular pageantry. Yet to the veteran British officers fighting under the relatively inexperienced Tarleton, it was anything but masterful. Ordered forward before Major Timothy Newmarsh had finished posting the officers of the 7th Fusiliers, the line's ragged disorder incensed Roderick Mackenzie, a lieutenant in the 71st regiment. In his post-war memoir, Mackenzie criticized the "un-officer-like impetuosity of directing the line to advance before it was properly formed, and before the reserve had taken its ground."[1]

But in Mackenzie's view, the decision to rush the infantry into battle without even a brief pause to reconnoiter Morgan's position was an error even more grave. "Had he done so . . . General Morgan's force and situation might have been distinctly viewed, under cover of a very superior cavalry; the British infantry, fatigued with rapid marches, day and night, for some time past . . . might have had rest and refreshment; a detachment from the several corps left with the baggage . . . would have had time to come up, and join in the action," wrote Mackenzie.[2] "Where then was the necessity for that hurry which he took his measures?" added Henry Lee. "That interval he might have advantageously employed in a personal examination of his enemy's position, and in disclosure of his plans to his principal officers."[3]

As the British line advanced, "in as good a line as could move in open files" according to Tarleton,[4] the Patriot skirmishers fired and retreated to Pickens's militia line. "McDowell and Cunningham gave them [the British] a heavy & galling Fire & retreated to the Regiments intended for their Support," Morgan reported.[5] Though the British artillery was now thundering, Pickens's militia held their line, firing only when the British infantry was in range. "The militia fired first," recalled Thomas Young. "It was, for a time, *pop-pop-pop*, and then a whole volley."[6] Continental soldier William Seymour, who was watching the action from the infantry line atop "Morgan Hill," recalled the militia "stood very well for some time till being overpowered by the superior number of the enemy they retreated, but in very good order, not seeming to be in the least confused."[7]

As Morgan had devised, the militia filed off, filtering back through the main Continental line. The British volley at the militia line, made downhill with their smoothbore muskets, had mostly missed high. In contrast, the fire of the American militia, with their handmade long rifles, was deadly. Ordered by Morgan to aim for the British officers, they performed to perfection. Mackenzie reported "two-thirds of the British infantry officers" wounded or killed by the militia sharpshooters, including himself. Also among the wounded was Major Newmarsh of the 7th Fusiliers, who could no longer lead his inexperienced troops.[8]

"The militia, after a short contest, were dislodged," Tarleton recounted. His main line now approached the Continental main line under Howard. But finding the Americans facing him in good order, Tarleton ordered a brief pause to reorganize. "The enemy seeing us standing in such good order halted for some time to dress their line which outflanked ours considerably," recounted Thomas Anderson, a Delaware soldier fighting with Howard.[9]

It was now about 7:15, just fifteen minutes into the fighting. "When the Enemy advanced to our Line they received a well-directed and incessant fire," Morgan agreed.[10] The contest became obstinate, and after approximately fifteen minutes of stiff resistance, Tarleton ordered up his reserve infantry, the 71st Highlanders under Major Archibald McArthur, to attack the Americans' western flank. According to his memoir, Tarleton also ordered his reserve cavalry, the two hundred mounted dragoons of his own British Legion, "to incline to the left, and to form a line, which would embrace the whole of the enemy's right flank."[11] With bagpipes blaring the Highlanders stepped forward, immediately bolstering the sagging British line, while Tarleton and his cavalry moved to the left, preparing to sweep behind the American western flank.

Although accounts vary, it seems to be around the time Tarleton was ordering up his reserve infantry, or perhaps a few minutes before, that he ordered the dragoons on his eastern flank to charge the militia on the Americans' east side, believing them to be retreating in panic. In this part of the fighting was James Collins. "Tarleton's cavalry pursued us; ('now,' thought I, 'my hide is in the loft;') just as we got to our horses, they overtook us," he recalled. But Morgan ordered a counterattack by William Washington's dragoons. Collins continued: "Col. Washington's cavalry was among them, like a whirlwind, and the poor fellows began to keel from their horses, without being able to remount. The shock was so sudden and violent, they could not stand it, and immediately betook themselves to flight."[12] Tarleton recalled his dragoons executed the order to attack the American east flank "with great gallantry, but were drove back by the fire of the reserve, and by a charge of Colonel Washington's cavalry."[13]

With the British 71st now aligned on the western flank, and British cavalry under Tarleton approaching that same side, Howard realized he was about to be outflanked on the west and ordered a company of Virginia militia under the command of Captain Andrew Wallace to turn toward the British line. But in the din and confusion of battle, the order was misunderstood. "First a part, and the whole of the company commenced a retreat," Howard recalled. "The officers along the line seeing this, and supposing that orders had been given for a retreat, faced their men about and moved on."[14]

While Howard was commanding the main Continental line, Morgan had been in the rear, helping to rally the American militia under Pickens. Although some of the militia did flee the field at this time, most remained, including young James Collins, bolstered by Washington's charge and the retreat of the British dragoons. Collins recalled, "We being relieved from the pursuit of the enemy began to rally and prepare to redeem our credit, when Morgan rode up in front, and waving his sword, cried out, 'Form, form, my brave fellows! Give them one more fire and the day is ours. Old Morgan was never beaten.'"

Pickens and his officers then led the militia in a wide sweep around the rear of Howard's Continental line, heading from east to west. Meanwhile, Morgan returned to the main line just in time to see Howard's western flank retreating. "Morgan, who had been mostly with the militia, quickly rode up to me and expressed apprehension of the event," remembered

Howard. "But I soon removed his fears by pointing to the line, and observing that the men were not beaten who retreated in that order. He then ordered me to keep with the men, until we came to the rising ground near Washington's horse."[15]

Beaten the Americans were not, but to the pursuing British infantry, their retreat had all the hallmarks of a rout. While Morgan retired to fix the place where the Americans would turn to face the enemy, the British soldiers surged forward, convinced the American retreat signaled their collapse and the moment of victory was upon them. But with many of their officers either dead or wounded, the attack was disorderly. Tarleton had lost control of his men. "The Enemy thinking that We Were broke set up a great Shout [and] Charged us With their bayonets but in no order," recounted Thomas Anderson.[16]

By now Morgan had chosen the point where the American Continentals and militia would turn to face the British charge. The British had gained the hill where the American line was originally posted and were rushing down the rear slope. From his post on the west, Washington had a commanding view of the scene and sent a message to Morgan: "They're coming on like a mob. Give them one fire and I'll charge about."

The booming voice of Morgan now rang out along the American lines. "Give them one fire and the day is ours," he commanded.[17]

"The enemy were now very near us," remembered Howard. But the American troops performed to perfection, wheeling in order at this decisive moment of the battle and firing on the dumbfounded British infantry. "Our men commenced a destructive fire, which they little expected, and a few rounds occasioned great disorder in their ranks," said Howard.[18] Sensing a tactical advantage, Howard ordered a bayonet charge, "which was obeyed with great alacrity." Wrote Morgan: "Howard . . . gave orders for the Line to charge Bayonets, which was done with such address that they fled with the utmost Precipitation."[19]

As Howard was ordering his bayonet attack on the British 71st, Washington and his dragoons had completed a sweep around the rear of the American line and commenced an attack on the 71st's flank and rear. "At the Same time that we charged, col. Washington charged the horse," Anderson recalled.[20] Thomas Young remembered that the dragoons, "about half-formed and making a sort of circuit at full speed, came up in the rear of the British line, shouting and charging like madmen. At this moment Colonel Howard gave the word 'charge bayonets!' and the day was ours."[21]

What had seemed a British victory just moments before now turned into a British rout. "We were in amongst them With the Bayonets, which caused them to give ground," recalled Anderson.[22] Of the decisive moment, Tarleton remembered, "An unexpected fire at this instant from the Americans, who came about as they were retreating, stopped the British, and threw them into confusion. Exertions to make them advance were useless."[23]

In his memoir, Tarleton makes a curious assertion of this moment in the battle. Recall that he had ordered his Legion dragoon reserve of approximately two hundred men to form a line on the far west of the American flank. But the cavalry had not joined the fighting. Loyalist historian Charles Stedman remarked diplomatically: "An order, it is said, was dispatched to the cavalry to charge the enemy when in confusion; but if such an order was delivered, it was not obeyed."[24]

Maybe it was the sudden appearance of Washington's dragoons that kept the Legion cavalry from joining the battle. Maybe it was due to their conflicted loyalties. In his account of the battle, Loyalist Alexander Chesney stated, "Colonel Tarleton charged at the head of his Regiment of Cavalry called the British Legion, which was filled up from the [American prisoners] taken at the battle of Camden . . . the prisoners on seeing their own Regt. opposed to them in the rear would not proceed against it and broke." But in their analysis of former Continental soldiers serving in the British Legion, historians Lawrence E. Babits and Joshua B. Howard report it's unlikely these former Continentals were concentrated in the dragoons, and even if they were, it was not their divided loyalties that prevented them from fighting but the success of William Washington's counterattack earlier in the battle, which they estimate inflicted a 78 to 95 percent casualty rate. "If the Legion dragoons in reserve saw this occur, it is no wonder they were unwilling to engage."[25]

Though the British continued to fight even after Howard's bayonet attack and Washington's cavalry charge, the appearance of the Patriot militia under Andrew Pickens caused the British infantry to break. Recall that Morgan and Pickens had been reforming the militia and moving them from east to west from behind the American line while Howard's right retreated then wheeled and fired. Seeing the British staggered by Howard's fire bolstered the militia's courage, and they now charged into the fray from the west.

"We pushed our Advantage so effectually, that they [the British infantry] never had an Opportunity of rallying," Morgan reported.[26] The British east and west flank collapsed. When historians write of Cowpens as a "double envelopment," considered the pinnacle of battlefield tactics, this is what they mean, that Morgan and his troops surrounded both flanks of the British army.

Exhausted by a long night's march, and overwhelmed by the Americans, the British now tried to escape. The Legion infantry and light infantry of the 71st, which had been fighting on the British east attempted to flee, but within two hundred yards they were subdued and captured by American dragoons. On the British west, the 71st Highlanders and the 7th Fusiliers tried to fight on, but when Georgia militia captured Major Archibald McArthur, his 71st Highlanders grounded their arms. Of the sixteen officers who had gone into battle with the 71st, nine were now either dead or wounded. McArthur surrendered his sword to Andrew Pickens. The recent recruits of the British 7th Fusiliers, now leaderless with their commander Major Timothy Newmarsh wounded in the first moments of the battle, threw down their weapons and cried for "Quarter." The American officers maintained discipline as the British surrendered. "Not a man was killed[,] wounded or even insulted after he surrendered," Morgan reported proudly to Greene.[27]

During the fighting, the two British field pieces had been brought up within thirty yards of the main line. As the British line collapsed and retreated, the British artillerymen remained stationed at their cannons, one on the British right and one on their left. Unlike their infantry counterparts, these artillerymen did not surrender or retreat, and they suffered for it. All were either killed or wounded, save one. "The men, provoked by his obstinacy, would have bayonetted him on the spot, had I not interfered, and desired them to spare the life of so brave a man. He then surrendered his match," recalled Howard."[28]

Tarleton made one last, desperate attempt to save his artillery, leading to one of the most iconic moments of the battle. Furious with his disobedient cavalry, he raced across the field to where they were gathered, garnering the fire of Patriot sharpshooters as he rode. Though Tarleton completed the ride unscathed, his horse was shot from beneath him. He appropriated the horse of his surgeon and continued to unsuccessfully harangue his cavalrymen, finally rallying about forty horsemen of the 17th Light Dragoons and fourteen mounted officers, most from his own Legion. With this force, he raced toward the artillery, attempting to rescue it, but the charge was repulsed by Washington's cavalry.

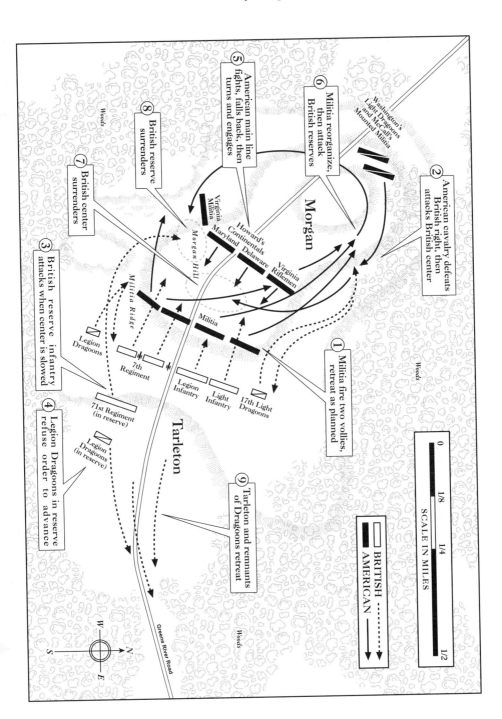

1. Militia fire two vollies, retreat as planned
2. American cavalry defeats British right, then attacks British center
3. British reserve infantry attacks when center is slowed
4. Legion Dragoons in reserve refuse order to advance
5. American main line fights, falls back, then turns and engages
6. Militia reorganize, then attack British reserves
7. British center surrenders
8. British reserve surrenders
9. Tarleton and remnants of Dragoons retreat

Washington's Light Dragoons and McCall's Mounted Militia

Morgan

Tarleton

Virginia Militia

Howard's Maryland Continentals Delaware

Virginia Riflemen

Morgan Hill

Militia Ridge

Militia

Legion Dragoons

7th Regiment

Legion Infantry

Light Infantry

17th Light Dragoons

71st Regiment (in reserve)

Legion Dragoons (in reserve)

Greene River Road

Woods

SCALE IN MILES
0   1/8   1/4   1/2

BRITISH
AMERICAN

Tarleton and his dragoons now rode from the battlefield. Washington spotted Tarleton escaping and ordered a charge against him, but in the din of battle, few of his men heard the command. Washington charged anyway, accompanied by a small contingent of cavalry. Some of the British officers, perhaps including Tarleton himself, now broke off from the British party to engage the pursuing Continentals. In the fight that ensued, Washington's sword broke at the hilt as he swung it at a British soldier. As his opponent raised his own sword toward his now defenseless adversary, Washington's black servant rode up and shot the British officer with his pistol, saving the American cavalry commander. Moments later, Washington was saved again by Sergeant Major Perry, who with his own sword deflected another blow aimed against his commander. Washington blocked a final blow, perhaps from Tarleton himself, with the hilt of his broken sword, before the British officers departed the field.

The story of Washington's "duel" with Tarleton is a glorious account of American bravery, probably too good to be true. Howard recalled the third officer "was believed to be Tarleton," but British accounts make no mention of a face-to-face duel. They do mention a Cornet Patterson, who was shot by an "orderly serjeant" as he fought Washington in the encounter. Nevertheless, the moment was immortalized in a famous painting by William Ranney, which hangs in the National Portrait Gallery and has become one of the most iconic images of the American Revolution.[29]

Washington's "duel" was the last action of the battle. The time was around 8 a.m.; in an hour of fighting, Tarleton's army was almost completely eradicated; those not killed were either wounded or taken captive. Morgan reported 110 British soldiers killed, including ten officers, and two hundred wounded, of whom all were taken prisoner. "We have in our Possession 502 non C[ommissioned] O[fficers] & P[rivates] . . . independent of the wounded . . . and 29 C[ommissioned] Officers." Other accounts differ slightly. Historian Christopher Ward lists British casualties at one hundred killed, including 39 officers, 229 wounded prisoners, and six hundred unwounded prisoners.[30] No matter the count, the results are the same: Tarleton's British force was defeated and captured, with only the recalcitrant Legion dragoons and the small guard accompanying Tarleton during his final charge, perhaps 140 men in all, escaping the field of battle.

In addition to the men killed, wounded, and/or taken prisoner, Morgan reported the capture of two standards (or regimental flags), Tarleton's two artillery pieces, thirty-five wagons, a mobile forge, and "all their Music," in addition to a hundred horses, eight hundred stand of arms, and seventy slaves.[31]

In contrast, Morgan reported only twelve Americans killed and sixty wounded, although historian Lawrence Babits believes this number only represents his Continentals and Virginia riflemen, not Carolina and Georgia militia casualties. Babits estimates twenty-four Patriots died at Cowpens, including both Continentals and militia, and 104 wounded. Suffering the worst was Robert Kirkwood's Delaware company. Fighting in the middle of the Continental line, the Delawares suffered a 25 percent casualty rate, more than any other American unit in the battle.[32]

But this was no time to quibble over figures. "The Troops I have had the Honor to command have been so fortunate as to obtain a compleat Victory," Morgan reported proudly to Nathanael Greene,[33] and indeed it was a victory that has cemented the Old Waggoner's status as one of our great American generals. According to his biographers, Morgan was so elated after the battle, he picked up his nine-year-old drummer boy, perhaps the same one who had warned him of Tarleton's pursuit a few weeks before, and kissed him on both cheeks. That same joy was still evident a few days later when he wrote to his friend William Snickers, "you remember that I was desirous of to have a stroke at Tarleton—my wishes are gratified & [I] have given him a devil of a whipping."[34]

The war would grind on. Even as Morgan paused to kiss his drummer boy's cheeks, celebrating his great victory, the British dead and wounded littered the Cowpens plain. Cornwallis was only twenty-five miles away, and Morgan knew that as soon as the British general learned of the morning's remarkable occurrence, he would redouble his efforts to drive Morgan from his flank.

But the history of the American Revolution must pause at Cowpens, for there a turning point was achieved. "Tarleton's defeat was the first link, in a grand chain of causes, which finally drew down ruin, both in North and South Carolina, on the royal interest," wrote David Ramsay, one of the American Revolution's earliest historians. And Henry Lee added in his memoir, "The victory of Cowpens was to the South what that of Bennington had been to the North," comparing the victory to the Battle of Bennington on August 16, 1777, widely considered a decisive turning point of the Saratoga campaign.[35]

Modern historians agree. "The victory (at Cowpens) was a 'Great Thing Indeed,'" writes John Buchanan. "Its primary consequence was the loss to

Cornwallis of his light troops, which would have a crucial effect on the balance of the campaign. Its secondary consequence was psychological. Morale soared."[36] Mark M. Boatner, the author of the *Encyclopedia of the American Revolution*, provides this summary, "Although the Battle of Cowpens saved half of Greene's army and destroyed a large part of Cornwallis's—depriving him of light troops when he needed them most—its farther reaching effects were to raise patriot morale when it badly needed raising. Southern militia started turning out in greater numbers, and the North started sending the support the South so badly needed. The substantial but not fatal British tactical reverse at Cowpens led Cornwallis into strategic errors that *were* fatal to the British at Yorktown."[37]

British army officer Charles Stedman was serving with Cornwallis at the time. A Loyalist from Philadelphia, Stedman would move to London following the war and publish a popular two-volume history of it. Of Cowpens, Stedman writes, "The defeat of his majesty's troops at the Cowpens formed a very principal link in the chain of circumstances which led to the independence of America."[38]

After the war, British commentary on the battle tended to attribute the loss to bad luck, not necessarily Morgan's stratagem, although neither Charles Cornwallis nor, in particular, Banastre Tarleton escaped critical wrath. "During the whole period of the war no other action reflected so much dishonour upon the British arms," Stedman continued. "Every disaster that befell lord Cornwallis, after Tarleton's most shameful defeat at the Cowpens, may most justly be attributed to the imprudence and unsoldierly conduct of that officer in the action."[39]

Most critical of all was Roderick Mackenzie. Wounded and taken prisoner after the battle, he would later publish a rebuttal to Tarleton's memoirs, incensed by what he considered Tarleton's self-serving portrait. Of Cowpens's consequence, Mackenzie surmised, "Had Earl Cornwallis not been deprived of his light troops, the blockade at York Town had never taken place; and the enemies of our country . . . would have sued for that peace."[40]

Criticism of Tarleton generally coalesced around three key points. First was that, finding Morgan arrayed for battle on the morning of January 17, after a difficult night march, he needlessly rushed his men into battle.[41] Second was his failure to consult his senior officers, McArthur and Newmarsh, "who held commissions long before our author was born, and who had reputations to this day unimpeached."[42] Had he done so, his critics argue, their discretion and understanding of sound battle tactics may have prevailed, and Tarleton would not have called up his reserves so quickly. "Here he violated the fundamental rules of battle. The reserve, as the term indicates, ought not to be endangered by the fire levelled at the preceding body; but, being safe from musketry by its distance, should be ready to interpose in case of disaster, and to increase advantage in the event of victory," observed Lee.[43]

But by far the most egregious offense was the failure to employ his considerable advantage in cavalry, on a field built for cavalry tactics. "The ground which he [Morgan] occupied . . . was an open wood, and consequently liable to be penetrated by the British cavalry: Both his flanks were exposed. . . . In such a situation he gave a manifest advantage to an enemy with a superior body of cavalry," Stedman noted.[44] "The most destructive [error] was in not bringing up a column of cavalry, and completing the rout, which, by his own acknowledgment, had commenced through the whole American infantry," seethed Mackenzie.[45]

Of course, Tarleton claimed he did order up his cavalry onto Morgan's west flank in the decisive moment of battle, but "the cavalry did not comply with the order."[46] And although at least some of Tarleton's cavalry were former Continentals, Stedman was among several British officers who found such claims dubious: "If such an order was delivered, it was not obeyed," he comments acidly.[47] Of the British cavalry's shameful retreat, Mackenzie wrote: "Two hundred and fifty horse which had not been engaged, fled through the woods with the utmost precipitation, bearing down such officers as opposed their flight."[48]

For his part, Tarleton's memoir attempted to defer at least part of the blame onto Cornwallis. There he reports that, as he escaped the field of Cowpens in disgraceful defeat, he learned with "infinite grief and astonishment, that the main army had not advanced beyond Turkey Creek."[49] Just as it is impossible to believe Tarleton's counterfeit incredulity in this passage, it is impossible to blame his defeat on Cornwallis's inertia. Even if Tarleton believed Cornwallis was in motion, it was his decision to engage Morgan in battle, though he had infinite opportunity to wait for Cornwallis's approach.

Nevertheless, his post-war aspersions served other political purposes, playing a minor but significant role in the feud between Cornwallis and Henry Clinton after the war. "We have here [in Cowpens], unfortunately, another fatal instance of the ruinous effect of risking detachments without being in a situation to sustain them, or [of] promising and not affording support," Clinton wrote in his own memoir of the war. "As a plan of coop-eration had been concerted between them [Cornwallis and Tarleton], and the advantages to be reaped from Lieutenant Colonel Tarelton's expected success in either defeating Morgan or driving him over Broad River so greatly depended on His Lordship's being near the fords, ready to fall upon him in his crossing, we naturally seek for His Lordship's reasons for being so tardy in his progress."[50]

Roderick Mackenzie, for one, was having none of it. "Of all men, Lieu-tenant Colonel Tarleton should be the last to censure Earl Cornwallis for not destroying Morgan's force," he countered.[51] His opinion on this was shared by many of Cornwallis's officers. "Under all these advantages in favour of Tarleton, and disadvantages against Morgan, Tarleton is com-pletely defeated and totally routed. Is it possible for the mind to form any other conclusion, than that there was a radical defect, and a want of military knowledge on the part of colonel Tarleton?" questioned Stedman.[52] And of a discussion with McArthur after the battle, John Eager Howard re-ported the British major complained the best troops in the British service had been put under command of "that boy" Banastre Tarleton "to be sacri-ficed."[53]

American general William Moultrie was a prisoner in Charleston at the time. "This defeat of Colonel Tarleton . . . chagrined and disappointed the British officers and Tories in Charlestown exceedingly," he wrote in his memoirs. "I saw them standing in the streets in small circles, talking over the affair with very grave faces. . . . Some of the old British officers who were made prisoners, and paroled to Charlestown, when they came down, were exceedingly angry indeed, at their defeat, and were heard to say, 'that was a consequence of trusting such a command to a boy like Tarleton.'"[54]

To the victors go the spoils. And the spoils of Cowpens would include not only the captured British soldiers, their baggage and stores, their arms and ammunition, their slaves, their standards, and their battered reputations but also a place of prominence in the annals of American military history. Today the Battle of Cowpens is still instructed at West Point, still pored over in minute detail by historians, and recounted tirelessly at the Cowpens National Battlefield, maintained by the National Park Service and visited by over two hundred thousand each year.

Even in its own time, Cowpens' glorious achievement was acknowl-edged. Upon receiving Morgan's battle report on January 23, Greene or-dered a celebration in the camp at the Cheraws. "We have had a *feu de joy*, drank all your Healths, Swear you are the finest Fellows, and love you if possible more than ever," Otho Holland Williams wrote to Morgan of the celebration.[55] To George Washington, in a letter that was also submitted to the Continental Congress, Greene wrote, "The victory was compleat, and the action glorious. The brilliancy and success with which it was fought, does the highest honor to the American arms and adds splendor to the character of the General and his Officers."

One of the most significant impacts of the battle was on the psyche of Greene himself, who would achieve mixed results using a "Cowpens" formation at the Battle of Guilford Courthouse on March 15, 1781. But Greene was no Morgan, lacking his common touch, and the larger scale of that battle was not suited to the tactic. Though much of the militia performed courageously at Guilford Courthouse, some ran under the British advance. The British army would not fall for the same trick twice and easily pushed through the militia lines. Despite Greene's almost three-to-one superiority in numbers, British assertiveness forced the Americans from the field, in what is widely considered a Greene defeat.

For its part, Congress was suitably impressed, publishing in its official motion on March 9, 1781, "that the thanks of the United States in Congress assembled be given to Brigadier General Morgan and the men under his command for the fortitude and good conduct displayed in the action at the Cowpens." In the notice, Morgan was awarded a congressional gold medal, one of only seven presented throughout the entire American Revolution. Nathanael Greene would also earn a gold medal for his service in the southern campaigns. Henry Lee achieved the honor, though for his heroism at Paulus Hook in 1779, not his service in the South. The other four winners were George Washington, Horatio Gates, Brigadier General Anthony Wayne, and John Paul Jones. For their valor at Cowpens, Congress awarded silver medals to William Washington and John Eager Howard and a sword to Andrew Pickens "in testimony for his spirited conduct in the action."[56]

But given the historical significance of Cowpens, even Morgan could not escape criticism. "The ground about the Cowpens is covered with open wood, admitting the operation of cavalry with facility, in which the enemy trebled Morgan. His [Morgan's] flanks had no resting-place, but were exposed to be readily turned; and Broad River ran parallel to his rear, forbidding the hope of a safe retreat in the event of disaster," wrote Henry Lee. "Erroneous was the decision to fight in this position, when a better might have been easily gained." Yet such armchair quarterbacking ignores the on-the-ground contingencies faced by Morgan in choosing to fight. And even Lee admits "Morgan's disposition for battle was masterly."[57]

Later, in response to precisely the kind of criticism Lee and others would level at him, Morgan rebutted:

> I would not have had a swamp in the view of my militia on any consideration; they would have made for it, and nothing could have detained them from it. And as to covering my wings, I knew my adversary, and was perfectly sure I should have nothing but downright fighting. As to retreat, it was the very thing I wished to cut off all hope of. I would have thanked Tarleton had he surrounded me with his cavalry. It would have been better than placing my own men in the rear to shoot down those who broke from the ranks. When men are forced to fight, they will sell their lives dearly. . . . Had I crossed the river, one half of the militia would have immediately abandoned me.[58]

Such recollection is probably a bit of armchair quarterbacking itself. On the field of battle, gathered around the campfires of the previous night, Morgan's circumspections surely lacked the assuredness he later gave them. Yet his psychological awareness was clearly prescient, in a manner unusual in battlefield commanders before or since. Morgan's "genius lay in reversing the strength of his linear formations and creating progressively stronger defensive lines," believes Babits. "Working within traditional European military thinking, Morgan constructed a mental, as well as a physical trap for Tarleton."[59]

But it was also a genius that extended beyond the battlefield, exemplifying the ideal partisan described by Saxe and Jenet. Morgan used critical thought and empirical analysis to peer inside the mind of both his opponent and his own men. As in New Jersey and Saratoga in 1777, he adapted his tactics based on his own strategic assets and employed the available terrain to his advantage, eschewing conventional tactics. Despite a lack of artillery and deficiency in cavalry, he used his available technology—the famed rifle of the America backwoods—to maximum advantage, and ultimately he rested his fate on his greatest asset of all—his experienced officers of the veteran Maryland and Delaware infantry, along with Washington and the talented militia general Pickens. Tartleton's British were superior in training, equipment, and troops. Morgan was superior in minds.

Part Three

RACE TO THE DAN

CHAPTER 9

TO THE END OF THE WORLD

As Daniel Morgan surveyed the rubble of the Cowpens plain on the morning of January 17, 1781, he knew Charles, Lord Cornwallis, was lurking somewhere less than thirty miles away, and with him the main body of his army, 1,150 crack British troops, soon to be reinforced by 1,500 more under the command of Alexander Leslie. Though the victory he had obtained was complete, one of the American Revolution's most glorious, he understood now was not the time for celebration; now was the time to run.

He ordered his men to quickly collect the weapons, baggage, and accoutrements littering the field. He put his prisoners under arms and made plans to transport them to safety. Morgan was determined not to repeat the mistake of King's Mountain, where all but a handful of the six hundred Loyalist prisoners captured there had escaped as they marched north under mostly indifferent militia guards. In the custom of the times, prisoners were typically exchanged, and the sparse ranks of the Continental army needed the British soldiers captured at Cowpens as tender for its own replenishment. And Morgan knew Cornwallis would be as anxious to recapture the British soldiers as he was to secure them, so he marched them off as soon as possible, ahead of his main force.[1]

To South Carolina commander Andrew Pickens and his militia, Morgan charged the morbid task of caring for the dead and wounded who could not be moved. Following his "duel," William Washington had regrouped his dragoons and set off to chase the escaping Tarleton, a search that would last most of the day. Though this pursuit almost immediately took a wrong turn, "the service, although baffled in its main object was by no means unproductive of advantages . . . on his return, sweeping the country on each side of his route, [Washington] succeeded in capturing . . . nearly one hundred more prisoners."[2]

Though he would evade Washington, the impetuous Tarleton was not yet done making mistakes. As he raced away from the battle with the forty loyal horsemen he had assembled for his last desperate charge, Tarleton "dispersed" a "party of Americans, who had seized upon the baggage of the British troops on the road."[3] Americans these men might have been, but they were in fact Loyalists who had been serving the British army as scouts and spies. As news of the battle's disastrous outcome filtered through the countryside, the Loyalists were "saving what they could of the officers' effects from the enemy, by appropriating it for their own use," wrote Greene's biographer William Johnson, tongue in cheek. Loyalist or not, as Tarleton and his men approached, "the wrath of the mortified dragoons was let loose upon all who were not fortunate enough to make good their retreat."[4] But this moment of wrath would have consequences in the days and weeks to come, convincing many of the region's Loyalists the British cause was lost, their officers vengeful and untrustworthy.

Shortly thereafter we have one more anecdote from the eventful tale of Thomas Young. Following the battle, Young and some of his fellow mounted militia pursued the retreating British "about 12 miles, and captured two British soldiers, two Negroes, and two horses laden with portmanteaus. One of the portmanteaus belonged to a paymaster in the British service and contained gold." Young was ordered to return to the American camp along with the British gold and prisoners but was apprehended by a party of British soldiers. "I drew my sword and made battle. I never fought so hard in my life. I knew it was death anyhow, and I resolved to sell my life as dearly as possible."

Young was cut on his hand, arm, and forehead. Now a prisoner, he was eventually taken to Banastre Tarleton. "I rode by his side for several miles. He was a very fine looking man, with rather a proud bearing, but very gentlemanly in his manners. . . . He asked me how many dragoons Washington had. I replied that 'he had seventy, and two volunteer companies of mounted militia—but you know how they won't fight.' 'By G-d!' he quickly replied, 'they did today, though!'"[5]

Young eventually escaped, as Tarleton made his way back to Cornwallis's camp, arriving there early the next morning. By now Cornwallis had already received news of the battle, perhaps from the recalcitrant Legion dragoons, who had ignored Tarleton's orders to charge into the battle and returned to British headquarters the night before. He could not have been in a pleasant mood as he received his young protégé. According to an American prisoner, who claimed to witness the interchange, Cornwallis "leaned forward on his sword" as Tarleton gave his account of the battle. "Angered by what he heard, he pressed forward so hard that the sword snapped in two." The normally reserved British lord was thrown into a rare fit of rage, and "he swore loudly he would recapture Morgan's prisoners no matter what the cost."[6]

Sensing Cornwallis's designs, Morgan and the bulk of his army marched north from Cowpens around noon, crossing the Broad River at Island Ford "before the close of day . . . and encamped for the night on its northern bank."[7] At Island Ford, Morgan sent scouts to look for signs of the pursuing British while he waited for his detachments to join him. First Pickens arrived, coming up that evening, then Washington, perhaps the next morning. "Long before daylight the next morning [January 18], Morgan had resumed his march. Anticipating difficulty, if not disaster, he took every precaution, and prepared for the worst." But later that morning, Morgan's scouts reported to him "not only that the enemy had not moved up to a late hour of the day, but that they did not intend to move until a junction had been effected with Leslie. Cheered by this encouraging news, Morgan pushed forward with renewed vigor."[8]

Morgan had his prisoners on his mind. He headed north toward Gilbertown, where the Overmountain Men had notoriously executed some of their prisoners after the victory at King's Mountain. From Gilbertown, roads led west into the mountains, or northeast skirting the North Carolina foothills toward the Moravian settlements near modern-day Winston-Salem, a stop on "The Great Wagon Road" leading north toward Virginia.

Morgan's biographer James Graham writes Morgan "kept his ulterior designs a secret to all but his principal officers, and gave currency to the impression that it was his intention to hold the country north of the Broad River."[9] Nineteenth-century historian David Schenck adds that Morgan "intended, if Cornwallis got between him and Greene, to retreat into or across the mountains, if necessary, and either fight at some strong pass or make his way by a circuitous route into Virginia."[10]

Morgan was assessing and reassessing his options, the strategic conditions fluid and much unknown. But the information about Cornwallis's delay affirmed to him his original instinct, marching the prisoners east toward the Moravian settlements and the Great Wagon Road, where they could then be transported safely into Virginia. To guard duty Morgan assigned Francis Triplett's Virginia militia, who had fought well at Cowpens but, with their enlistment ended, now wanted to return home. With Triplett's militia, he sent some cavalry under Col. William Washington and Carolina militia under Andrew Pickens to join the guard duty, ordering them to "move higher up the country."[11]

Following along the foothills of western North Carolina, the prisoners and their guards traveled on a northerly course, crossing the Catawba River at Island Ford and the Yadkin at Shallow Ford. Meanwhile, Morgan also turned east toward the Catawba River, though marching on a more southerly course to shield the prisoner train, his "Flying Army" now mostly just his Maryland and Delaware Continentals.

On the morning of January 19, two days after the battle, Cornwallis started his pursuit of Morgan, Leslie's reinforcements finally joining him the previous day. His force now numbered 2,550 men, mostly British regulars, though including 450 trained and experienced Hessians, along with 256 North Carolina volunteers.[12] With this army, he would commence the invasion of North Carolina he had long planned. To Clinton, he submitted a mostly ambivalent report on the battle, admitting Tarleton's advantages at Cowpens "left him no room to doubt of the most brilliant success," but laying most of the blame on an incomprehensible twist of fate: the enemy's unexpected turn caused the "utmost confusion," as occasionally occurs in the chaos of war.[13]

Despite Cornwallis's anger at Tarleton, the Cowpens defeat put him in a precarious position. He had served as a staunch advocate, promoter, and mentor to Tarleton's increasing status throughout the southern expedition; his reports to both Clinton and Germain on Tarleton's performance had been almost embarrassingly enthusiastic. It was he, after all, who had ordered Tarleton to pursue Morgan and entrusted him with command of the light troops. And though delayed by circumstances he deemed out of his control, he *had* agreed with Tarleton on a coordinated plan of attack. And perhaps most importantly, he still needed Tarleton, for Cornwallis was not about to let the setback at Cowpens delay his invasion of North Carolina. With his light troops decimated, and much unknown ground still to cover,

Cornwallis would require the services of Tarleton and his Legion dragoons to act as guides and scouts, no matter their questionable loyalties, now more than ever.

Admitting the almost total loss of cavalry, and that "it is impossible to foresee all the consequences that this unexpected and extraordinary event may produce," Cornwallis nevertheless assured Clinton "that nothing but the most absolute necessity shall induce me to give up the important object of the winter's campaign."[14] But at some psychological level, he understood the movement he was now initiating would displease his commander; he would not write to Clinton again for three months.

As Cornwallis started after Morgan, his plan was to "march by the upper in preference to the lower roads leading into North Carolina, because, fords being frequent above the forks of the rivers, my passage there could not easily be obstructed and . . . I was the more induced to prefer this route as I hoped in my way to be able to destroy or drive out of South Carolina the corps of the enemy commanded by General Morgan." Likewise, he "hoped by rapid marches to get between General Greene and Virginia and by that means force him to fight without receiving any reinforcement from that province, or failing that, to oblige him to quit North Carolina."[15]

It was not an unrealistic plan, given the circumstances, and parts of it almost worked, although, like most plans, its efficacy lay in its preparation and details. Though his winter campaign relied on North Carolina's Loyalist populace for provisions and intelligence, Cornwallis had done little to scout the territory he would soon travel, though in fairness his pursuit of Morgan had altered his planned route. Still, this weakness—one of thoroughness perhaps, especially in comparison to Greene's more comprehensive geographic approach— impaired him immediately. Setting out toward Cowpens in pursuit of Morgan, Cornwallis took the wrong road.[16] For intelligence he was now relying almost entirely on dragoons from Tarleton's Legion, the local population either too scared or too Patriot to provide assistance. "In this critical situation, Lt. Col. Tarleton's misfortune at the Cowpens on 17th January at once determined our *numerous Friends* what part they should take, and all that could, deserted from Us, and our hopeless cause," wrote British brigadier general Charles O'Hara, who had arrived with Leslie's reinforcements in command of the Brigade of Guards and was now traveling with Cornwallis.[17]

On January 20, the British army paused while Tarleton "was directed to pass the Broad river with the dragoons and yaegers [German riflemen], to obtain intelligence of General Morgan. . . . He recrossed the river in the evening, having received information, that Morgan, had quitted the field of battle, to pass his corps and prisoners at the high fords of the Broad." This news "induced Earl Cornwallis to cross Buffaloe creek and Little Broad river."[18]

By now, Cornwallis had lost two full days blundering through the Carolina countryside, in addition to the day he had spent waiting for Leslie. During this period, his thinking appears indecisive, even muddled. On the next day, January 21, Cornwallis sent the following letter to Francis, Lord Rawdon:

> The late affair has almost broke my heart. Morgan is at Gilbertown. I shall march tomorrow . . . to attack or follow him to the banks of Catawba. General Howard remains at Cherokee Ford with all the baggage, knapsacks included, ready to meet us at Ramsoure's. I was never more surrounded with difficulty and distress, but practice in the school of adversity has strengthened me.[19]

That Cornwallis letter began with an admission of emotional distress ("The late affair has almost broke my heart") followed by one of psychological isolation ("I was never more surrounded with difficulty and distress") suggests his mental state. Cornwallis's biographers Franklin and Mary Wickwire acknowledge their subject was capable of the occasional mental fugue. "In a prolonged endeavor, it almost seemed sometimes as though he lacked some mental staying power, a form of patience. . . . Certainly he seemed sometimes to take too long to arrive at decisions."[20] In that light, his admission to Rawdon could be an acknowledgment of such a mental lapse; while his closing—"practice in the school of adversity has strengthened me"—suggests he had finally gathered some inner resolve to push past the malaise of the previous few days.

Also, the letter acknowledged that, whether by design or happenstance, by Morgan's stratagem or the deceptions of his local guides, Cornwallis was fooled. If the previous two days had been wasted marching the environs of Cowpens aimlessly, seeking Morgan, the earl had finally achieved clarity: "Morgan is at Gilbertown." And even if this information was two days old, at least it was reliable, giving Cornwallis definitive direction: toward Ramsour's Mill.

The nineteenth-century historian William Johnson castigates Cornwallis for this delay: "Had Cornwallis immediately in receiving intelligence of the disaster [at Cowpens] . . . put in motion one thousand infantry and a few pieces of light artillery . . . it is unquestionable that he must have overtaken General Morgan."[21]

The truth was Morgan had, yet again, outfoxed the British army by crossing the Broad River to the north, where Loyalist support was minimal and the roads provided him more options for escape. But also true is that, even if Cornwallis had started in the right direction, his army's movement was too slow, their baggage too cumbrous, for him to have caught the nimble Morgan, especially after his delayed start. Why didn't Cornwallis begin his pursuit of Morgan immediately? "For his baggage he had nothing to apprehend, since he could still have left a sufficient guard for its protection, and the army of General Leslie was encamped the night before at so short a distance as to have joined him early on the 18th," ponders Johnson.[22]

Historian Charles Heaton suggests Cornwallis was constrained by the military conventions of the British army. "A British military officer often linked honor for himself and his comrades closely to adherence to doctrine and tradition. Officers who deviated from doctrinal norms were often ostracized, while those who conformed to expectations regarding doctrine and honor frequently received effusive praise for their actions, regardless of strategic, or tactical success."[23]

We hear echoes of Heaton's argument in the post-war criticisms of Henry Clinton. Writing of Cowpens, he says: "We have here, unfortunately, the fatal instance of the ruinous effect of risking detachment without being in a situation to sustain them or [of] promising and not affording support."[24]

Cornwallis was surely sensitive to such considerations at this time. After all, he had just been burned by Tarleton's recklessness at Cowpens and was rewarded with the decimation of his light troops. O'Hara suggested Cornwallis was torn by strategic considerations at this time: "With all these Storms gathering round Us some desperate Vigerous measure however desperate was to be adopted . . . but where and how to direct our opperations were the great points to be consider'd, as it was evident every material, possibly fatal consequences might attend any steps that could be taken—circumstanc'd as we were all was to be risked, and as the only event that could possibly tho' in a small degree for the moment, retrieve our affairs in this Quarter, was the beating or driving Greene's Army out of the Carolinas."[25]

To achieve this, he needed Leslie's reinforcements, and so he waited for Leslie before moving. Burned once by sending a detachment after Morgan, he had no appetite for doing it again, and probably somewhere in the back of his mind, Clinton's conventionalities influenced his decisions. But three days into the pursuit, he was adjusting again. The problem was the baggage. The British army was designed for war in Europe, where the urbanized landscape provided good roads and established magazines. "By the mid-eighteenth century, warfare in Europe had become almost ritualistic in its formality. Armies maneuvered like huge chess pieces," writes historian John Morgan. "It was warfare that required vast logistics."[26]

Cornwallis and many of his officers and soldiers had a great deal of experience campaigning in America. Having served in the campaigns of 1776, 1777, and 1778, they were well adapted to living without tents and foraging for some portion of their provisions. Cornwallis had brought his army into the field with what was, by previous American campaign standards, minimal baggage—each regiment was allowed only one four-horse wagon for a medicine chest, sick men, forage, and other absolute necessities. Most officers were allowed only what baggage could be carried on a pack horse, with only Cornwallis himself, his subordinate general officers, and regimental commanders allowed wagons. There were also ammunition wagons, hospital wagons and, most important of all, the provision train, hauling the food and rum that kept the army alive.[27]

On campaigns in New York, New Jersey, and Pennsylvania, soldiers often carried only a musket and ammunition, a blanket, a haversack filled with a few days' provisions, and a canteen of water, leaving their knapsacks with spare shoes and clothing on baggage wagons that caught up with them every few days. Doing without those wagons, the soldiers under Cornwallis carried their knapsacks on their backs, adding several pounds. One man in five also carried a tin camp kettle, and at least two in five carried hatchets that were essential for making brush shelters in lieu of tents. The individual burden could reach fifty pounds.[28]

Even though this was what amounted to the "bare essentials" for Cornwallis and his men, it was still too much for the terrible roads, frequent fords, and rotten weather. The army's baggage and its transport was quickly becoming a problem in the North Carolina wilderness, seriously limiting Cornwallis's mobility.

At Cherokee Ford, not far from King's Mountain, Cornwallis left some of his baggage behind with Brig. Gen. John Howard, with instructions for

Howard to follow the main army to the Catawba, as he had indicated in his letter to Rawdon. To Germain he wrote, "great exertions were made by part of the army, without baggage, to retake our prisoners and to intercept General Morgan's corps on its retreat to the Catawba." But in fact, the only portion of the army completely without baggage was Tarleton's Legion dragoons and other cavalry, who spent the days scouting Morgan's position but returned to the British camp each night, eliminating any advantage they may have gained during the day.[29] The rest of the army was still accompanied by wagons.

With baggage or not, depending on Cornwallis's definition, the effort was too little too late. By British army standards, he was traveling light, even lighter after leaving Cherokee Ford, but he was still too slow to catch Morgan. Cornwallis was at King's Mountain when he "learned that he had been deceived, and that Morgan had eluded him."[30] Still he pressed on. From January 19 to January 22, Cornwallis marched thirty-one miles. "The King's Troops, after their ineffectual pursuit, pointed their course toward the Catawba," noted Tarleton. Despite his efforts to accelerate his march, "the train of waggons that now attended them met with great obstacles on the march, which considerably hindered the progress of the army."[31]

Morgan crossed the Little Catawba River (now called the "South Fork" of the Catawba) and reached Ramsour's Mill on January 21, the same day Cornwallis was writing to Rawdon that "Morgan is at Gilbertown." Two days later, on January 23, Morgan successfully crossed his army over the Catawba River at Sherrills Ford.

Even with a head start, the march was harrowing. "A very rainy season had rendered the numerous streams difficult to ford, and the roads heavy and fatiguing to travel," writes Graham. "His troops were harassed by the hard duty of the preceding fortnight and were unequal to their usual exertions when rested and refreshed." Of the march from Cowpens to Sherrills Ford, "we had very difficult marching, being very mountainous, the inhabitants . . . being very poor," recalled Delaware sergeant William Seymour, who had survived Cowpens and was still with Morgan. To facilitate his progress, Morgan destroyed the British baggage he had captured at Cowpens, "but the muskets and ammunition were clung to . . . to these causes of delay, was added that growing out of the necessity of collecting provision and forage for the daily wants of the army."[32]

Yet Morgan pressed on, driving his men relentlessly. "It was in such circumstances that Morgan was at his best," writes biographer Don Higginbotham. "Morgan seemed indefatigable, helping his men here and there, and cheering them on with praise for their industry and spirit," all the while the sciatic pain in his joints that had been bothering him throughout the winter was becoming more and more relentless due to the cold, wet weather and strenuous activity.[33]

"I arrived here this morning," Morgan wrote to Greene from Sherrills Ford later on January 23. "The prisoners crossed at the Island Ford, seventeen miles up the river. . . . Lord Cornwallis, whether from bad intelligence, or to make a show, moved up towards Gilbertown, to intercept me, the day after I had passed him." Morgan's plan was "to stay at this place till I hear from you, in order to recruit men and to get in a good train. . . . I have got men that are watching the enemy's movements, and will give you the earliest accounts. But I think they will be this way, if the stroke we gave Tarleton don't check them."[34]

As Morgan had raced across western North Carolina, many of his militia had left him, either detached to the prisoner guard or simply melting away to return to their homes and family. Such was the nature of militia service in the southern campaigns. Now across the Catawba, Morgan set out to raise the local militia on the east side of the river, to guard the fords and reconnoiter Cornwallis's position while he waited for Greene's instructions.

These efforts, however, aggravated his painful physical condition. "After my late success and my sanguine expectations to some thing clever this campaign must inform you that I shall be oblig'd to give over the persuite, by reason of an old pain returning upon me. . . . It is a ciatick [sciatic] pain in my hip, that renders me entirely [in]capable of active service," he wrote Greene on January 24.[35]

It was the next day, January 25, when Morgan learned Cornwallis finally reached Ramsour's Mill, four days behind him, having marched only thirty-six miles in the three days since he had left some of his baggage behind at Cherokee Ford.[36] Stedman writes with Loyalist hyperbole that "so closely had he [Morgan] been pursued, that the advance of the British troops arrived at the banks of that river [the Catawba] . . . only two hours after the last of Morgan's troops had crossed."[37]

Pure balderdash, although historian M.F. Treacy argues that if "Cornwallis with a corps of light troops had advanced on January 26, he could in all probability have destroyed Morgan, for on that day the Catawba was still passable."[38] Morgan clearly feared this possibility, suggesting Treacy is right about the fords. "I receive intelligence every half hour of the enemies

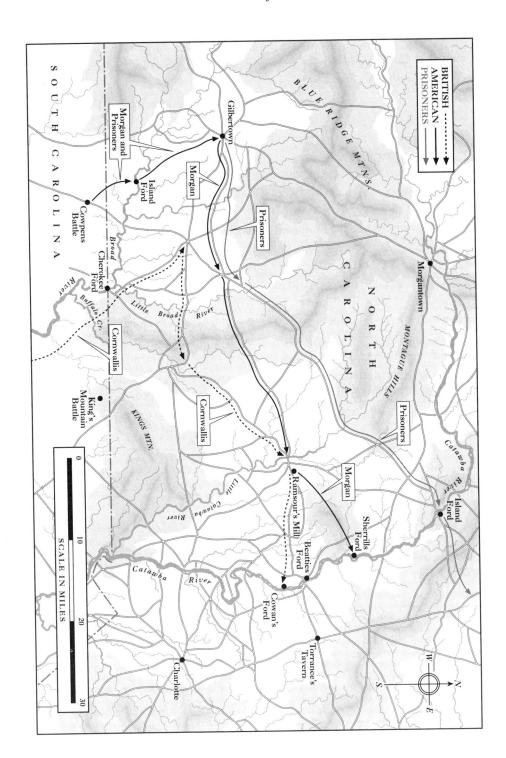

rapid approach," he wrote to Greene on January 25. "In consequence of which I am sending off my waggons. My numbers at this time are too weak to fight them."[39]

Morgan was waiting on the arrival of North Carolina general William L. Davidson, who was raising the local militia in Mecklenburg and Rowan Counties. Davidson would eventually find eight hundred men, although it would take him several days. Again, lack of good intelligence probably prevented Cornwallis from taking advantage of Morgan's weakness. After arriving at Ramsour's Mill, he did send out an advance party toward Morgan's position on the Catawba, alarming Morgan, but this party soon returned to the British camp.[40] Having lumbered through the North Carolina wilderness for the last six days, only to be continually frustrated by the burdens of his baggage and wagons, and the slow progress of his conventional troops, Cornwallis decided to stop and regroup, not press forward across the Catawba River into the unknown. Again, his conventionalities guided him; after the disaster at Cowpens he was in no mood for risky detachments.

Located about twenty miles north of the South Carolina line and thirty-four miles northwest of Charlotte, Ramsour's Mill was a small settlement near an important crossroads leading from the North Carolina foothills east toward Salisbury, then the largest town in western North Carolina. Mills were popular gathering places in the Carolina backcountry. It was at Ramsour's Mill on June 20, 1780, that one thousand Loyalists were attacked by a smaller party of four hundred Patriot militia at the "Battle of Ramsour's Mill." Often described as more brawl than battle, for many of the men there did not have weapons and fought only with their hands, the fight was still deadly, leaving about 140 killed and two hundred wounded.

Ramsour's Mill was located about twenty miles west of Beatties Ford, one of the main Catawba River crossings. The site provided Cornwallis a convenient location to camp and take advantage of the mill while his army refitted for their push across the Catawba.[41] Miraculously, a supply of leather was discovered nearby, giving Cornwallis the opportunity to resole his soldiers' shoes, "as the like opportunity may not happen for some time."[42]

Arriving at Ramsour's with Morgan already across the river seems to have burdened Cornwallis's already fragile spirit. Writing again to Rawdon on January 25, the day he arrived there, Cornwallis admitted: "My situation is most critical. I see infinite danger in proceeding but certain ruin in retreating. I am therefore determined to go on."[43]

But he could not go forward as he had before. Not if he intended victory. For victory required speed and decisiveness, and in spite of minimizing its baggage at Cherokee Ford, his army still could achieve neither. "Lord Cornwallis, considering that the loss of his light troops could only be remedied by the activity of the whole army, resolved to destroy all the superfluous baggage," wrote Stedman.[44]

Although we are not certain of the exact date, probably either January 26 or 27, Cornwallis ordered a fire. If the dangers he saw ahead were "infinite," then the baggage had become a symbol for the ruin he otherwise feared—for his army, for his own resolve, and for his military career. And if we accept this theory, it is not surprising that, according to both Stedman and Tarleton, it was Cornwallis himself who first reduced the "size and quantity of his own [baggage]" by throwing it into the fire, setting "an example which was cheerfully followed by all the officers under his command, although by doing so they sustained a considerable loss."[45]

Up in flames went the senior officers' wagons, the regimental baggage wagons, the hospital wagons, even most of the provision wagons. The number of pack horses was further reduced. An extra ration of rum was issued out before the remaining stores of that precious beverage were destroyed. "The supply of rum for a time will be absolutely impossible," Cornwallis told the men in general orders, "and that of meal very uncertain. To remedy the latter it is recommended either to bruise the Indian corn or rasp it after it is soaked." But the general had "not the smallest doubt that the officers and soldiers will most cheerfully submit to the ill conveniences which must naturally attend a war so remote from water carriage and the magazines of the army."[46]

Stedman and O'Hara wrote approvingly of Cornwallis's resolution in this critical moment of the campaign, and Cornwallis would later report to Germain, "I must in justice to this army say that there was a most cheerful and general acquiescence" to the burning of the baggage.[47] And no more do we hear from Cornwallis about his broken heart, nor his fear of ruin, at least in the letters that have survived.

His entire army converted into a "light" force, legitimately this time, Cornwallis was now ready to resume his pursuit, both logistically and psychologically. "In this situation without Baggage, necessaries, or Provisions of any sort for Officer or Soldier . . . with zeal and Bayonets only, it was resolv'd to follow Green's Army to the end of the World," O'Hara would dramatically conclude.[48]

But never again would he have the same opportunity to catch Morgan as he had squandered on the way to the Catawba. And though his historians may credit his baggage for the delay, sharing the blame may be his state of mind.

And then, once more, it started to rain.

CHAPTER 10

HORSES IN DEEP WATER

O N JANUARY 28, the baggage bonfire probably occurring the day before, Cornwallis and his army marched from Ramsour's Mill toward Beatties Ford, another of the prominent fords over the Catawba River in south-central North Carolina, though they did not yet cross the river.[1] "I approached the river by short marches so as to give the enemy equal apprehension for several fords," Cornwallis recalled.[2] That night the main part of the army camped within ten miles of the Catawba.[3]

The rains that had hindered Cornwallis's march since early January had recommenced, and most sources attribute this latest delay to a flood. "I employed a halt of two days in collecting some flour and in destroying superfluous baggage," Cornwallis would later report to Germain. "In the mean time the rains had rendered the North Catawba impassable."[4] This account is supported by Stedman who adds, "A heavy rain . . . swelled the river so much as to render it impassable . . . and it continued for two days."[5]

Joseph Graham was a North Carolina militia officer stationed on the Catawba. "It is stated by the historians that the river was swollen so as to impede the passage of the British," Graham recalled in his memoir. "The fact is, it was fordable from a week before until two days after this time, though a little deeper than usual."

Likely the truth is somewhere in between: though a local like Graham may have known the river was still fordable, those unacquainted with the native environs, like Cornwallis, would have been intimidated by the rising waters, although here again is evidence of Cornwallis's intelligence networks failing him. Nevertheless, with the main fords now guarded by Patriot militia, Cornwallis paused to scout the area, looking for an optimal place to cross. "The situation of the public fords rendering them formidable, inhabitants and spies were employed to discover the state of the private passes through the river, that the main column of the army might attempt some place not strongly guarded," reported Tarleton.[6] In this delay, Cornwallis seems prudent, not hesitant, though we can only imagine the psychological toll this postponement imposed on the British troops after the wasted dramatics of the bonfire.

One intrigue burdening Cornwallis during this delay was camp gossip about Tarleton's mistakes at Cowpens, the same type of innuendo we have already heard from Mackenzie, McArthur, Moultrie, and Stedman about faulty troop dispositions and failure to use his cavalry properly. As these criticisms filtered back to Tarleton in the days after the battle, he exhorted his mentor Cornwallis: either provide him an "approbation" or Tarleton would request a court martial, knowing full well that process would "require his leave to retire til inquiry could be instituted, to investigate his conduct."[7] For all practical purposes, this would discharge Tarleton from the North Carolina invasion, an option Cornwallis could now ill afford.

With no alternatives, Cornwallis provided Tarleton the "approbation" he demanded, writing to him on January 30: "You have forfeited no part of my esteem as an officer by the unfortunate event of the action of the 17th: The means you used to bring the enemy to action were able and masterly, and must ever do you honor. Your disposition was unexceptionable; the total misbehavior of the troops could alone have deprived you of the glory which is so justly your due."[8]

Cornwallis's biographers call it "a curious letter, totally uncharacteristic of Cornwallis, and seems almost curt."[9] Tarleton would eventually repay Cornwallis for this kindness with the critical aspersions of his memoir. But in the present, the letter was enough to convince Tarleton to stay, ending his demands for a court martial. While Cornwallis waited for the river to fall, Tarleton was active along the banks of the Catawba, scouting the fords and reconnoitering enemy positions.

Nathanael Greene finally received word of Morgan's miraculous victory at Cowpens on January 23, six days after the battle. That day Morgan's aide, Edward Giles, arrived at Greene's camp with Morgan's battle report. It was the same day Morgan and the Flying Army successfully crossed the Catawba River at Sherrills Ford. Greene had spent the previous weeks attending to his army, drilling and training, and lobbying for more men, more ammunition, and more supplies with his relentless correspondence. Henry Lee and the South Carolina militia leader Francis Marion commanded his other detachments in the field, and to them he directed orders and advice.

The army's jubilation at news of the Cowpens victory, the *feu de joy* fired in Morgan's honor, Greene's letters to George Washington and Congress, and the awards and accolades the Cowpens players were soon to receive have already been reported. Greene could perform calculations along parallel, opposing, and intersecting lines, and while he joined his troops in celebrating the Cowpens victory, he also deliberated its consequences.

Almost immediately he foresaw the eastward movements of the two armies—Cornwallis and Morgan's—though it is likely Giles reported to him Morgan's intentions by voice, which were not printed in Morgan's report for security reasons. Upon receiving Morgan's account of the battle, he sent orders to have the Continental army's prisoners at Salisbury and Hillsboro, along with provisions stored there, moved to safety in Virginia, and to assist Morgan with the transport of his prisoners if and when the opportunity arose.[10]

Though Greene contemplated a surprise attack on Ninety Six to divert Cornwallis from his pursuit of Morgan, the expiration of his Virginia militia's enlistment, and their determination to return home, convinced him to abandon the idea. Mostly he wrote, far and wide, to everyone he could think of, pleading for more supplies and more reinforcements. Greene's biographer William Johnson reports Greene wrote Edward Carrington at this time, "to hold his boats in readiness on the Dan," though this correspondence is not included in Greene's collected letters; perhaps it went privately, by way of Giles, who was soon headed north to deliver news of the Cowpens victory and other Greene orders.[11]

Over the following days, Greene continued to consider some sort of action in Cornwallis's rear, but as news of Cornwallis and Morgan's movements east toward the Catawba trickled into camp, he finally resolved to join the branches of his army, probably at some point on January 27. The troops at the Cheraws he would leave under the overall command of General Isaac Huger, the veteran South Carolina general, with orders to move northward toward "Salisbury as fast as possible." Huger would put these men in motion on January 29.[12]

Greene would oversee operations on the Catawba himself. On January 28, his preparations made, Greene rode out of the camp accompanied only by a guide, an aide, and three dragoon guards.[13] In a campaign of uncommon and unusual decisions by Greene, this was one of his most dangerous. His hundred-mile journey would take him across contested territory with the barest of escort, through a countryside torn apart by civil war and abundant with lawless hooligans from both sides of the conflict. We recall his journey south in November and early December with a similarly small entourage. But that journey was through friendly territory, not a war zone.

Were he alive today, the general might argue he took these measures to expedite his movements, that only by traveling light could he reach Morgan's side in the shortest amount of time. "Whatever dangers might otherwise attend the journey of General Greene across the countryside, it was greatly diminished by the celerity of his movements," agrees Johnson.[14] Yes, there were strategic reasons for adopting such measures, but there must have been psychological ones as well. Whatever the case, it is an unusual instance of a commander in chief traveling treacherous ground essentially alone. And this appetite for seclusion would reveal itself again in even more dangerous fashion.

"Partizan strokes in war are like the garnish of a table, they give splendor to the Army and reputation to the Officers, but they afford no substantial national security," Greene had written to the South Carolina militia leader Thomas Sumter on January 8, only a few weeks earlier.[15] Yet we now see Greene behaving boldly, even recklessly, in partisan fashion, taking inordinate risks with his own security, defying military conventions, for the sake of coordinating his detachments. "Don't be surprised if my movements don't correspond with your Ideas of military propriety," Greene would explain to a fellow officer a few months later, explaining his decision to return to South Carolina following the Battle of Guilford Courthouse. "War is an intricate business, and people are often saved by ways and means they least look for or expect."[16]

We can reconcile these opposing viewpoints through situational contingencies: his admonishments to Sumter were an attempt to control a subordinate though not particularly obedient officer; his dangerous ride across the Carolinas was an effort to relieve the ailing Morgan and direct a delaying action that would allow his two detachments to reunite in some degree of safety. No doubt, he foresaw the danger to the American cause if Morgan was apprehended and was determined to prevent such disasters himself.

And in the study of Greene we can never hold him stringently to his own words; some contradiction can always be found. But neither can we deny an instinctive ingenuity, born out of empirical knowledge achieved through a long career in war, but also the intellectual environment of his upbringing and his inherent talents. Most assuredly there was no dog-eared copy of Saxe in the pocket of Greene's officer jacket as he raced dangerously across the Carolinas in solitary fashion, yet Saxe would recognize the officer on his ride, and probably even admire him.

While Greene rode west toward the Catawba, Morgan tried desperately to rally the local Patriot militia and guard the Catawba's fords, fearing an attack by Cornwallis at any moment. Though he was anxious to get his Flying Army out of harm's way, he feared Cornwallis could easily cross and apprehend him unless the British army faced some resistance at the Catawba.[17] These efforts were hindered by his physical condition, for Morgan was essentially now an invalid. On January 24, he wrote Greene complaining of the "ciatick pain" in his hip, "that renders me entirely incapable of active service." In a letter dated January 28, he admits to Greene he is "Obliged to lie in a house out of Camp not being able to Engage in the Badness of the Weather," adding, "However nothing shall be left undone in my power to secure this part of the country and anoy the enemy as much as possible."[18]

His force at this time was not much more than three hundred men, essentially the Maryland and Delaware Continentals, along with Washington's dragoons. And Morgan reported "near fifty men disabled" in his letter to Greene of January 24.[19] To defend the fords and scout the countryside Morgan would rely on the militia of General William Davidson, whose authority embraced the "old superior court districts of Salisbury and Morganton, now composing the fourth and fifth divisions of North Carolina militia."[20]

Davidson was born to Irish immigrants in Lancaster County, Pennsylvania, and moved to what is now southern Iredell County, North Carolina, as a young child. Educated in Charlotte, he was an ardent Whig and served in the militia prior to joining the Continental army in 1776, commissioned as a major in North Carolina's Fourth Regiment. The regiment traveled north and served under Washington at Germantown, where Davidson was promoted to lieutenant colonel for his bravery in that battle, then wintered at Valley Forge.

When the North Carolina troops were sent south in late 1779, Davidson requested a furlough, and he was later unable to rejoin his regiment, which was surrounded and eventually captured in Charleston during the British siege. Without a command, Davidson joined the Salisbury District militia, where he was immediately appointed second-in-command by its general, Griffith Rutherford. Wounded in a skirmish at Colson's Mill, Davidson was not at the Battle of Camden, where Rutherford was captured. Then made brigadier general of the Salisbury militia, Davidson commanded his troops in conjunction with William Davie in the active campaigning around Charlotte in September 1780 that eventually forced Cornwallis to abandon his position there.[21]

Davidson was briefly at Daniel Morgan's camp on the Pacolet River in the weeks before Cowpens, delivering 120 militia, but left to raise more men in his home district and missed the battle. After Cowpens, he immediately "ordered out the next detachment" of his district, but by January 28 he had raised only five hundred men, "two hundred and fifty of which are without flints." With these men Morgan ordered Beatties Ford guarded, leaving Sherrills Ford open for the local population fleeing the advance of Cornwallis's army. At some of the private fords, Morgan ordered trees felled in the road, ditches dug, and parapets constructed, "so as to make them impasseable."[22]

Serving as Davidson's adjutant, or principal administrative officer, was Joseph Graham. Born of Scots-Irish descent in Pennsylvania in 1759, Graham moved south with his family during the 1760s, first to the region around Spartanburg, South Carolina, then to Mecklenburg County, North Carolina. Like Davidson, he was educated in Charlotte. Commissioned a lieutenant in the North Carolina Rangers in 1778, Graham joined the Continental army later that same year, serving as a sergeant in the North Carolina Fourth Regiment. In 1780, he volunteered again for the militia and became captain of a mounted unit.

Graham's most memorable service was with William R. Davie, during the campaigning around Charlotte and Camden in the summer and fall of 1780. At Charlotte in September 1780, he commanded a rear guard action against Tarleton's Legion cavalry, enabling Davie to escape Cornwallis's pursuit after Charlotte eventually was taken by the British. Graham was wounded nine times in the action, shot three times, and saber-slashed six, then left on the field for dead. But he recovered in two months and joined Morgan with Davidson at the Catawba. After the war, during the 1820s,

Graham began writing about his military experiences, leaving a valuable account of the Race to the Dan.[23]

Davidson ordered Graham to raise a mounted unit. Of this unit Graham provides the following remarkable portrait of a Southern militia brigade:

> In a few days he [Graham, referring to himself in the third person] succeeded in raising a company of fifty-six, mostly enterprising young men who had seen service, but found it difficult to procure arms. Only forty-five swords could be produced, and one-half of them were made by country blacksmiths. Only fifteen had pistols, but they all had rifles. They carried the muzzle in a small boot, fastened beside the right stirrup-leather, and the butt ran through the shot-bag belt, so that the lock came directly under the right arm. Those who had a pistol, carried it swung by a strop about the size of a bridle rein on the left side, over the sword, which was belted higher than the modern mode of wearing them, so as not to entangle the legs when acting on foot. They had at all times all their arms with them, whether on foot or on horseback, and could act as infantry or cavalry, and move individually and collectively, as emergencies might require. With those arms, and mounted generally on strong and durable mounts . . . they were ready for service, without commissary, quartermaster, or other staff.[24]

By January 29, Davidson had raised eight hundred men, including the fifty-six described here so memorably by Graham. He now had two hundred men at Tuckasegee Ford and seventy men at Tool's Ford. At the smaller Cowan's Ford, also called "McCowns," he placed twenty-five guards. The remaining militia, including Graham's mounted unit, he kept with him, guarding the main crossing at Beatties.[25]

Scouts from both sides were now swarming up and down the riverbanks, looking for strategic advantage. On the morning of January 30, Graham's cavalry crossed the river "and ascertained that the enemy was encamped within four miles [of Beatties Ford]. Within two miles they discovered one hundred of their cavalry, who followed them to the river but kept at a respectful distance," fearing an "ambuscade."[26]

Later that day, Nathanael Greene arrived at the Catawba with his small entourage. Many historians have noted Greene's determination to avoid battle if he lacked a decisive advantage. "It would always be Greene's first and highest object to preserve his army," writes historian Albert Louis Zambone, in his outstanding biography of Daniel Morgan. "If there was no army in the South then there would be no southern governments, no South Carolina, no North Carolina."[27] Greene understood the Continental army stood as a political symbol of the American cause. If it were ruined, he believed, the populace would soon return to the status quo they had known for so many decades under British rule.

At the Catawba, he sensed no strategic advantage. "I wish to avoid an action until our force is collected," he wrote to Huger. "It is necessary we should take every possible precaution to guard against a misfortune." Still, in Cornwallis's determination to pursue the Continental army, Greene saw some glimmer of an advantage. "I am not without hopes of running Lord Cornwallis if he persists in this mad scheme of pushing through the Country."[28] And when Greene heard of Cornwallis's baggage fire, he is said to have uttered, "Then he is ours."[29] Something in the news sprouted in Greene the seed of a plan that would grow and thrive, watered by Cornwallis's own apprehension, until its tendrils reached all the way to Yorktown.

But for now, those plans were only tiny grains, not yet budded, and there were other circumstances to consider. Greene had only recently received word of a British force landing at Wilmington, North Carolina. In late December 1780, turncoat British general Benedict Arnold had invaded Virginia with a force of 1,600 British Provincial troops. In early January, Arnold and a part of his army raided Richmond, where Governor Thomas Jefferson had recently relocated the state government from the more vulnerable Williamsburg. Though Jefferson escaped, with many of the colony's documents, Arnold marched through the middle of town before seizing military stores, destroying a foundry, and burning various warehouses, mills, and buildings.

After raiding Richmond, Arnold marched to Portsmouth, where Clinton had ordered him to establish a British base, hoping to rally the Loyalists in the region. Without good intelligence, Greene feared the move on Wilmington was part of a coordinated action between Cornwallis and Arnold, with an objective of trapping Greene between the two British armies. Shortly after arriving on the Catawba, Greene wrote to Huger, "The Enemy appear determin to cross and from different accounts have in contemplation visiting Salisbury. If they cross and push that way they must have a plan of cooperation in view with General Arnold at Cape Fear."

In fact, Cornwallis had no such intention, and the British invasion at Wilmington was only a token force under command of Major James H. Craig, part of a detachment sent from Charleston to support Cornwallis's invasion plans. Craig's mission was to hold the port at Wilmington as a supply depot and to rally the local Loyalists.[30]

Yet the ever-cautious Greene was determined to avoid any such trap. The next day, January 31, Greene ordered the Continental troops at the Catawba to move east toward Salisbury under the command of John Eager Howard. They would leave early the next morning, on February 1. The river was dropping; Greene and Morgan agreed the British would soon attempt their crossing. Later that morning, Greene, William Washington, and Morgan rode south to Beatties Ford to meet with Davidson in a scene captured memorably by Graham:

> They and General Davidson retired with him out of camp, and seating themselves on a log, had a conversation of about twenty minutes. . . . About the time General Greene had arrived, the British vanguard of about four or five hundred men appeared on the opposite hill beyond the river. Shortly after their arrival, some principal officer, with a numerous staff, thought to be Lord Cornwallis, passed in front of them at different stations, halting and apparently viewing us with spy-glasses. In about an hour after Greene's departure, General Davidson gave orders to the cavalry and about two hundred and fifty infantry to march down the river to Cowan's Ford, four miles below Beatties. . . . 'That though General Greene had never seen the Catawba before, he appeared to know more about it than those who were raised on it,' and it was the General's opinion that the enemy was determined to cross the river; and he thought it probable their cavalry would pass over some private ford in the night; and in the morning when the infantry attempted to force a passage, would attack those who resisted in the rear.[31]

Greene's efforts to scout the rivers and roads of central North Carolina were now paying dividends. Davidson's observation, recounted by Graham, that Greene knew more about the Catawba than "those who were raised on it," indicates Greene had thoroughly digested the report of Thaddeus Kosciuszko's Catawba River expedition issued almost two months before and was now employing it to his strategic advantage.

Morgan and Washington now returned to the Continental troops retreating toward Salisbury. But Greene was not quite ready to surrender the
vicinity of the Catawba. He still hoped to rally the local militia to dispute
Cornwallis's advance, giving Morgan's Flying Army more time to reach
safety.

"The enemy are laying on the opposite side of the river and from every
appearance seem determined to penetrate the country," he wrote on January
31 to the officer of the Salisbury militia, the letter addressed generically
because Greene did not even know the man's name. "Let me conjure you
my countrymen, to fly to arms and to repair to Head Quarters without loss
of time and bring with you ten days provision. You have every thing that is
dear and valuable at stake, if you will not face the approaching danger your
Country is inevitably lost."[32] To the Salisbury militia, and other militia in
the vicinity, he ordered them gathered at the property of David Carr, about
sixteen miles east of the Catawba on the main road to Salisbury. Davidson's
militia was ordered to defend the Catawba as long as possible, then retreat
to Carr's once Cornwallis had crossed the river. His orders issued, the plan
made, Greene now made a decision that "was very near terminating his
military career."[33]

In an active combat zone, with enemy patrols swarming the area, the
countryside in literal chaos as frenzied locals attempted to flee the coming
British invasion, Greene decided to remain behind to command the Patriot
militia himself. Accompanied by only a small mounted guard, he repaired
to Carr's plantation to await the militia's arrival.

Of this decision, we shall soon give further deliberation. For now we return to Cornwallis, who "having procured the best information in my
power, I resolved to attempt the passage at a private ford."[34] His destination? Cowan's Ford, exactly where Greene had surmised, which Cornwallis
still believed was lightly guarded, not realizing Greene had ordered Cowan's
reinforced earlier that day.

"On the evening of the 31st, a large proportion of the King's troops received orders to be in readiness to march at one o'clock in the morning."
Lieutenant Colonel James Webster was directed to move at daybreak with
a part of the army and all of its remaining baggage to Beatties Ford, six
miles upriver. Their orders were to "make every possible demonstration, by
cannonading and otherwise, of an intention to form a passage there."[35]

At 1 a.m., Cornwallis ordered his guides to take him to Cowan's. With
him was the remainder of the army, including notably the British Guards

under O'Hara, and two three-pounder cannons. Tarleton reports that, "owing to the intricacy of the roads, and the darkness of the morning, one of the three pounders was overset, and some time caused a separation of the 23rd regiment, the cavalry, and the artillery men from the main body." But the Brigade of Guards, and the Hessian regiment of Bose, reached the river before dawn.[36]

Awaiting them on the other side that morning were men like Robert Henry, another teenage militia soldier with an amazing story to tell. Henry had been wounded in the Battle of King's Mountain but had recovered and returned to a normal teenage life. At school on January 31, Henry's schoolmaster, Robert Beatty, announced that Cornwallis was camped about seven miles away, and "Tarleton was raging through the country catching Whig boys to make musicians of them in the British army."

Beatty dismissed class to join the fighting himself, and later that night Henry joined in with a band of Whig militia, including his brother, Joseph Henry, which crossed the Catawba in canoes and found their way to Cowan's Ford.[37] Also at Cowan's that night was Joseph Graham, who arrived there with Davidson "about dusk in the evening, and after camping, it was too dark to examine our position." Nevertheless, Graham provides a detailed description of the ford and the conditions there:

"At Cowan's Ford, the river is supposed to be about four hundred yards wide, of different depths, and rocky bottom. That called the wagon ford goes directly across the river; on coming out on the eastern shore, the road turns down, and winds up the point of a ridge. . . . That called the horse ford (at the present time much the most used) comes in on the west at the same place with the wagon ford, goes obliquely down the river about two-thirds across, to the point of a large island, thence through the island and across the other one-third to the point of a rocky hill. Though longer, this way is much shallower and smoother than the wagon ford, and comes out about a quarter of a mile below it."[38]

Assuming the enemy would attempt to cross at the horse ford, Davidson set up most of his men on an overlooking hill. But Robert Henry and his militia comrades were stationed at the end of the wagon ford, where Henry took a position next to the "getting-out place of the Ford." It was a position he was pleased with, "for in shooting, if I would miss my first aim, my lead would range along the British army obliquely and still do damage, and that I could stand it until the British would come to a place the water was riffling over a rock, then it would be time to run away." Looking around him from his shooting perch, Henry was pleased to see his schoolmaster, Robert Beatty, not far away.

The night was quiet. "Shortly after dark a man across the river hooted like an owl, and was answered; a man went to a canoe some distance off, and brought word from him that all was silent in the British camp. The guard all lay down with their guns in their arms, and all were sound asleep," Henry recalled in his memoir. All except one, a last sentinel named Joel Jettson, who at daybreak "discovered the noise of horses in deep water."[39]

CHAPTER II

PEALS OF THUNDER

CORNWALLIS WAS AT THE HEAD of the advance that reached Cowan's Ford just before dawn on the morning of February 1, 1781. "It was evident from the number of fires on the other side that the opposition would be greater than I expected," he would recall. But there was no more time for delay. "As I knew that the rain then falling would soon render the river again impassable and I had received information the evening before that General Greene had arrived in General Morgan's camp and that his army was marching after him with the greatest expedition, I determined not to desist from the attempt."[1]

Leading the charge across the river he placed the Brigade of Guards in two columns under the command of Charles O'Hara. "It is impossible to conceive a more awful appearance than the many very formidable obstacles that opposed themselves to us in the Passage of the Catawba," O'Hara wrote memorably of his perspective that morning. "A Broad, Deep and Rapid Water, full of very large Rocks, the opposite shore exceedingly high and steep, covr'd with the largest Timber."[2]

To guide O'Hara's guards across the river, the British had designated a local Tory guide, his name Dick Beal in the account of Robert Henry, or Frederick Huger in the account by Joseph Graham, "who lived within two miles of the place." Graham recalled Cornwallis had his infantry formed in front, with "fixed bayonets, muskets empty, carried on the left shoulder at a slope, cartridge-box on the same shoulder, and each man had a stick about the size of a hoop pole eight feet long" to help stabilize them as they marched through the water.[3]

Roger Lamb was a British officer in the rear of the column, guarding the artillery. Cornwallis, "according to his usual manner, dashed first into the river, mounted on a very fine spirited horse," Lamb recalled.[4] Was this the noises of horses in deep water that awoke the sleeping Robert Henry? Unfortunately, Lamb's account is suspect, no other British source describes Cornwallis as leading the charge across the river, though it is a breathtaking image, Cornwallis as embodiment of *homme de guerre*, charging into unimaginable danger. Nevertheless, some noise alerted General Davidson's militia on the other side of the river. Henry and his comrades rose quickly, wiping the sleep from their eyes at the sound of the approaching British, and hurried to their stands on the riverbank.

O'Hara's guards plunged into the river, leading the British advance. Trying to maintain their ranks as they fought the current of the river, "they marched on with the utmost steadiness and composure."[5] The morning was cloudy, with fog hanging on the water, limiting the visibility of Davidson's sentinels. Graham reported the Patriot militia did not start firing until the enemy "were near one hundred yards in the river." From his stand on the bank at the wagon ford, Henry "heard the British splashing and making a noise as if drowning. I fired, and continued firing."[6]

"The enemy stood on the hills of the opposite shore," recalled Lamb, "so they had every advantage over us to facilitate their firing." Cornwallis's horse was shot from under him, but the general "escaped unhurt," Lamb reported, and whether or not Cornwallis was leading the advance, he was indisputably charging across treacherous waters in the face of enemy fire, sharing equally in the danger he required of his beloved troops. It is a moment impossible to imagine of Henry Clinton or the other senior British generals, perhaps solidifying Cornwallis's reputation as England's great general of the American Revolution, despite his many miscalculations. Certainly, it is Cornwallis's greatest act of personal courage in the southern campaigns, *alea iacta est* indeed.[7]

Recall there were two paths at Cowan's Ford, the horse path and the deeper wagon path. Davidson had posted the majority of his troops at the exit of the shallower horse path, assuming the British would come that way. But somewhere near the middle of the five-hundred-yard crossing, the British took a wrong turn, following the wagon path. For this mistake,

Stedman blamed the Tory guide, who abandoned the army in the shooting. Without guidance, the British column marched directly across the river "to the nearest part of the opposite bank. This direction, as it afterwards appeared, carried the British troops considerably above the place where the enemy's picquets were posted."[8]

Seeing the enemy were marching on the wagon path, Davidson ordered Graham to reinforce Henry and the pickets posted there, but Graham and his mounted men lost precious time in the ride. When they got to the bank where the wagon path exited the river, the British column was within fifty yards. But Graham and his men "took steady and deliberate aim and fired. The effect was visible. The three first ranks looked thinned and they halted." Commanding the British vanguard was a Colonel Hall, who rallied his wavering troops, but not before being shot from his horse by one of Graham's riflemen. "At the flash of the gun, both rider and horse went under the water, and rose downstream. It appeared that the horse had gone over the man. Two or three soldiers caught him and raised him on the upper side. The enemy kept steadily on, notwithstanding our fire was well maintained."[9] This may have been the rider shot from his horse Lamb reported as Cornwallis. Again, no other sources repeat Lamb's account of Cornwallis being dismounted. Still, it is a measure of Lamb's esteem for Cornwallis, his troops' devotion toward him, that Lamb believed it Cornwallis.

In the rear of the column, Lamb and his guard for the British cannon were now taking heavy fire. "Just in the centre of the river, the bombadier who was employed in steering one of the three pounders, unfortunately let go his hold of the helm of the gun, and being a low man, he was . . . immediately carried headlong down the river. . . . I knew that if this artillery man was either killed or drowned, his loss would be great indeed, as we had no man at hand that could apply his place in working the gun." Lamb was "determined to save his life or perish in the attempt. I therefore quitted my hold on the right hand man of my division, and threw myself on my belly on the surface of the water, and in nine or ten long strokes I overtook him." The artillerist was exhausted, having been carried downstream "heels over head," but Lamb got him on his feet and led him back to the cannon.[10]

By now the advance of the British column had reached the Patriot shore. By all accounts, they crossed with discipline and cool courage, maintaining ranks as much as possible. "The Spirit of the Officers and Men upon that occasion, deserve the highest praise," wrote O'Hara. "Under every possible disadvantage, contending against a powerful current that carried many of the strongest Men down the stream, under a very heavy Fire. They were never thrown into the smallest confusion."[11]

"The enemy kept steadily on," agreed Graham. Robert Henry was now standing next to schoolmaster Robert Beatty, "who fired, then I fired, the heads and shoulders of the British being just above the bank."

With their cartouche boxes tied to their necks to keep their ammunition dry, the British columns had not fired a single shot as they crossed the river. "As each section reached the shore, they dropped their poles and brought their muskets and cartridge-boxes to their proper places, faced to the left, and moved up the narrow strip of low ground, to make room for the succeeding section, which moved on in the same manner. By the time the front rank got twenty or thirty steps up the river, they had loaded their pieces and began to fire up the bank."[12]

Henry and Beatty were still at their posts not far away. "I observed Beatty loading again; I ran down another load—when he fired, he cried, 'It's time to run, Bob.' I looked past my tree, and saw their guns lowered. . . . They fired and knocked some of the bark from my tree."[13]

The bank where the British came out of the water was so steep, Graham reports, they "had to pull up by the bushes." Davidson had now followed his mounted unit down to the wagon path with the rest of his militia. As the British army gained the bank, he ordered his men to retreat one hundred yards to a nearby ridge, where they commenced a heavy fire, before taking cover among the trees.[14] Beatty was hit in the hip as he and Henry tried to retreat and fell, shouting for Henry to run. "I then ran at the top of my speed about 100 yards," Henry recalled, before he stopped and "fired about 50 yards at the British. They fired several guns toward the place where I was; but their lead did not come nearer to me than about two rods."[15]

Henry escaped through the woods to safety. Davidson was not so lucky. "The enemy was advancing slowly in line, and only firing scatteringly, when General Davidson was pierced by a ball and fell dead from his horse," Graham recalled. The Patriot militia, which until then had been retreating from the riverbank in good order, finally broke ranks and fled when Davidson fell, except Graham's cavalry, which "moved off in order."

Davidson had been shot with a small rifle ball, near the nipple of the left breast, and "never moved after he fell." The Tory guide Frederick Huger was known to possess a rifle that shot just such a ball, and the killing was attributed to him locally. (Never mind that Stedman reports the Tory guide

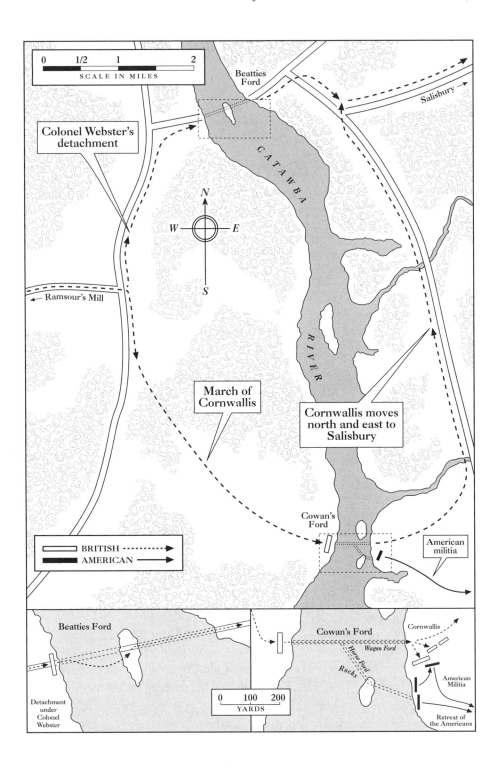

abandoned the British army midriver.) Graham reports that after the war, Huger fled the vicinity and never returned, first becoming a fugitive from justice in Tennessee, then making the "first American settlement on the Arkansas River . . . married and raised a family there."[16] Though killed at Cowan's Ford, William Davidson's legacy would live on through his sons and family. After the war, the family moved to Tennessee on land that had been awarded to Davidson for his service in the American Revolution, eventually forming Davidson County, home to the city of Nashville. Davidson's son, also William Davidson, donated the land on which Davidson College is located. The prestigious school, on the outskirts of Charlotte, is named in honor of the heroic general of the American Revolution.[17]

The British had gained the bank and scattered the militia, but their losses were severe. In his letter to Germain, Cornwallis reported only four deaths and thirty-six wounded. In return, the British, "killed near fifty upon the spot," Stedman reported, making the encounter a tactical victory, at least from the British perspective.[18] But in his memoir Henry makes it a point to dispute the British casualty figures. "The water at the ford was fully waist-band deep, and in many places much deeper, with a very heavy pressing current, and when a man was killed or badly wounded, the current immediately floated him away, so that none of them that were killed or badly wounded were ever brought to the shore." The next day, Henry and his militia comrades "took our canoe to cross the river to the Lincoln side," when "it was proposed that we would go to James Cunningham's fish-trap, to see if there were any fish in it. When we arrived at the fish trap, there were 14 dead men lodged in it, several of whom appeared to have no wound, but had drowned."[19] Two months later, Graham would see a more accurate account of British casualties in the Charleston *Gazette*, listing thirty-one killed, including two officers, and thirty-five wounded.[20]

But this collateral damage was of small concern to Cornwallis, who was in no mood to pause and collect his dead now that he was finally across the river that had detained him for almost a week. While crossing at Cowan's with his crack units, he had dispatched Lieutenant Colonel James Webster to Beatties Ford with the rest of the army and their remaining wagons and artillery. Webster's orders were to create a diversion, firing artillery and ammunition at the enemy side, while Cornwallis attempted his crossing at Cowan's. "Four pieces of artillery fired smartly for thirty minutes and his front lines kept firing by platoons, as in field exercises," reported Graham. Though the British bombardment caused no real damage at Beatties Ford, the Patriot militia there nevertheless dispersed after hearing of Davidson's death.[21]

After the crossing, Cornwallis learned Morgan's Continentals were in retreat toward Salisbury. Morgan had sent them off early that morning, and with only brief stops, they marched over thirty miles that day, "every step being up to our Knees in Mud—it raining on us all the way," recalled Thomas Anderson.[22] His fellow Continental William Seymour remembered they "continued our march . . . in a very unpleasant condition, it having rained incessantly all night, which rendered the roads almost inaccessible."[23]

Despite this head start, Cornwallis was determined to unite the two branches of his army before resuming his pursuit. He ordered Tarleton to pursue the fleeing militia with the cavalry but delayed the rest of his detachment to wait for a junction with Webster. However, Webster's crossing at Beatties Ford "had become tedious and difficult by the continuance of the rain and the swelling of the river," and it wasn't until dark that the two branches of the British army finally reunited, "about six miles from Beattie's Ford."[24] Given the events to come, one might argue Cornwallis's conservative instincts hindered him again. Yet his army had marched most of the night before, then performed a harrowing river crossing under enemy fire. Surely, they deserved a night's rest. Meanwhile, Morgan and his Continentals were slipping farther and farther away.

But not Nathanael Greene, for earlier in the day he had ridden from his camp at Oliphant's Mill, a Patriot supply post seventeen miles upriver from Cowan's Ford, to the property of David Carr, about sixteen miles from the river "on the road between Batey's Ford and Salisbury." This was where he had ordered the local militia to reconnoiter for the next phase of the resistance operation,[25] but when he arrived at Carr's alone, for he had sent the last of his aides out to the road to gather information, there was no one to meet him. "His danger was more imminent at this point than he apprehended," admits historian David Schenck.[26]

Ignoring Greene's orders, or not receiving them all, most of the militia who remained in the area had congregated at a place called Torrance's Tavern, also seen as "Torrence's" or "Tarrant's" Tavern in some sources. Torrance's was also located on the main road to Salisbury, about ten miles east of the Catawba. According to Graham, the tavern was kept by Torrance's widow because her husband was killed at the battle of Ramsour's Mill on June 20, 1780.

Also at Torrance's was an ever-increasing congregation of terrified settlers, their wagons, carts, and baggage flooding the main road as they tried
to escape the wrath of the approaching British army. Although the British
artillery bombardment at Beatties Ford that morning had done little damage, the "repeated peals of thunder" were "heard over the country to the
distance of twenty-five miles" with alarming effect on the local population.
"Hitching up their teams in great haste, and packing up their most valuable
goods and some means of sustenance, the men who were not in service and
women and children abandoned their homes. . . . In one hour after the firing, the whole country appeared in motion, but unfortunately too many of
them fled into the Salisbury road."[27]

Tarleton's British cavalry was now scouring the countryside, and soon
they learned of the militia gathering at Torrance's. It was raining now, vio-
lently according to Tarleton's memoir. The five hundred Patriot militia accumulated at Torrance's "being wet, cold and hungry . . . began to drink
spirits, carrying it out in pailsful. The wagons of many of the movers, with
their property, were in the lane, the armed men all out of order and mixed
with the wagons and people, so the lane could scarcely be passed." It was
around midday when this quagmire of terror, chaos, and debauchery received news of Tarleton's approach.

Though Tarleton reported the "militia were vigilant" at Torrance's and
"were prepared for an attack," the scene described by Graham was bedlam.
Some Patriot militia formed for battle at discovering Tarleton's approach,
but others ran, "some with their pails of whiskey." When Tarleton and his
corps charged through the crowded lane, "the militia fled in every direction.
Those who were on horseback and kept to the roads were pursued about
half a mile. Ten were killed, of whom several were old men, unarmed who
had come there in the general alarm, and a few were wounded, all with
sabres." Tarleton would recall that he and his cavalry, charging through the
center of the morass, "with irresistible velocity, killed near fifty on the foot,
wounded many in the pursuit, and dispersed above five hundred of the
enemy," though he admits that seven of his own men were killed or
wounded, and twenty British horses lost, in the skirmish. Worst of all was
the effect on the terrified refugees, among whom Tarleton's attack "diffused
such a terror" that the British army was not shot or sniped at throughout
the rest of their march through the countryside to Salisbury.[28]

Butchering defenseless old men was far from a courageous act of war,
but Cornwallis seemed eager to restore the battered image of his disgraced

protégé. "The Spirited behaviour of Lt. Co. Tarleton & the Officers & Soldiers of the British Legion in the Attack of a large body of Infantry posted behind Rails & in Strong Houses, does them Infinite Honour," he would write in after orders distributed at camp the night following the action at Torrance's Tavern. "It is proof they are Determin'd to preserve the reputation Which they have so deservedly Acquir'd in the Course of this War."[29] Proof of something perhaps, though honor doesn't spring to mind. But remember Cornwallis had issued his "curious" affirmation of Tarleton's conduct at Cowpens just two days before in response to Tarleton's threats to seek a court martial.

ALONE GREENE WAITED for his militia to arrive at David Carr's property, just six miles east of Torrance's Tavern. There he stayed for the rest of the afternoon and evening of February 1. Though he was within easy striking distance of Tarleton's mounted scouts, Tarleton was "unaware of Greene's proximity and of the fact that twenty of his troopers could easily have led Greene captive into the British Camp." To the fact they did not, writes historian David Schenck, "perhaps Divine Providence was more conspicuously displayed."[30]

Also conspicuously displayed was a curious recklessness by Nathanael Greene. His seclusion at Carr's is usually treated only as a footnote in American Revolution history, if it is addressed at all. Yet for the Greene enthusiast, it presents a conundrum of all we know about his typical cautiousness. Alone at Carr's for the afternoon and evening, the normally hyper-vigilant Greene was unusually separated from his scouts and attendants, unable to issue orders or receive intelligence. Surely, as the day progressed, he must have realized his plans had collapsed, that the militia wasn't coming. The accounts, however, suggest an unusual passivity on Greene's part, almost a sense of stasis.

From Greene himself we have no explanation for this unusual behavior, at least not in the papers that have persevered through time, leaving us only our imagination to consider the interior forces at play. If Greene felt the militia defense required the leadership of a Continental officer, he had good options at his disposal. Even with Morgan incapacitated, John Eager Howard was more than qualified. Some logic compelled him to believe his army's jeopardy so great, the militia resistance so crucial to its security, that only he was qualified to command it. True, the officer was the ultimate weapon of partisan war. "The First of all qualities is *Courage* [italics original]," wrote Saxe, in describing that officer's disposition. "He should possess a talent for sudden and appropriate improvisation."[31]

But what if Greene had been captured or killed at Carr's? His army now separated dangerously in two detachments and on the run, his men exhausted, hungry, and near naked, Greene's loss would've been a devastating blow to Patriot morale, perhaps the final domino to fall in Cornwallis's long-delayed conquest of the South. Just from earlier in the day, we see the devastating effect the loss of William Davidson had on militia organization in the Catawba region. Surely, the impact of Greene's loss would've been exponentially larger.

We can explain Greene's dangerous ride across the Carolinas by the strategic expediency of directing the American resistance at the Catawba himself. With Morgan ailing and his two detachments dangerously exposed, the fate of his army rested on a successful delay, requiring his presence there. But the strategic expedience of his remaining at Carr's, alone and dangerously exposed, is more difficult to justify, especially after he must have realized his plans for a militia rearguard action had collapsed.

To explain Greene's behavior then, we look to less rational dimensions of the human mind. Was it simple exhaustion? Remember Greene had ridden three days from the Cheraws, only to arrive in the face of the British advance. Though a talented general, Nathanael Greene was only human, and perhaps his judgement was clouded by fatigue, the desire for a few hours of rest overcoming prudent decision making.

Or was it the solitude he craved? Like the writer who ignores family, friends, and career to escape into the loneliness of his study, longing only to play with words and ideas in search of some original revelation, perhaps Greene now saw opportunity for precious moments alone, no matter the danger. Of the truth in these theories, we will never know. That men in war—driven by desire, fear, guilt, exhaustion, and emotion—sometimes make irrational decisions is no great epiphany. Yet it is all I can offer here, the rest only mundane speculation.

Sometime around midnight, Greene received a message that the militia had dispersed through the countryside. Alone again, he mounted a horse and rode to Salisbury through the night. According to William Johnson, Greene stumbled into Steele's Tavern in Salisbury after his midnight ride. "It was impossible not to perceive in the deranged state of his dress and the stiffness of his limbs, some symptoms of his late rapid movements and exposure to the weather." Also at the tavern was Dr. William Read, who was in charge of the Continental army hospital at Salisbury. "To the inquiries of Dr. Read, who received him [Greene] on his alighting, he could not refrain from answering, 'Yes, fatigued, hungry, and pennyless.' This reply did not escape the quick ears of his benevolent landlady; and he was scarcely seated at a comfortable breakfast, when she presented herself . . . and exhibited a small bag of specie in each hand. 'Take these,' said she, 'for you will want them, and I can do without.'"

Read left his own memoir of the war, and though he does not describe the encounter with the flourishes of Johnson, he does say he encountered Greene early that morning "actually alone, the most fatigued man he ever saw."[32]

Fatigued is a word that could also describe Cornwallis's army. Cold, hungry, and angry are others. In the previous two weeks, they had suffered a devastating defeat, losing a large portion of the army; floundered through the Carolina wilderness over bad roads of mud and many obstacles; destroyed the majority of their baggage and accoutrement, including most of their rum; been rained on incessantly; and been lethally sniped at while attempting a treacherous river crossing. Surely, they might be forgiven their sour mood.

Finding out that Morgan and his Continentals were two days ahead of them from the banks of the Catawba couldn't have improved their disposition. In fact, after marching through most of the night, the Continentals under the command of John Eager Howard had arrived in Salisbury early that same morning, February 2, around the same time Greene himself arrived in the town.

Cornwallis's biographers, Franklin and Mary Wickwire, observe their subject didn't possess much taste for the kind of "total warfare" made famous by the Civil War general William Tecumseh Sherman, among others. According to them, Cornwallis "never quite understood that to quell revolutionaries—men fired with dedication to an ideal above themselves—he had to be as ruthless as they; he had to use terror, oppression, confiscation, and brutality on a grand scale."[33]

But as they passed through Rowan County, the British army came closest to adopting the total warfare tactics that, had they been applied more broadly, might have won the war. Rowan was the North Carolina county to which the British attributed much of the fierce resistance they had experienced in Charlotte five months before, believing it "the most hostile part of North Carolina."[34]

On February 1, it had rained "at times all day, and in the evening it fell in torrents," wrote Graham, but the morning of February 2 was clear, "though the roads very bad with the rain that had fallen the preceding night."[35] In an angry mood, the British army marched ten miles that day, burning Torrance's Tavern and several homes along the way. In war, the British generally abhorred rape and execution as official policy, but fire was another matter. In his memoir, William R. Davie laments that the "barbarous practice" of arson "was uniformly enacted by the British officers in the Southern States. However casual the rencounter might be, when it happened at a plantation, their remaining in possession of the ground was always marked by committing the House to the flames."[36]

Without their baggage and wagons, the army now was literally living off the land, and they pillaged and burned as they marched toward Salisbury. Cornwallis did not approve. After camping that night at Nelson's plantation, he issued the following after orders: "Lord Cornwallis is highly displease'd that Several Houses was set on fire during the March this day, a Disgrace to the Army; & that he will punish with the Utmost Severity any person or persons who shall be found Guilty of Committing so disgraceful an Outrage."[37]

But these strong words did little to quell his army's rage the following day. To expedite his march over the muddy roads on February 3, Cornwallis ordered his engineers to open "a kind of track in the bushes on each side of the road for a single file. The wagons, artillery and horsemen only kept the road," Graham reports. "But by the time they were within eight miles of Salisbury, their line of march was extended four miles."[38] With his troops spread out in such a broad swath across the countryside, smoke from burning homes rising on the horizon behind them, and no Patriot militia to delay their march, Cornwallis could do little to control the pillage, despite his orders. A few days later he would issue the following edict: "It is with great Concern that Lord Cornwallis acquaints the Army that he has lately receiv'd the most Shocking Complaints of Excesses Committed by the Troops. He calls in the most Serious manner on the Officers Commanding Brigades & Corps to put a Stop to this Licentiousness, which must inevitably bring Disgrace & Ruin on his Majestys Service." Of particular concern were reports of "Negroes Stragling from the Line of March, plundering and Using Violence to the Inhabitants."[39]

Cornwallis and his angry men would arrive in Salisbury around three o'clock on February 3, still a day behind Morgan's Continentals. After arriving in the town on February 2, the Flying Army had pushed on seven miles north to the Trading Ford, one of the main crossings of the Yadkin River, camping on the western bank that night.

For those unacquainted with the geography of North and South Carolina, the Yadkin River and the Pee Dee River are one and the same. Its headwaters start in the Blue Ridge Mountains, not far from present-day Boone and Blowing Rock, North Carolina. Flowing south by southeast into the North Carolina Piedmont, it passes by modern-day Winston-Salem before continuing south to Salisbury and toward South Carolina. At its confluence with the Uwharrie River near present-day Badin, North Carolina, the name of the river changes to the "Pee Dee," before flowing into South Carolina and emptying into the Atlantic near Georgetown, South Carolina. The two different names are attributed to different Native American tribes that once called the river basin home. *Yadkin* is a Siouan name, its meaning unknown. The word *Pee Dee* comes from the Pee Dee tribe, which once lived along its lower reaches.

By the 1780s, Salisbury had emerged as the most important town in western North Carolina, due to its location on the Great Wagon Road, just south of the Yadkin River. At this time, it was larger by far than the tiny hamlets of Charlotte to the south and Hillsboro to the northeast. Travelers on the wagon road considered Salisbury the first important trading center after crossing the Appalachians and descending into the Carolinas. In 1765, Governor William Tryon reported more than a thousand immigrant wagons had passed through the town that fall and winter. Merchants and industry had set up shop in the town to take advantage of this immigrant transit. The city was host to a shoe manufacturer, prison, hospital, and armory prior to the revolution. Most Salisbury households took in boarders to accommodate the travelers; in 1762 the town operated sixteen of these public houses.[40]

Both Daniel Morgan and Nathanael Greene were well acquainted with Salisbury. Morgan had passed through the town in October 1780, camping there briefly before moving on to Charlotte with his light troops. Similarly, Greene had passed through Salisbury on December 1, 1780, as he rode south to take command of the Southern Army from Gates in Charlotte. Instantly understanding the strategic significance of the town's location to the nearby Yadkin, Greene ordered a prisoner stockade, hospital, and several

supply magazines established there later that month. Recall he also commissioned General Edward Stevens to conduct a thorough survey of the
Yadkin River, with special consideration as to how boats could be employed
to transport men and supplies.[41] Through this survey, Greene knew the
river would rise precipitously two days after a major rain, making it imper-
ative to cross within two days of the torrential rains of February 1.[42]

With Morgan and the Flying Army pushing north to the Trading Ford
on the morning of February 2, Greene lingered in Salisbury that day to oversee the removal of the supplies stored there. Generally, he was dissatisfied
with their condition, complaining to Baron Steuben, "in moving the Stores
from Salisbury I found upwards of 1700 stand of Continental Arms in one
Store, kept for the use of the Militia, in the most miserable order you [can]
imagine. Such distribution of publick stores is enough to ruin a nation."[43]

In between inspections, and with his normal industry and caution seemingly restored, Greene also managed to send off a flurry of correspondence
from Salisbury. To General Isaac Huger, now in command of the remainder
of the Southern Army, he ordered a march "up the East side of the [Yadkin]
river," realizing a junction on the west side was now impossible. Most significant was a letter sent that same day by Greene's aide, Major Ichabod
Burnett, ordering Colonel Henry Lee to join Greene immediately. In the
interim between Cowpens and Cowan's Ford, Lee continued to campaign
with Francis Marion in eastern South Carolina, conducting a bold but unsuccessful attack on the British garrison at Georgetown on the night of
January 24. But with Washington's cavalry now down to only sixty men,
Greene was anxious to have Lee's Legion with him as soon as possible.
Burnett enticed Lee to hurry with the admonishment that, unless Lee
moved to join Greene "immediately," he would "lose the opportunity of acquiring wreaths of laurel."[44]

Thanks to his industry, Greene was successful in getting most of the
stores out of Salisbury before Cornwallis arrived, and he joined Morgan at
the Trading Ford later that day, where he found his men and the Continental supplies already crossing the river. There is some historical debate
as to how or who procured the boats necessary for the Yadkin River crossing. On January 1, Greene had ordered Thaddeus Kosciuszko to begin construction of boats for use on the Yadkin/Pee Dee River.[45] These were
flat-bottomed "batteaus" that could be loaded on wagons, similar to the
ones he had ordered made by Edward Carrington on the Dan. Kosciuszko
had commenced this construction at the confluence of the Pee Dee and

the Rocky River, not far from modern-day Wadesboro, North Carolina, and Greene had ordered these boats north on January 30.[46]

According to some historical accounts, including that of historian Christopher Ward, normally considered sacrosanct, it was these batteaus used by Greene and Morgan in transporting the Flying Army across the Yadkin.[47] Yet on February 1, Huger wrote Greene that the location of Kosciuszko and his boats was at that time unknown.[48] For final proof that Kosciuszko's boats were not the ones used by the Continentals on the Yadkin, we have Greene's correspondence with Huger on February 5, where he writes, "I hope Col. Kosciuszko has not fallen into the enemies hands, which I much apprehend, if he set out to join me." Though lost, Kosciuszko was eventually found, rejoining Greene and the Continentals on February 8 at Guilford Courthouse.[49] We will assume Ward, writing long before Greene's collected papers were assiduously assembled during the late 1990s and early 2000s, did not have access to this letter.

More likely is the theory that Stevens had compiled an audit of available boats when he conducted his survey of the Yadkin back in December. Though Greene's orders to Stevens did not specifically request such an audit, it is probable such information was generally known. The Trading Ford had been used extensively by the Continental army throughout the war, both in moving troops to Charleston for the defense of that city, and in the retreat from Camden in 1780. Morgan's biographer James Graham writes that, in fact, it was Daniel Morgan who had procured the boats for the Yadkin River crossing, arranging for their procurement at the same time he was establishing defenses on the Catawba.[50]

Whatever the origin of the boats, Morgan spent most of February 3 employing them. With the river rising, Washington's cavalry and the mounted militia were still able to swim across the Yadkin, but the boats transported infantry, baggage, and the Continental stores. A few days later, General Edward Stevens wrote to Thomas Jefferson, "The Great Quantity of Rain that fell the night before raised the River in such a manner as made it difficult to Cross even in Boats."[51] Nevertheless, by that evening, Greene, Morgan, and the Continentals were safely camped on the other side.

Cornwallis arrived in Salisbury earlier that evening, after his desperate march of twenty miles, his angry columns spread out through the countryside. Tarleton writes that at Salisbury, "some emissaries informed him [Cornwallis], that General Morgan was at the Trading Ford, but had not passed the river; Brigadier-general O'Hara was directed to march to that place, with the guards [British Guards], the Bose, and the cavalry." O'Hara raced forward to the Trading Ford, only to find the Continental army safely across. "General O'Hara having made a fruitless effort to get possession of the flats and large boats upon the river, took post with the infantry on the ground which commanded the ford and ferry, and sent the cavalry back to Salisbury."[52] There they must have informed Cornwallis of the news he already suspected: Greene, Morgan, and the Continental army had escaped him again.

CHAPTER 12

CAPITAL MISFORTUNES

Greene, Morgan, and the Flying Army may have made it safely across the Yadkin River by the evening of February 3, but some of their wagons had not. When Charles O'Hara approached the Trading Ford that night, these wagons were guarded by about 150 Patriot militia, including Joseph Graham.

"It was getting dark when he [O'Hara] came near," Graham recalled. As the British approached the militia took cover at a nearby branch feeding into the river. "The American position was low along the branch, under the shade of timber; that of the advancing foe was open and on higher ground, and between them and sky, was quite visible. When they came within sixty steps, the Americans commenced firing, the enemy returned it and begin to form in line." As O'Hara extended his left flank beyond the Patriot right, Graham ordered a retreat, "after having fired, some two, some three rounds." Graham reported the loss of two men in the skirmish but believed the British might have lost "ten or twelve."[1]

For his part, O'Hara only reported, "we arrived a few hours after him [Greene] before he had completed his passing, and beat up his Rear Guard, who after giving a few Shots in the language of this Country, Split and Squander'd—that is run away."[2]

Greene's escape with the river's "Flatts and Ferrys" now moored securely on the opposite bank of the river, the impudence of the Patriot militia, and the fact "The Yadkin which had increased some days past from heavy rains, swelled so much as to be impassible," put O'Hara in a foul mood. He could see the Patriot camp on the other side of the river, and in frustration, he ordered his artillery to open up on it.

For the most part, this cannonade was only sound and fury. Though the two cannon Morgan had captured at Cowpens had been sent ahead to safety, he had set up his camp "behind a rising ground, while the rocks on the margin afforded shelter to his sentinels." But closer to the river was a small cabin. Dr. William Read was in the Continental camp and reported that "In this [cabin] general [Greene] had taken up his quarters" and was "busily engaged in preparing his dispatches" while surrounded by his staff. "All this time the artillery was playing furiously, but [Greene's cabin] seemed to attract no one's attention. At length, however, whether from intelligence or conjecture, their rage seemed to vent itself exclusively at our cabin, and the balls were heard to rebound against the rocks directly in the rear of it." Though the British artillery barrage sent the cabin's "clap-boards flying from it in all directions," Greene "wrote on, nor seemed to notice any thing but his dispatches . . . his pen never rested but when a new visitor arrived, and then the answer was given with calmness and precision, and the pen immediately resumed."[3]

Of more concern to Greene and his officers than the British artillery barrage was the condition of Daniel Morgan. That night Read found him lying in his tent "on leaves, under his blanket. On enquiry, the General said he was very sick, rheumatic from head to feet." When Read advised Morgan to leave camp "and retire to some place of safety, and warm quarters," Morgan replied, "I do not know where that is to be found until I reach Virginia."[4]

Greene's correspondence from his February 3 camp on the Yadkin River takes on extra context with Read's tale of cannonballs screaming overhead. To North Carolina governor Abner Nash, he sent his usual exhortations for troops and supplies, warning that there would be little he could do to protect North Carolina's "Lower Country" without additional support. "Decided measures are necessary to be taken, for reinforcing this Army, and the arrangements of the Commissary and Quarter Masters department are not less requisite than men."[5]

Greene commanded Andrew Pickens to raise men "on the other side of the Catawba" for the purpose of harassing Cornwallis's rear and prepare them to be engaged "some given time."

FOLLOWING HIS BRAVERY AT COWPENS, Pickens had been promoted to brigadier general in the South Carolina militia by Governor John Rutledge, and he still commanded a small contingent of South Carolina and Georgia militia that traveled north with Morgan's Flying Army. Given Davidson's death, and the lack of a suitable replacement readily available, Pickens was to "assume the command" of the North Carolina militia until "a more perfect arrangement could be made."[6] Greene would also write South Carolina partisan general Thomas Sumter that same night with plans to coordinate militia operations between Sumter, Pickens, and Francis Marion "against the enemy in South Carolina" or with the "continental Army," as circumstances might dictate.[7]

To Baron Steuben, commanding the Continental forces in Virginia, more lamentations about the lack of supplies and troops, with special contempt for those who were available to serve but wouldn't. "O that we had in the fields as Henry the Fifth said, some few of the many thousands that are Idle at Home," he wrote. The lines from Shakespeare's *Henry V* Greene paraphrases here are "O that we now had here/But one thousand of those men in England/That do no work to-day."[8] Was it O'Hara's cannonballs screaming overhead that brought the Bard to mind? Greene believed Cornwallis contemptuous of him and his ragged army, much as the Dauphin of France had been contemptuous of Henry. Perhaps to Greene, O'Hara's cannonballs formed an allusion to the tennis balls the Dauphin sent Henry as an insult: "When we have march'd our rackets to these balls/We will, in France, by God's grace, play a set," Henry replied.

Greene planned to form a junction with Huger and the rest of the Continental army by February 5 somewhere on the east side of the Yadkin River. All of the army's "heavy baggage" and wagons had now been ordered on the road toward Guilford Courthouse.[9]

With the Yadkin River cresting, and all the boats that could be found on the other side, Cornwallis needed another way to cross the Yadkin to continue his pursuit of Morgan and Greene. He was now convinced Greene's objective was to unite his army and retreat across the Dan River to safety in Virginia. In this assumption, he was probably influenced by news Greene was sending supplies and stores collected in Salisbury, and others in magazines kept at the Moravian settlements around Salem, north to safety.[10]

As we shall soon see, Cornwallis's assumption that Greene would retreat across the Dan River would ultimately prove correct, though as usual, his intelligence in this particular case was lousy. Relying on reports "from our friends," or Loyalist spies, who crossed the river in canoes, Cornwallis "concluded that he [Greene] would do every thing in his power to avoid an action on the south side of the Dan." These friends, or perhaps others, also assured Cornwallis the lower fords of the Dan were not fordable by foot or horse in the winter. "It being my interest to force him to fight, and being assured that the lower fords [of the Dan] are seldom practicable in winter and that he could not collect many flats at any of the ferrys, I was in great hopes that he would not escape me without a blow."[11]

With his assumption the lower fords were an impossibility, Cornwallis believed Greene would head for the Dan's upper fords, where his army could march or swim their horses across. This assumption, fueled by the misinformation of his second-rate spies, would prove disastrous. Only with an active, reliable intelligence network, or perhaps the good fortune to intercept correspondence on the issue, could Cornwallis know Greene had already inventoried and collected the flats on the Dan River's lower crossings. But such a network was not a luxury to Cornwallis in the southern campaigns, though the critic could argue he never devoted much attention to building one.

And Cornwallis's critics abound, none more acrimonious than Clinton, who would later disapprove of his junior officer's strategy. "Lord Cornwallis' great exertions had hitherto certainly merited every praise," Clinton begins with what is perhaps faint praise of this decision at Salisbury, "but it should be at the same time recollected that every step they [Greene's Continentals] took drew them nearer to their magazines and friends. . . . On the contrary, the King's troops were now advanced into an exhausted, hostile country above 200 miles from theirs, without means of collecting supplies. . . . Under such circumstances as these . . . it is presumable His Lordship might have thought himself justified in relinquishing his fruitless pursuit and returning to restore tranquility to South Carolina."[12]

Nothing in the written record suggests any thought of retreat ever crossed Cornwallis's mind. To his interior deliberations at this time, his biographers the Wickwires suggest Cornwallis now indulged his natural inclinations to advance rather than retreat, despite the perils he faced. "If he retreated," they write, "he might as well not be there at all. . . . The mere existence of a British force in the South was pointless: to be worthwhile it must do something to speed the reestablishment of royal government in America." They suggest this could have been achieved in one of two manners:

by decisively defeating the Continental army or rallying the Loyalists to His Majesty's cause. But months of partisan conflict in South Carolina had convinced him the latter strategy was practically futile. That left one option: destroy Greene.

Greene understood this instinctively. "If Lord Cornwallis knows his true interest he will pursue our army. If he can disperse that, he compleats the reduction of the State: and without that he will do nothing to effect," he wrote to Huger.[13] Greene had long believed that the fate of the American cause rested with the fate of the Continental army. Writing to George Washington in 1779, Greene observed, "The great object of the Enemies attention is and ever ought to have been our Army. . . . Destroy that, and the Country is conquerd; or at least this is the most ready way to affect the reduction of the United States. They have seen that taking Cities and marching through Governments answerd no other purpose than that of giving them an opportunity to plunder the Inhabitants with more security than by little parties."[14]

Using this understanding to dangerously extend Cornwallis's supply lines seems to have been on Greene's mind: "It is not improbable from Lord Cornwallises pushing disposition, and the contempt he has for our Army, we may precipitate him into some capital misfortune," he explained to Huger.[15] However, Greene had not yet made the decision to retreat from North Carolina. He was still hopeful he could make a stand against Cornwallis somewhere north of the Yadkin if he could gather local militia, or perhaps get reinforcements from Virginia, although his optimism about either of those contingencies was diminishing.[16] And so in this moment we see Greene contemplating two different contingencies at once, placing his pieces on the board, setting traps he may or may not require.

No matter Clinton's preferences, which Cornwallis probably instinctively understood, even if he had no way of confirming them from the field, he would not turn back. Instead he dispatched Tarleton's cavalry, supported by the 23rd Regiment, on an expedition north to scout the Yadkin's upper fords, anxious to get his army between Greene and the Dan River. Tarleton's expedition was delayed when Patriot militia "broke the bridge" on nearby Grant's Creek, but "as soon as the bridge was repaired" he "made a long patrole with the cavalry," of the Yadkin's western bank north of Salisbury.[17]

Morgan, meanwhile, was moving with great celerity, abandoning camp on the Yadkin early in the morning of February 4 with the baggage and a detachment of guards. For now, the "light infantry," some composition of the Maryland and Delaware regulars who had fought and traveled with Morgan for the last several months, would stay with Greene. Morgan's destination was Guilford Courthouse, a crossroads on the main road from Salisbury to Hillsboro, where Greene had also ordered Huger. There Greene intended "to try to collect the Militi[a] about Guilford if possible; and if we can find a good position, prepare to receive the enemies attack,"[18] he explained to Huger.

The small community of Guilford Courthouse was the seat of Guilford County, which had been established by the North Carolina General Assembly in 1770 from land taken from Orange County to the east and Rowan County to the west. Though named for Frederick North, the Earl of Guilford, King George III's current prime minister, the county was formed as a concession to its ardent Whig population, who had demanded from the legislature a more centrally located county seat than either Rowan or Orange afforded.

The courthouse itself was a simple, one-story wooden structure in what was then roughly the geographic center of the county. It had been built on a tract of land purchased by Alexander Martin and Thomas Henderson in 1774, and over time the surrounding area would become known as Martinsville. In 1781, the courthouse was part of a tiny cluster of buildings including a jail and a coppersmith shop, surrounded by scattered homes, the population of the entire settlement no more than two hundred.[19] Nevertheless, it was the closest thing to a local landmark, a place all local militia would've known, and also about halfway between the Trading Ford and the North Carolina town of Hillsboro, where the Continental army had formerly had their headquarters and still maintained some magazines.

Although Guilford County was a hotbed of Patriot activity, the western part of the county was also home to a thriving settlement of Quakers, the same denomination into which Nathanael Greene had been born. An early history of Guilford County described the Quaker dwellings as "comfortable homes, hiproofed, with dormer windows, built of brick or frame material . . . spacious fields of wheat, corn, buckwheat and patches of flax and cotton surrounded the homes. Sometimes a hundred bee hives added another charm to the garden, with its lilacs, roses, sweet lavender and daisies."[20]

Greene's relationship with his Quaker brethren was complicated, to say the least. After his father's death, Greene drifted from the religion. Yet the Quaker tenets on discernment, or the centered search for truth, obviously influenced Greene's long-time interest in the Enlightenment concept of

ot cannot

rational empiricism. And Quakerism's moral doctrine also remained an influence, serving as an anchor for his military and public life. "Life is difficult to tread with Publick Approbtion and self satisfaction," he would note to his brother, Christopher. "But conscious Virtue is a never failing source of human happiness amidst the frowns of a Jaring [jeering] World."[21]

After the Battle of Guilford Courthouse on March 15, 1781, Greene would address his Quaker brethren of the New Garden Monthly Meeting near the courthouse, calling on their moral virtue for assistance in relief of the battle's wounded and begging their embrace of the Patriot cause. "I was born and educated in the professions and principles of your Society; and am perfectly acquainted with your religious sentiments and general good conduct as citizens," he wrote. "I respect you as people, and shall always be ready to protect you from every violence and oppression which the confusion of the times afford but too many instances of. Do not be deceived. This is no religious dispute. The contest is for political liberty, without which cannot be enjoyed the free exercise of your religion."[22] The address would endure as one of the adult Greene's few reflections on his Quaker heritage.

Morgan marched the forty-seven miles to Guilford Courthouse in forty-eight hours, arriving on the evening of February 6. As usual, it was raining. Adding to the misery was Morgan's rapidly deteriorating physical state. The sciatica that plagued him was now joined by a painful case of hemorrhoids, or "piles" in the vernacular of the day, which left him hardly able to ride. "This is the first time I ever experienced this disorder," he would complain to Greene, "and from the idea I had of it, [I] sincerely prayed that I might never know what it was."[23]

At least this time Morgan had access to good roads. Traveling through this same vicinity on horseback during the winter of 1849, though in the opposite direction, the writer Benson J. Lossing found himself "upon a fine ridge road a greater portion of the way, and the snow produced but little inconvenience." As the name suggests, the ridge roads were constructed along the top of the ridges that covered this part of central North Carolina. "Although the whole country is hilly upon every side, these roads may be traveled a score of miles, sometimes, with hardly ten feet of variation from a continuous level. These ridges are of sand, and continue, unbroken by the ravines which cleave the hills in all direction for miles, upon almost a uniform level. The roads following their summits are exceedingly sinuous, but being level and hard, the greater distance is more easily accomplished than if they were constructed n straight lines over the hills. The county has the appearance of vast waves of the sea suddenly turned into sand," described Lossing.[24]

While Morgan marched to Guilford Courthouse, Greene stayed behind at the Yadkin with the light infantry to organize militia and monitor Cornwallis. From the east side of the river Greene received reports that the British army was "very busy yesterday in preparing to cross." This was the same day Cornwallis had detached Banastre Tarleton north, seeking shallower fords upriver. Still, with the Yadkin River "falling so fast, that it might be forded this morning," Greene retired from the Yadkin on the night of February 4.[25]

Though his destination was Guilford Courthouse and a junction with his army, Greene took a more northerly course with the light infantry than the direct route taken by Morgan and the baggage. The early Greene historian William Johnson has suggested this was part of a deliberate effort to deceive Cornwallis, for "it drew the eye of the enemy toward the upper fords of the Dan, as the route by which he meditated an escape."[26] If true, there is nothing in Greene's collected correspondence to support this assertion. Still, let us not discount the idea that Greene's movements served multiple purposes, and he at least hoped his northward movement would deceive or confuse Cornwallis. Still, Johnson admits, Greene's primary strategy at this time was to meet and fight the British. "This had always been his first object and leading desire, should he ever be placed in a condition that would render it prudent. His other designs were but alternative and auxiliary."[27]

Camping "25 Miles from the Trading Ford" on February 5, Greene wrote Colonel James Martin, commanding officer of the Guilford militia, ordering him to assemble the militia of Guilford and neighboring counties, with six days' provisions. In his pension application, Martin would remember Greene ordered him to: "raise and call upon the Guilford Militia en masse and to equip themselves as the military laws directed . . . but guns were wanted by a number of the men and I had to have recourse to impress and borrow as many as I could get and I could only raise about 200 to go with me to camp, and they, hearing that the British were marching toward us in Guilford, it struck such terror on them that some number of them deserted." Nevertheless, Martin and his small group of followers would join Greene as ordered at Guilford Courthouse and serve with him throughout the retreat to the Dan.[28]

The following two days, February 6 and 7, Greene camped on Abbotts Creek, a community in what is now northeastern Davidson County, North Carolina, where a Baptist church had been established in 1756.[29] Roughly due south of the Moravian settlement at Salem, North Carolina (now Winston-Salem), the Abbotts Creek location allowed Greene to monitor Cornwallis's activity. "The enemy have not crossed [the Yadkin River], on the contrary it is said they have all left the Trading Ford," he reported to Huger on February 7. Though he'd received reports Cornwallis was moving "up to the Shallow Ford," Greene admitted that "which way they have marched I cannot learn."[30]

Greene's base at Abbotts Creek has long been ignored by historians. Early histories published in the 1780s by David Ramsay and William Gordon don't mention it. Neither does John Buchanan in *The Road to Guilford Courthouse*, considered the great, latter-day account of the campaign. In his seminal account from 1941, *War of the Revolution*, historian Christopher Ward erroneously reports both Morgan and Greene marched briefly to Abbotts Creek, before proceeding to Guilford Courthouse. Greene biographer George Washington Greene notes "Greene was watching the movements" of Cornwallis from "the forks of Abbott's Creek, not far from Salem," but never comments on the unusualness of his forward position.[31]

It is only with the publication of his collected correspondence in the late 1990s and early 2000s that his movements during this stage of the Race to the Dan have become more widely known. Though Greene at Abbotts Creek did not exhibit the same reckless disregard for his personal safety as he did at Carr's plantation only a few days before, it is still an unusual case of a Continental major general, in this case commanding an entire theater of operations, acting as a partisan officer at a forward operating base in an active war zone. Attended to only by a small detachment of infantry, separated from his main body of troops, to which he would've had only communication by courier, he collected intelligence and perhaps propagated disinformation—hallmarks of *petite le guerre*. Of his motivations for subjecting himself to this danger, we can only speculate, as we have in the past. Acting with such temerity is certainly unusual behavior for a major general on either side of the conflict. Yet, as Greene has already admonished us, we must not be surprised if his movements don't correspond with our ideas of military propriety.[32]

From Abbotts Creek, he continued to address the local militia, urging them to cross the Yadkin and join him toward Guilford. His plan was still to form a junction at Guilford Courthouse with Huger and the rest of the Southern Army. With militia support, he wrote in his address, Greene had "no doubt of stopping Lord Cornwallisses progress." But by now, even the indefatigable Greene seemed resigned to the militia's desertion. If nothing else, Greene urged them to move all provisions and horses out of the enemy's way. Denying them horses was particularly important, he wrote, because it prevented the British "from moving with such amazing rapidity, as they may, when they can mount their infantry."[33]

As Greene believed, Cornwallis had departed Salisbury on the morning of February 6.[34] His destination was, in fact, the Shallow Ford on the upper reaches of the Yadkin, to the west of the Salem settlement. Tarleton's advance party had scouted the ford, and "finding no obstacles to impede the course of the main army to the upper fords, and no probability of opposition in the crossing of the Yadkin above the forks . . . sent a written report of his discoveries" to Cornwallis.[35]

Whether intended or not, Greene's northerly course toward Abbotts Creek probably did help convince Cornwallis the Continental army's destination was the upper fords of the Dan River, as his spies had suggested. Therefore, a move north toward the Shallow Ford would actually play to his strategic advantage, giving him a more direct route to the upper fords despite the Continental army's head start. Even if Greene could reunite the two branches of his army, Cornwallis believed he could still get between the Continental army and the Dan River if he pushed his men vigorously. That this strategy moved him farther and farther away from his supply lines and reinforcements seemed not to be much on his mind.

Aware of Greene's spies, Cornwallis tried to disguise his departure from Salisbury as much as possible, ordering his army to observe "the Strictest Silence in getting off their Ground & during the March."[36] Though he had been delayed three days at Salisbury, his time there was not entirely wasted, for his hungry army had discovered and devoured a small herd of cattle found near the Yadkin Ford on February 4;[37] on February 5, they received a proportion of flour, apparently the fruits of a foraging party Cornwallis had dispatched throughout the countryside earlier that day.

Despite his orders, Cornwallis struggled to maintain discipline on the march. Writing the night of February 6, he requested all officers "seize any Militia or followers of the Army who go into Houses & Commit Excesses; & Report them to Headquarters as soon as the Troops come to their Ground. Any Officer who looks on with Indifference & does not do his

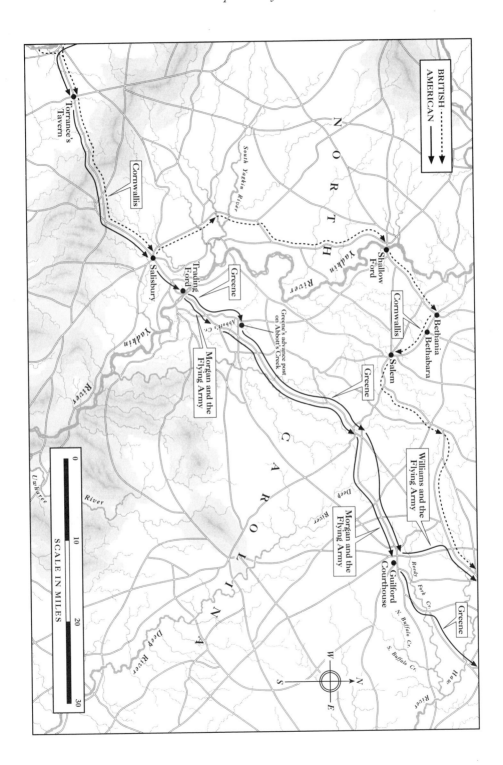

Utmost to prevent the Shamefull Marauding Which has of late prevaild in the Army Will be Consider'd in a more Criminal light than the persons who Commit those Scandalous Crimes, which must bring disgrace & Ruin on his Majestys Arms."[38]

Meanwhile, Greene's efforts to organize a militia resistance were mostly ineffectual. Of Pickens's efforts to raise militia in Cornwallis's rear, he had received "no accounts."[39] Still, the indomitable Joseph Graham, after learning of Cornwallis's march north, had "on his own responsibility . . . decided to take the route of the enemy" with his militia company, "thinking some opportunity might offer of attacking him [Cornwallis] in detail."

On the night of February 7, Graham and his militia arrived at a farm, "within ten miles of Shallow Ford. There he learned that the rear of the enemy had passed this place a little before sunset, and that the men were much scattered on their march, and appeared fatigued. The man of the house thought they were upwards of two hours in passing, most of the cavalry being in front."[40]

The following morning, February 8, Cornwallis and his army crossed the Yadkin at Shallow Ford, having marched forty miles from Salisbury in approximately forty-eight hours, through the muck and mire of sodden red clay roads.[41] They must have crossed in the darkness of early morning, because Graham and his militia arrived at the Shallow Ford "at the first cockcrowing" where "not a human being was to be seen. The enemy had all passed over in the night."

Graham and twenty of his best men scouted ahead. After riding about three miles, and passing a party of Loyalists, they came up behind a party of "fifty dragoons, marching slowly in compact order," which they followed for about two miles, but "finding that they kept the same order, it was thought imprudent to go further." But on their return to the Shallow Ford they captured "three men in red coats," and a little farther down the road they captured another Briton and a Hessian, apparently deserters. "The Briton surrendered, but the Hessian held his piece at a charge and would not give up." He was cut down and killed. Graham took three more prisoners, six in all, before recrossing the ford and retiring with his cavalry.[42]

Not all of the Patriot militia was as noble or as brave. A few days later, Greene would receive a letter "From the Residents of Salem, North Carolina," complaining of the "Excess of some Georgia & South Carolina People traveling thro' here," elements of Pickens's militia. "The Robberies committed in our Neighbourhood, the unreasonable Treatment we just now receive of a couple of hundred militia of another County, come here under Pretence of going to join Your Excellency's Army." According to the letter, these militia bands stole brandy, beef, flour, corn, sale, and horses, with "horrid Imprecations, striking the people . . . & threatning not to leave this place before they have killed a Number of us, besides many Pretences to pick a Quarrel or invade Peoples Properties."[43]

But with the British army now across the Yadkin, spreading fear and terror throughout the countryside, there was little Greene could do to unite the militia, let alone control marauding elements of it. Instead, Greene and his light infantry finally abandoned their base at Abbotts Creek and marched for Guilford Courthouse, arriving at the Continental camp there on February 8, the same night Cornwallis camped at a place called Lindsays Plantation three miles from the Trading Ford on the east side of the Yadkin River.[44]

At Guilford Courthouse, Greene would finally be reunited with Huger and the rest of his army, which had arrived at the tiny settlement around four o'clock in the afternoon of February 7 and was "encamped in the woods, a few hundred yards in the rear of the Court House."[45] Even better news was that Colonel Henry Lee and his Legion were in the vicinity and approaching camp from their location at Bell's Mill, not far from Abbotts Creek. And the recently-lost-but-now-found Colonel Thaddeus Kosciuszko had also appeared at camp, having "run the gauntlope [gauntlet]"[46] on his journey from the Rocky River, though of the boats he was supposed to be bringing with him we have no final account.

Though Greene was relieved to have the two divisions of his army united, he was shocked by the condition of Huger's men. William Seymour, who had been with Greene since departing the Yadkin River, described Huger's division as "in a most dismal condition for the want of clothing, especially shoes, being obliged to march, the chief part of them, barefoot from Chiraw Hills."[47] Luckily six hundred shirts and three hundred shoes had also arrived in camp the day before, a help though "not half enough," as reported by Seymour.

Now Greene would pause to take an accounting of his army, and as usual, the general was disappointed. His whole army numbered 2,036 men. Of those, only 1,426 were reliable Continentals. And what kind of resistance could these soldiers provide if many were without shoes or decent clothes? His militia was reluctant and antsy. Only two hundred men from the area around Guilford Courthouse had joined him; the rest were the remnants of Pickens's division from Cowpens, perhaps many of the same men who had raided the Moravian settlements, along with a few reluctant holdouts from Davidson's Mecklenburg and Rowan regiments.[48] From Baron Steuben he received word that reinforcements were delayed and had not yet left Virginia.[49]

And most significantly, perhaps, was the physical condition of General Daniel Morgan, who was in such pain and discomfort that he "felt himself quite unable to encounter the hardships and fatigues which must necessarily follow."[50] The Old Waggoner begged for his discharge, which Greene considered reluctantly. As he contemplated his options, the always unpredictable Greene yet again did something unusual: he called a council of war.

CHAPTER 13

COUNCIL OF WAR

On January 10, Greene had boasted in a letter to Alexander Hamilton that "I call no councils of war: and I communicate my intentions to very few. . . . If I cannot inspire the Army with confidence and respect by an independant conduct I foresee it will be impossible to instill discipline and order among the troops."[1] Even as recently as February 8, Greene had reminded Henry Lee, "I am an independent spirit, and confide in my own resources," responding to a stratagem Lee had proposed for raiding the British outposts in South Carolina and Georgia.[2]

Greene had learned caution for the council of war during the early days of the American Revolution, where as a member of George Washington's many councils, he had observed the advice given there usually tended toward retreat or inaction. Too often, he felt, these meetings resulted only in pointless arguments and bad advice, sapping the army's zeal.[3] And in the southern campaigns, we see many instances of Greene relying on his own counsel, most notably in the decision to split his forces, sending Morgan west over the Broad River in December, but also, in a decisive moment to come, when he turned his army away from Cornwallis and marched to South Carolina in the aftermath of the Battle of Guilford Courthouse.

So it was something of an anomaly that, faced with the decision on whether to stand and fight the approaching Cornwallis or flee northward across the Dan, Greene now called a council of war. Attending there, probably in the small wood structure of Guilford Courthouse itself, was Greene, Huger, Daniel Morgan, and Colonel Otho Holland Williams. This was a small assembly only of Greene's senior officers, with some notable exclusions, including John Eager Howard, Henry Lee, and William Washington, who were all in camp.

Its proceedings on February 9 began by noting, "The Commanding Officer informs the Council that by the field Returns which were given in this Day his Army does not consist of more than 1426 Infantry Men, many of whom are badly armed and distressed for Want of Clothing. Exclusive of this Force there is Militia consisting [of] six hundred Men, but badly armed." In contrast, "The Force of the Enemy, from the best intelligence that can be obtained amounts to twenty-five hundred or three thousand men."[4]

General Greene, it seems, wanted this council to be about math. After all, from what we know about Greene's deliberations at this time, it wasn't that he didn't want to fight. Since arriving on the Catawba, he had persisted tirelessly in efforts to raise enough militia to engage Cornwallis. But those efforts had failed, and now the numbers simply didn't add up. An important variable in this equation was the availability of stores and provisions. In the interim between crossing the Yadkin and arriving at Guilford Courthouse, the supplies and ammunition collected at Salisbury and Salem had been sent north to safety in Virginia.[5] Other stores were available at Hillsboro, but those couldn't be transported to Guilford Courthouse in time to feed and provision his army in the face of Cornwallis's advance.

Facilitating the decision to retreat was news from Edward Carrington, who had now joined Greene's command at Guilford Courthouse. Carrington reported that everything was prepared for a passage over the Dan's lower, deep water fords. "The boats were not actually collected at the point of transportation," writes William Johnson, "for that also would have unmasked the general's designs; but they were secured at convenient distances, so as to admit of their being collected at a few hours warning."[6]

According to Carrington's account, there were six suitable boats on the Dan, in addition to "wide and shallow flats" at the ferries themselves, "which it was not possible to carry against the River." One of the boats was at Dixon's ferry, "from which place, Cornwallis well prepared for rapid movement, was not much more distant than Greene." The other five were located between Dixon's and Boyd's ferry, about twenty miles downriver.[7]

Carrington's news, delivered to Greene and his officers, must have given Greene some measure of satisfaction. Greene could be pedantic in his correspondence and, we assume, some of his personal interactions. Born with a facile and astute mind, yet sensitive to his lack of formal education, Greene's habit of advertising his intelligence to others hints at the influence of an inferiority complex. Word of the secured boats on the Dan could only emphasize the confidence and respect he hoped to instill in his subordinates through his "independant" conduct, a fact he must've smugly recognized somewhere deep in his insecure soul. And why not take a moment to remind his senior officers he was thinking several moves ahead? The plans to assemble the boats on the Dan, coupled with his efforts to scout the Catawba and Yadkin Rivers during the relatively inactive month of December, had proven integral to January and February's operations. Certainly, Cornwallis had shown himself incapable of such foresight during the North Carolina campaign; Gates, as well, before the Battle of Camden. And though Morgan may have well been Greene's superior in the realm of battlefield tactics, he could not touch Greene's superiority at logistics and planning.

In this situation, the council of war was called, and with the army's escape awaiting them on the Dan, thanks to Greene's foresight and Carrington's industry, the decision Greene wanted was made. You may read in some historical accounts, particularly those of the nineteenth century, where conceptions of honor and courage are tied more closely to an earlier chivalric code, a different interpretation, that it was Greene who wanted to stand and fight, and his officers who discouraged him. But make no mistake, if Greene wanted to fight, he would've fought. Of the council, Henry Lee describes, "Taking into view his comparative weakness, General Greene determined to continue his retreat to Virginia,"[8] as if the other participants were mere spectators in Greene's deliberations. This council of war was about his decision to retreat and the political risks he foresaw in it.

All of these negatives—the numbers of the Continental army compared to the British, the lack of reinforcements and supplies—led Greene and his officers to the inevitable conclusion: "The Question being put, whether we ought to risque an Action with the Enemy or not; it was determined unanimously that we ought to avoid a general Action at all Events, and that the Army ought to retreat immediately over the Roanoke River," Lee continued.[9]

This was the answer Greene wanted, but he needed the council's endorsement for political cover. Greene was keenly aware the reputation of a

Continental officer often rested on the outcome of such decisions, for he had seen similar ones turn sour. Greene himself had been humiliated when a decision he supported to hold Fort Washington during the New York campaign in 1776 was made by one of Washington's councils of war. The fort was stormed and seized by the British on November 16, 1776, resulting in the loss of three thousand Continental soldiers, one of the worst American disasters of the war.

"How many long hours a man may labor with an honest zeal in his Country's service and be disgraced for the most trifling error either in conduct or opinion?" Greene had posited to Hamilton, in a letter where this precise topic seemed very much on his mind. (The same letter where he pronounced: "I call no councils of war.") In response to his own question, Greene paraphrased Enlightenment philosopher David Hume, noting, "Hume very justly observes no man will have a reputation unless he is useful to society. . . . Therefore it is necessary for a man to be fortunate as well as wise and just."[10]

At this council, Greene's reputation seemed much on his mind, and with good reason, for he understood his retreat into Virginia could be perceived as his abandonment of North and South Carolina, giving courage and incentive for those states' Loyalist populations to rally around the British occupation force, precisely as the British had planned. Yet he sensed instinctively fortune was not on his side, at least for the moment, and prudence demanded his withdrawal. No matter his emotional instinct to fight, Greene's priority remained the preservation of his army, despite the retreat's political ramifications.

With these dangers to consider, both military and political, it's no wonder Greene enclosed the proceedings of the council in a letter he sent to George Washington later that day. And following the council, Greene immediately wrote North Carolina governor Abner Nash, explaining the decision in terms of the numbers, and assuring him "Should I leave the State, I shall return the moment I find the army in a condition to take the field." The letter must have been a bittersweet exercise for Greene, for it allowed him the opportunity to scold Nash for North Carolina's failure to deliver men and arms in its own defense: "There are few militia collected nor can I see the least prospect of collecting any considerable force," he informed the man who was, theoretically, in charge of doing just that. "Your Excellency must take such steps for the preservation of public Stores and other matters that concerns the interest of the State." Also, he could not resist a dig at Nash for the poor condition of the arsenal he had found at Salisbury, apparently still very much on his mind: "Such a waste of arms and ammunition I have seen in different parts of this State, is enough to exhaust all the Arsenals of Europe," he scolded, revealing the pedantic tendencies already noted.[11]

The time had come for decisive action, for by now Cornwallis was camped only twenty-five miles away at Salem, North Carolina, one of the Moravian settlements clustered around the present-day city of Winston-Salem. The Moravians were a Protestant sect formed in the present day Czech Republic in the 1400s which then migrated across Europe, including England, and eventually to the American colonies, where they first formed a spiritual and cultural center in the town of Bethlehem, Pennsylvania.

Moravian society was characterized by a communal system where all individual efforts were directed toward the benefit of the community as a whole. Close spiritual ties were maintained by the "choirs," in which members of the community lived with others of like circumstance. Children, women, and men were divided into groups based on their sex, age, and marital status; members of the same "choir" participated in common work and worship. This system enabled Moravian communities to thrive in frontier settings, where the work of all provided for sustenance and safety in times both good and bad.

With a well-deserved reputation for industry, culture, and craftsmanship, the Moravians were recruited by John Lord Carteret, the second Earl of Granville, who offered them a hundred-thousand-acre tract on his land in central North Carolina, centered around what is now Forsyth County; the Moravians would come to call this tract "Wachovia" and settled there in the 1750s, establishing the town of Bethabara as their first settlement. By the time of the American Revolution, several other Moravian communities had been created, including Salem, the largest settlement, established in 1772.

Despite earning a reputation as a center for industry and trade, with a rich cultural life, including music and public education for their children, the Moravian settlements were still small by 1781. Salem itself had only 167 residents, though "barely a hundred adults." In general, the Moravians had remained neutral during the American Revolution, causing both British and American partisans to regard them suspiciously.[12]

Marching through the Moravian settlements, the British army first arrived at Bethania around noon on February 9. Though the settlement's population was only ninety-one people, several British officers, along with a German reformed minister who was probably serving as the chaplain for the Hessian Bose Regiment, were quartered in the village. Here the British seized cattle, sheep, chickens, and geese, along with seventeen horses for the artillery. Meanwhile the British Legion was ordered to the nearby village of Bethabara, population eighty-one, where they took three hundred pounds of bread and one hundred gallons of brandy. No wonder Banastre Tarleton fondly remembered his passage through the Moravian settlements: "the mild and hospitable disposition of the inhabitants, being assisted by the well-cultivated and fruitful plantations in their possession, afforded abundant and seasonable supplies to the King's troops during their passage through this district."[13]

Of the British army's march through Bethabara on the morning of February 10, one resident recalled, the "English army was passing through our town from eight o'clock in the morning until nearly two in the afternoon." With the British rum rations diminished after Cornwallis had ordered their barrels smashed back at Ramsour's Mill, the earl vigilantly guarded the town's liquor supply, placing "a guard near the tavern, where the road turns toward Salem, and another guard was placed in front of the tavern. Another guard was paced at the still-house," a Moravian observer noted.

The British vanguard reached Salem later that same morning, around 10 a.m., though the army's last columns would not complete their march through town until four o'clock that afternoon. Cornwallis, several of his officers, and North Carolina's exiled Royal governor Josiah Martin met with town leaders before rejoining the column and camping east of the town at the plantation of Friedrich Müller, where their camp reportedly extended about two and a half miles. This is where the British army lay as Greene called his council of war.

Cornwallis was now within a day's march of Greene's Continentals. The decision to retreat now resolved, Greene moved quickly to prepare his departure from Guilford Courthouse. The Southern Army's destination was Boyd's Ferry, near the modern-day town of South Boston, Virginia, about ten miles from the North Carolina line, and Irwin's Ferry about four miles downstream from Boyd's, the deep-water ferries where Carrington would collect the boats and flats he had assembled on the Dan River.[14]

The distance was only seventy miles but required travel over the region's sludgy red clay roads in the midst of a sodden winter. By now, through the intelligence of his spies and his own evaluation, Greene knew Cornwallis thought him headed to the Dan's upper fords, believing there to be insufficient transport elsewhere on the river. To buy his army time, Greene planned to continue this deception, forming a "light corps" to make a feint toward the upper fords, masking his movement toward the lower ones.

It was a bold plan, both dangerous and strategically expedient, for Greene knew "the lure of an offer of battle . . . would always draw his adversary's attention the contrary way."[15] To set the trap, he needed his most capable partisan officer to command the light corps. Of course, Daniel Morgan was his first choice for the job. Though Morgan had already informed Greene of his intention to leave the Army,[16] Greene still "requested" Morgan take the assignment. "With a heavy heart he [Morgan] declined the proffered command and repeated his desire for leave to retire until sufficiently recovered to justify his return to duty."[17]

According to Henry Lee, Greene at first refused to accept Morgan's answer. "Greene listened with reluctance to the excuse, and endeavored to prevail on him to recede from his determination," Lee recalled. When Morgan would not relent, Greene called on Lee to press the argument: "Lieutenant-Colonel Lee, being in habits of intimacy with Morgan. . . . Many commonplace arguments were urged in conversation without success," remembered Lee, who even went so far as to suggest "that the resignation of a successful soldier at a critical moment was often attributed, and sometimes justifiably, to an apprehension that the contest would ultimately be unfortunate to his country." Yet, despite a brief reconsideration by Morgan, who "discovered a faint inclination to go through the impending conflict," the Old Waggoner finally returned to his original position. The Race to the Dan, which Morgan had initiated at his masterpiece of Cowpens, would now proceed without him. Morgan again repeated his "request to retire," which Greene now reluctantly granted.[18]

Coincidentally, the Rowan County militia had just sent a request to Greene to send Morgan to replace Davidson as their commander. "The general is so unwell he could not discharge the duties of his appointment if he had it," Greene wrote in reply.[19] The following morning, February 10, Morgan departed from Guilford Courthouse, his body so wracked with pain he had to ride in a carriage instead of horseback.[20]

It was a humbling departure for the hero of Cowpens. Morgan would return to his home in Frederick County, Virginia, a place he called "Soldier's Rest," where he would recuperate in time to take part in some minor actions of the American Revolution later that year. But never again would he command the starring role he had played so expertly at Cowpens. Though he has been a bit of a cypher during the second half of our story, his body tormented by pain, his influence on Greene can't be ignored. His strategy for using the militia in battle at Cowpens would influence Greene heavily at the Battle of Guilford Courthouse in a few short weeks. Certainly, he is today regarded as Greene's master in terms of battlefield orchestration, along with the camaraderie he enjoyed with his troops, a comportment Greene could never manage with his rank and file.

Replacing this great man in command of the Flying Army would be no easy task. According to James Graham, it was Morgan's "instance and recommendation" that influenced Greene into selecting Colonel Otho Holland Williams for the job.[21] No doubt Morgan did have some influence, though Williams was certainly qualified on his own merits. Recall that upon his arrival in the South, Greene had made Williams his adjutant general, a mostly thankless role charged with making sure orders were properly transmitted down the line.

Like Greene, Williams had natural talent for these administrative tasks. From Christmas Day, 1779, until April 1780, Williams had served in a temporary appointment as adjutant general of the Continental army on George Washington's staff while also maintaining his position as commander of the Sixth Maryland Regiment. When the Maryland and Delaware troops were selected to march south under Kalb in April 1780 to relieve Charleston (a destination they never reached), Williams was named deputy adjutant general for Kalb, a position he retained when Gates assumed command of the Southern Army later that summer.

But also like Greene, to label Otho Holland Williams a "paper pusher" is to discredit his remarkable combat experience, both before the Race to the Dan and during it. Like Morgan, Williams's first commission was in one of the rough-and-tumble rifle companies of the colonial frontier—the First Regiment of Maryland rifle company, formed in June 1775, in which Williams served as a lieutenant. "We can therefore reasonably assume that his leadership style developed under tough, experienced frontier leaders, and that he must have served competently with the rugged frontiersmen that made up these units," writes his biographer, John Beakes. "It also seems reasonable that he would not have been accepted by such a unit without some knowledge of the frontier rifle and backwoods battle tactics."[22]

It was as an officer in this company that Williams was wounded and captured during the attack on Fort Washington on Manhattan Island, during the New York campaign of 1776. Williams was among the riflemen bravely defending the north side of the fort from an attack by Hessian units. Of these riflemen, Washington would later recall, "they fought with a degree of veteran bravery and tho' but a handful, they maintained their ground a considerable time, notwithstanding the most rigorous efforts to force them. All who were spectators upon the occasion have declared this, and the Enemy themselves have not refused them applause."[23]

There is a natural tendency to confuse Otho Holland Williams with John Eager Howard. Both were senior officers in the Maryland infantry, and both are known by their three names. After all, Howard had served with distinction at Cowpens, coolly commanding the Continental infantry in one of the war's most crucial moments, a service which earned him a silver medal awarded by the Continental Congress. Meanwhile, Williams had been trudging north from the Continental camp at the Cheraws in relative obscurity, missing the decisive moments at Cowpens, Cowan's Ford, and at the Yadkin. But Otho Holland Williams was Howard's senior, both in terms of age and rank. After his capture at Fort Washington, Williams was promoted to full colonel during his long captivity; he was paroled on December 17, 1777, and finally exchanged and returned to the American ranks on January 16, 1778, fourteen months after his capture. Howard, meanwhile, was a lieutenant colonel, a subordinate rank to Williams. And Williams enjoyed more of a peer relationship with both Morgan and Greene thanks to his service experience earlier in the war, both in campaigns and as a member of Washington's staff.

Williams was no Morgan, however, for he lacked the easy camaraderie Morgan could command with his troops. "As a soldier, he may be called a rigid, not cruel, disciplinarian," recalled Lee, "obeying strictly his superior, he exacted obedience from his inferior." In a later assessment several years after the war, George Washington would write that Williams "is a sensible man, but not without vanity." Beakes acknowledges the pressures of his administrative duties could sometimes make Williams quarrelsome.

Despite these common flaws, Williams was respected and liked by his fellow officers. "His countenance was expressive, and the faithful index of his warm and honest heart," wrote Lee, who recalled his comrade as about five foot ten, "erect and elegant in form, made for activity rather than strength." Pleasing in his address, "he never failed to render himself acceptable, in whatever circle he moved, notwithstanding a sterness of character, which was sometimes manifested with too much asperity. . . . He possessed that range of mind . . . which entitled him to the highest military station, and was actuated by true courage which can refuse as well as give battle. . . . During the campaign of General Greene, he was uniformly one of his few advisers, and held his unchanged confidence."[24]

So in Otho Holland Williams Greene's answer was found. In the ranks of Greene's Continental officers, Williams was a close second, if not an equal, to Morgan in Greene's trust. And to him fell one of the most important roles in the campaign so far, upon which lay the fate of Greene's Continental army, if not the southern states. Otho Holland Williams was named commander of the light corps. The Race to the Dan would now commence its final leg.

CHAPTER 14

TO THE DAN

As usual, Greene was a blur of stratagem and correspondence in the moments and hours after the council of war. In addition to his letters to North Carolina governor Abner Nash and George Washington reporting his reasons for abandoning North Carolina, he also wrote South Carolina militia general Thomas Sumter, begging for militia support, and Virginia Governor Thomas Jefferson, requesting the same. "If I should risque a General action in our present situation, we stand ten chances to one of getting defeated, & if defeated all the Southern States m(ust) fall," he explained to Sumter.[1]

By the morning of February 10, preparations for the retreat were made. To the "light corps" under the command of Otho Holland Williams he would use as a shield and diversion for Cornwallis's pursuit, Greene assigned 240 cavalry soldiers from William Washington's First and Third Regiments and Henry Lee's Legion. Its infantry was composed of 280 Maryland, Delaware, and Virginia Continentals under the command of John Eager Howard, mostly the same men who fought with Morgan at Cowpens; sixty Virginia riflemen led by Captain David Campbell; and 120 from "Henry Lee's Partizan Infantry." Seven hundred men in all, a group Greene would call "the flower of the army."[2]

The orders for these men, Greene reported to George Washington, were to "harrass the enemy in their advance, check their progress and if possible give us an opportunity to retire without general action."[3] While Daniel Morgan rode away from Guilford Courthouse in his carriage, Greene was putting the main body of his army in motion on the direct road to Boyd's Ferry.[4] Ahead of this main body, Greene had sent a party forward to collect the boats on the Dan, and with them was his engineer, General Thaddeus Kosciusko, who was ordered to erect a breastwork at Boyd's Ferry to protect the boats and provide cover for the safe passage of the army if necessary.[5]

As noted, Cornwallis had camped the night before on the east side of Salem, twenty-five miles away. Had he lost yet another chance to catch Greene by stopping for the night instead of pushing forward to Guilford Courthouse in a forced overnight march? Perhaps, believed Greene biographer William Johnson: "It is true, that in the end, this halt proved destructive to his views," though with his "antagonist now formed a junction with his main army . . . prudence dictated the necessity of determining his force, and their views, before he approached within striking distance."[6]

According to Henry Lee, Williams stayed on the ground that morning while Greene moved off, allowing his light corps to finish their breakfast before leaving Guilford Courthouse on an "intermediate road" on the direct route for the Upper Dan. "This movement was judicious and had an immediate effect."[7]

Almost immediately elements of Cornwallis's advance came into contact with Williams's detachment. After some desultory rifle fire, the British scouts took cover to await orders. "His lordship, finding a corps of horse and foot close in front, whose strength and object were not immediately ascertainable, checked the rapidity of his march to give time for his long extended line to condense," writes Lee.[8] Lee's account suggests that Cornwallis himself was in command of the British advance forces on February 10, although historian John Buchanan reports with more credibility that it was O'Hara.[9]

Primary British accounts of these movements are sparse. Cornwallis's correspondence provides little perspective on this period, and the British narratives of Stedman, Tarleton, and O'Hara only describe them broadly, without pausing to note the activities and incidents of individual days. They were, of course, in a desperate pursuit, with little time to reflect or record their thoughts, although that didn't stop Nathanael Greene, who still managed to maintain his correspondence during the retreat, though even his normally heavy production was diminished significantly. For details, we rely then mostly on Henry Lee, an eyewitness account, though written decades later, along with Greene's correspondence and the accounts collected by Greene's early biographers.

Still, it does seem from Cornwallis's actions that he was almost completely fooled by Greene's strategy to deceive him with a light corps, as those sources suggest. William Johnson writes it was an "acknowledged fact" that Williams's light detachment completely hoodwinked the enemy.[10] George Washington Greene imagines Cornwallis's thoughts upon encountering Williams's detachment: "'It is Greene's rear,' thought Cornwallis, 'and I have him in my grasp.'"[11] Whatever the case, Cornwallis lost more precious time during the day as he attempted to assess the enemy and their objectives.

Part of the confusion may be attributed to Cornwallis's own strategies. By the night of February 10, Cornwallis had advanced his camp from the outskirts of Salem to a place called Millar's Plantation.[12] According to Greene biographer William Johnson, Cornwallis had received intelligence there were still Continental provisions stored in Hillsboro, which was also the capital of North Carolina's Patriot administration. Believing "the repository of the state stores and records . . . would claim the protection of the American army,"[13] Cornwallis planned to make a feint toward Hillsboro with a portion of his army on a direct route that bypassed Guilford Courthouse, hoping Greene would delay his retreat to turn and defend the town.

The British records make no mention of this feint toward Hillsboro. Neither Stedman, O'Hara, nor Tarleton describe it in their post-war accounts, and Cornwallis never mentioned it in his later correspondence. However, sometime during the morning of February 11, Greene wrote to Colonel John Gunby, guarding the Continental stores at Hillsboro, that he had reliable intelligence the British were moving in that direction. Greene ordered Gunby to remove all the public stores in Hillsboro to Taylor's Ferry on the Roanoke River, fifty miles northeast. Throughout the course of the day, Greene sent two more letters to Gunby with similar instructions, suggesting that, at the least, Greene believed Cornwallis was making some march toward Hillsboro, supporting Johnson's account.[14]

And if this account is accurate, we can presume Cornwallis had separated his army into at least two detachments on February 10, one marching toward Millar's Plantation to execute the deception toward Hillsboro, the other an advanced guard, probably under O'Hara, reconnoitering Williams's light brigade. Lee reports Williams considered a surprise attack on the British rear during the day on February 10, and perhaps it was this separation of Cornwallis's force into two detachments that briefly tempted him, though prudence soon won him over. "He adhered, therefore, to the less dazzling, but more useful system," of keeping his force between Greene and Cornwallis, "his attention, first on the safety of the main body," recalled Lee. Later in the day on February 10, Williams found a road that veered to the left, or northwest, placing him between Greene to his east, or on his right, and Cornwallis to his left, or west. "This was exactly the proper position for the light corps," Lee wrote, "and Williams judiciously retained it."[15]

Lee writes that his Legion, which was composing the rearguard of Williams's light corps, and the British vanguard under O'Hara were "in sight during the day" of February 10. However, after some brief rifle fire during the initial encounter, there appears to have been little skirmishing that first day, the two armies content to scout one another's positions. On the morning of February 11, Williams wrote to Greene from a location seven miles northwest of Guilford Courthouse: he had received a report earlier that morning the British army had advanced "six miles from Salem by early Yesterday' afternoon, but was still not sure of their route," suggesting the previous day's contact had been with a British detachment, not the main force.[16]

And though the day had been relatively serene, the night was long and dangerous. Williams's troops hadn't eaten all day, but it was the fatigue that depleted them, "so much more operative is weariness than hunger," that each man not on duty surrendered to "repose as soon as the night position was taken." But Williams did not want to be caught off guard and employed "numerous patrols and strong pickets" during the night, "not only for their own safety, but to prevent the enemy from placing himself, by a circuitous march, between Williams and Greene," Lee reports.

If February 10 had been the opening leg of the Race to the Dan, with Williams's rearguard and O'Hara's vanguard probing for tactical advantage, the real action started on February 11. Williams broke camp at the "hour of three," so that his troops could "gain such a distance in front as would secure breakfast" for his soldiers, "their only meal during this rapid and hazardous retreat."[17]

Cornwallis and the British army were moving early as well. This was the morning Cornwallis probably attempted his feint toward Hillsboro. Meanwhile, the British vanguard found a "causeway leading to the desired route" of Dix's Ferry and got in the rear of the American troops, though unbeknownst to Williams or Lee.

After a rapid morning's march, Williams sent forward some of his staff to begin preparations for breakfast, leaving small cavalry patrols under the command of a Lieutenant Carrington (*not* Colonel Edward Carrington, procurer of Greene's boats) in his rear to guard against surprise attack. "The morning was cold and drizzly," Lee recalled. "Our fires, which had been slow in kindling, were now lively: the meat was on the coals, and the corn-cake in the ashes." At this moment, a countryman approached the camp in haste with a message for the "General." Escorted to Williams, the civilian told the colonel the British "had got into our road" and just one half hour before he had seen them advancing, only four miles away.

Williams took the news calmly, not wanting to interrupt his men's breakfast at what might have been the ravings of an overwrought farmer, or possibly the deliberate deceptions of a spy. Instead, he ordered Lee to scout the road in his rear to determine the accuracy of the civilian's report. Lee dispatched a Captain Armstrong, with "one section of the horse," to investigate the report and returned to his breakfast, but shortly thereafter another report arrived from Lieutenant Carrington, communicating the "unusually slow progress of the British van-guard." Williams now ordered Lee to take command of the scouting party himself, and with the "coun-tryman" informant as his guide, Lee traveled down the road in search of Armstrong.

"Lee proceeded, in conformity with the advice of the countryman," for two miles, but seeing no British, decided to return to his breakfast, believing his guide, "however well affected, was certainly in a mistake." By now he had found Armstrong, whom he left behind as a rearguard with three dra-goons, mounted on "the swiftest horses," and the countryman guide to con-tinue their search for the British. But the countryman protested. He had considered himself safe with the whole detachment, but now being left with only four dragoons, "whose only duty was to look and fly," he de-manded for himself one of the Legion's fine horses. Admitting the man's logic, Lee gave him the horse and pistol of his bugler, a boy named James Gillies. Now defenseless, Gillies was sent back to camp on the countryman's inferior horse to inform Williams "how far the lieutenant-colonel had pro-ceeded without seeing a portion of the enemy, and of his intention to return after advancing Armstrong still further in the front."

Lee now ordered his men into the woods, where they must have been separated. A few minutes later, he heard the sound of muskets, "and shortly after the clangor of horses in swift speed declared the fast approach of cavalry." It was Armstrong with his small party, now being closely pursued by a troop of Tarleton's dragoons. For them Lee felt no apprehension, but for the safety of his bugler, Gillies, atop the countryman's slow pony, "every feeling of his heart became interested."

Lee waited in the woods for the pursuit to pass, halting one of his lieutenants to scout for additional British cavalry coming up the road. He was "determined to rescue his bugler," yet wanted the charging British dragoons to take "the utmost allowable distance, that they might be deprived of support." Now hastening his progress with the remainder of his party, he soon came upon the British dragoons, who by this time had unhorsed Gillies and sabred the defenseless young man several times while he lay "prostrate on the ground."

In a fury, Lee led his men in a charge against the British. "The enemy was crushed on the first charge; most of them were killed or prostrated." During the fight, the British commander was recognized by some of Lee's soldiers as a Captain Miller, who had participated in the slaughter of Continental soldiers at the Waxhaws on May 29, 1780, the infamous British atrocity responsible for Tarleton's "Bloody Ban" nickname and the term "Tarleton's quarter," an epithet for the merciless butchery of unarmed or wounded men.

After the skirmish, Captain Miller escaped with a small segment of his men. Lee ordered a pursuit, giving his soldiers the order to provide no quarter to Miller. "This sanguinary mandate, so contrary to the American character, proceeded from a view of the bugler," explained Lee, "a beardless, unarmed youth, who had vainly implored quarter, and in the agonies of death presented a spectacle resistless in its appeal for vengeance." Meanwhile, Lee ordered some of his soldiers to deliver the severely wounded Gillies back to the American camp for medical attention.

Lee's soldiers soon captured Miller and two of his dragoons and brought them before Lee. In his "sanguinary" mood, Lee reprimanded his men for not executing his orders to kill Miller and now ordered his execution. But the British officer pleaded his case, explaining to Lee that he had tried to stop his "intoxicated" dragoons from slaughtering the bugler without effect; furthermore, he argued, his own humanity during the Waxhaws was well known to some of the Americans that had escaped.

Miller's arguments convinced Lee to relent, and he ordered the prisoners taken to the American camp. However, along the way they overtook the party transporting Gillies, who confirmed to Lee his "former impressions" of the British atrocity, apparently right before dying. The boy's deathbed account reignited Lee's zeal for vengeance. "Descending a long hill, he [Lee] repeated his determination to sacrifice Miller in the vale," and had just handed him a pencil, "to note on paper whatever he might wish to make known to his friends," when just at that moment his rearguard communicated the approach of the British vanguard by pistol shot.

Miller and his men were now sent to Colonel Williams, who "put his corps in motion, and forwarded the captured officers and soldiers to head-quarters, ignorant of the murder of the bugler, and the determination of Lieutenant-Colonel Lee."[18]

The murder of the defenseless Gillies and capture of Captain Miller is a chilling account from Lee's memoir, a book full of such accounts and vivid detail. Henry Lee is occasionally accused of not letting accuracy stand in the way of a good story, but here he recounts the dark horrors of war and how those horrors can drive even a "gentleman" like Lee to murderous vengeance.

Lee recounted that his Legion killed eighteen British dragoons in the engagement over the prostrate bugler, leaving their bodies on the road to be buried by "order of Lord Cornwallis as he passed." Though we will never know the accuracy of this account, we do have a report from Williams to Greene dated February 11 that "Colonel Lee with a Troop of Dragoons" met an advance from the enemy and "Captured 3 or 4 Men whom I send you." William Seymour, marching in Williams's column, wrote that after receiving intelligence the British army was approaching from their rear, "Colonel Lee detached a party of horse to intercept them, who meeting with their vanguard, consisting of an officer and twenty men, which they killed, wounded and made prisoners, all but one man."[19] But Seymour made no mention of the slaughtered Gillies. Tarleton reported the encounter as well, though not surprisingly, he gave a completely different account of the action, reporting only that Lee was "repulsed with some loss," though admitting one of his officers, with three soldiers, continued the pursuit too far and were made prisoners. As for the "beardless bugler," whom Lee records as the only American casualty, "his corpse was necessarily deposited in the woods adjoining the road, with the hopes that some humane citizen might find it."[20]

In his report from the night of February 11, Williams informed Greene the "Lord Cornwallis & the whole British army" was within six or eight miles of his camp, suggesting whatever detachments Cornwallis had made as part of his alleged feint toward Hillsboro earlier in the day, his entire army was now reunited. "Colonel Tarltons Legion is close in our rear," reported Williams. "I will endeavor to avoid him."[21]

Avoid him they did, though it wasn't easy. As the retreat continued, Lee's rearguard and the van of O'Hara were within musket shot of one another several times, providing temptation to the Patriot marksmen. But they were "restrained with difficulty from delivering their fire," Williams fearing such skirmishing might ignite a larger engagement that would threaten the light corps and allow Cornwallis to get on Greene's rear. According to Lee, Williams's refusal to allow his troops to engage had a curious effect on the British. "The demeanor of the hostile troops became so pacific in appearance that a spectator would have been led to consider them members of the same party. Only when a defile or a water-course crossed did the enemy exhibit any indication to cut off our rear; in which essays, being always disappointed, their useless efforts were gradually discontinued."[22]

The retreat pressed on, engendering the limits of human misery and endurance with each step. In the mornings, the men would cut their feet on the sludge and muck of the region's red clay roads frozen over into sharp edges the night before, while their "unsubstantial garments, wholly unsuited to the season,"[23] provided little relief from the wet and cold. "The miserable situation of the troops for want of clothing has rendered the march the most painfull imaginable," Greene would soon report to George Washington, "several hundreds of the Soldiers tracking the ground with their bloody feet."[24]

After their breakfast, the men marched the rest of the day and deep into the night with only their dreams and fantasies of the following morning's meal for sustenance. "You must understand," explains William Seymour, "that we marched for the most part both day and night, the main army of the British being close in our rear, so that we had not scarce time to cook our victuals, their whole attention being on our light troops."[25] During the day, the frozen roads would thaw "into a heavy mire, and with horses' feet and wagon tracks cutting into it all the way, every step was made with efforts equally exhausting to man and horse."[26] At night Greene's army slept four men to a blanket, though Lee reports the light corps "was rather better off." Their officers slept three to a blanket, while the fourth whose "hour admitted rest" must "keep upon his legs to preserve the fire in vigor." Williams's detachment never slept in their tents, Lee tells us, so this fire was the only protection "from rain and sometime snow."[27]

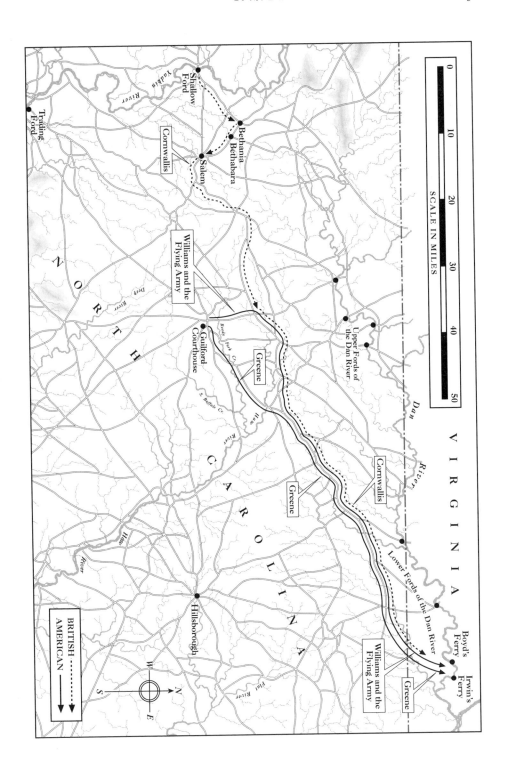

Officer and soldier alike suffered from sleep deprivation; on the fourth day of the march, Greene would report he had not slept more than four hours since departing Guilford Courthouse. In one letter, he admits to Williams his sleep was interrupted by what he believed was a British officer lurking through the Continental camp in the dark. In another letter, written long after the retreat, Greene would recall a restless night spent with South Carolina governor-in-exile John Rutledge. The two had stopped at a meager house along the retreat route, where they shared a bed. During the night, each accused the other of kicking in their sleep. The kicking continued until they discovered they had been joined by the family's hog, seeking shelter from the rain and cold.[28]

The British army, of course, faced the same challenges, though they were better shod and "well clothed," at least according to their American historians.[29] But the British pursuit was hampered by other burdens. According to their provost marshal records, the British were accompanied by up to one hundred American prisoners, most of them men captured during the raid at Torrance's Tavern. Along with these prisoners were a large number of camp followers, mostly women, who still accompanied the British army despite Cornwallis's attempts to shed them back at Ramsour's Mill. This human accoutrement probably slowed the progress of the British army as much as the lack of clothing and provision delayed the American.[30]

UNFORTUNATELY, we have few reports of the Race to the Dan dated from February 12 and 13. Henry Lee continued to provide anecdotal accounts, though the dates recorded in his memoir sometime don't correspond to other sources. Lee records the death of Gillies as occurring on February 13, though Williams's letter to Greene clearly dates the encounter to February 11. From what appears to be later that same evening, either the eleventh or the thirteenth, Lee describes another memorable skirmish in his memoir.

Lee writes that he had discovered, "from conversation with his guides, that a by-way in front would lead him into Williams's rear before the close of the evening, and to save a considerable distance, determined to avail himself of the accommodation." Lee and his cavalry had missed their breakfast that morning due to the encounter with Captain Miller and the death of Gillies, so when they came upon an "abundant farm," Lee decided to stop there for dinner.

Believing the British were still marching on the nearby main road, and that the "obscurity of the narrow road" taken by Lee provided him some safety, Lee posted only a few guards at "intermediate points, rather than to give notice when the British should pass along than to guard the Legion from surprise." As Lee and his soldiers sat down to dinner, "our horses were unbridled, with abundance of provender before them. . . . The hospitable farmer had liberally bestowed his meat and bacon, and had given the aid of his domestics in hastening the much-wished repast." But just at this moment, Lee heard the fire of the advance guards, "certain signal of the enemy's approach." Somehow, slipping the notice of Lee's scouts, the British vanguard had turned onto the same road and was now approaching.

Between the farm and the approaching British was a creek, "which in consequence of the late incessant rains, could only be passed by a bridge." Lee now ordered his cavalry to rise from their comfortable meal and support the guards; meanwhile, his infantry scurried toward the bridge. "The bridge was gained, and soon passed by the corps of Lee." But the British were now in hot pursuit. Lee reports the British gave chase, "through cultivated fields for a mile," until Lee's Legion once more entered the main road to Irwin's Ferry and managed to get away. "Thus escaped a corps, which had been hitherto guarded with unvarying vigilance, and whose loss would have been severely felt by the American general, and which had been exposed to imminent peril from a presumption of certain security," scolds Lee to himself. "A soldier is always in danger, when his conviction of security leads him to dispense with the most vigilant precautions."[31]

Whether it was this encounter, or some other intelligence gained by Cornwallis, he was now aware of Greene's deception, that the Continental army was headed toward the Dan's lower fords, and he shifted his route to follow Greene on the road toward Irwin's Ferry. The relentless pursuit was taking a toll. Greene's volunteer militia were not up to the tension and started to desert. In a letter dated February 12, Greene's only correspondence from what must have been a long, weary day, he complains to North Carolina militia general John Butler, "the militia have been so inattentive to their own interest that not more than one hundred & fifty Men are left with this Army to render the Regular Troops the least assistance."[32] By the next day, he reported to Williams that all but eighty of the North Carolina men had deserted. "Majors and captains are among the deserters."[33]

Without correspondence from Cornwallis or his senior commanders, we must rely on deduction to assess their strategy during this time. From the accounts of Lee, Williams, and Greene, we know the British stayed in close pursuit of the American rear during the final two days of the race. From Lee, we know the British at first attempted to use the crossing of water to gain some strategic advantage, though these "essays, being always disappointed," were gradually discontinued as the march ground on. And we know the nights were wildly dangerous, with British scouts and detachments seeking some strategic advantage, their Continental counterparts on constant watch and patrol.

But the British still showed no inclination to attack Greene from behind or try to cut him off with their cavalry or some other stratagem. This suggests Cornwallis still believed he could pin Greene against the Dan River, either remaining unaware of the boats collected at the deep-water fords or believing he could apprehend Greene before the Americans could attempt a crossing. Cornwallis's lack of intelligence let him down as well; in a confusing landscape of unknown roads, Cornwallis had no other option but to pursue. From the British orderly book of February 12, instructions read only that the troops were to march "under Arms" at "half past Six oClock tomorrow Morn," and from the following day, February 13, only that the march the following morn was to begin earlier, at "1/2 past five oClock."[34]

"It is very evident the enemy intend to push us in crossing the river," Greene wrote to Williams on February 13,[35] and indeed from the evidence at hand, that is the only deduction we can make of Cornwallis's strategy from our modern perspective. Marching in unfamiliar country, on a primitive and confusing road system, with unreliable intelligence and wavering Loyalist support, Cornwallis appeared unwilling to risk any elaborate plan to apprehend Greene before he reached the Dan.

"I was in great hopes that he [Greene] would not escape me without receiving a blow," Cornwallis would write in his report to Germain. "Nothing could exceed the patience and alacrity of the officers and soldiers under every species of hardship and fatigue in endeavouring to overtake him, but our intelligence upon this occasion was exceedingly defective, which, with heavy rains, bad roads and the passage of many deep creeks and bridges destroyed by the enemy's light troops, rendered all our exertions in vain."[36]

Of this period Tarleton also writes little, noting only "on the road many skirmishes took place between the British and American light troops, without great loss to either party, or any impediment to the progress of the main body."[37]

By the night of February 13, despair was setting in. Writing to Greene around seven o'clock that evening, Williams admitted he was "concern'd to hear by the Express . . . that you were yet 25 miles from the ferry. . . . My Dear General at Sun Down the Enemy were only 22 miles from you and may be in motion now or most probably by (3) oClock in the morning. . . . Rely on it, my Dear Sir it is possible (for you) to be overtaken before you can cross the Dan even if you had 20 Boats." Williams swore to Greene his relentless efforts to delay the British advance but admitted he could not "help being uneasy."

Williams's letter from this desperate night goes on to describe the fatigue of both his men and horses. He admitted some of his men were deserting him. In this dire situation, he saw no other option but offering Cornwallis battle to give Greene and the rest of the army time to cross. "I'm confident we may remain in the State but whither it will not be at the risque of our Light Corps and whither we shall not be wasted by continual fatigue you can determine," he concluded, practically begging Greene for further guidance before the decisive moment he anticipated was at hand.[38]

At what must have been just a short time after Williams wrote this somber letter, his men observed fires glowing in the distance ahead. Williams's heart sunk, believing the fires were from Greene's camp. With the British in close pursuit, Williams and Lee believed finally they would be forced to turn and fight to give Greene and the rest of the army any chance of escape. "No pen can describe the heart-rending feelings of our brave and wearied troops," agrees Lee. "Not a doubt was entertained that the descried camp was Greene's; and our dauntless corps were convinced that the crisis had now arrived when its self sacrifice could alone give a chance of escape to the main body."

But something wasn't quite right, for Williams had received correspondence from Greene earlier in the day that they had already passed this point. Suspiciously approaching the campfires, the whole corps rejoiced to discover that the camp was where Greene had halted two nights before, on February 11, and the burning fires had been tended by residents of the surrounding countryside as a welcome for the weary light corps.

As relieved as they were to discover their mistake, they could not stop to enjoy the fires, for Cornwallis was too close behind. Williams did permit his men to stop briefly, "at the first convenient spot," but by midnight the troops were again in motion, "in consequence of the enemy's advance on our pickets." They were getting close now to the Dan, and "animated with the prospect of soon terminating their present labors, the light troops resumed their march with alacrity."[39]

Around 4 a.m. the next morning, February 14, Greene wrote to Williams. He was "preparing for the worst," he told his trusted aide and urged him to follow the route of the army to join him as quickly as possible, "as a division of our force may encourage the enemy to push us further than they will dare to do, if we are together."[40]

Then at 2 p.m. later that afternoon, Greene wrote Williams again. "The greater part of our wagons are over [the Dan], and the troops are crossing." The plan had worked. Greene had finally reached Irwin's Ferry earlier that day with the boats and flats awaiting him. At 5:30 that afternoon, Greene informed Williams that the troops were all across, "the stage is clear," and Greene was ready to receive Williams and give him a "hearty welcome." According to the historian William Gordon, the light corps cheers at receiving this last message were so loud they could be heard by the British vanguard commanded by O'Hara, who realized immediately what it meant—their quarry had escaped across the river.[41]

At the glorious news, Williams moved ahead with the infantry and Virginia riflemen of the light corps, leaving Lee and his Legion behind to act as a rear guard. Williams and his party arrived at the banks of the Dan later that night, after a march of forty miles that day. Nathanael Greene awaited them on the Dan's southern bank, eager to thank them for their gallant defense during the retreat, and soon they were safely across the river. The infantry of Lee's Legion arrived shortly thereafter, followed finally by Lee's cavalry.

Lee writes he was greeted at the river by Lieutenant Colonel Carrington, who had begun the preparations for this remarkable escape nearly two months before. "The horses were turned into the stream," Lee recalled, "while the dragoons with their arms and equipment, embarked in the boats. . . . In the last boat, the quarter-master general, attended by Lieutenant-Colonel Lee and the rear troops, reached the friendly shore. . . . Thus ended, on the night of the 14th of February, this long, arduous, and eventful retreat."[42]

Part Four

AFTERWARD

CHAPTER 15

FAVOURABLE OPPORTUNITIES

The Race to the Dan was over. Cornwallis's British army had pushed Greene's American army out of the Carolinas. Charleston, the most important city in the South, was firmly in possession of the British throne, and South Carolina was under British military administration, ruled from a series of outposts stretching across its frontier. Georgia and Florida also were under British control. As he had retreated across North Carolina, Greene tried desperately to rally the North Carolina militia, but after the death of general William Davidson, these "Patriots" had shown little interest in rallying to the American cause, leaving Greene no option but to abandon the colony.

Cornwallis cast the American retreat in this light. In his proclamation issued to the people of North Carolina a week later, he wrote, "Whereas it has pleased the divine providence to prosper the operations of His Majesty's army in driving the rebel army out of this province, and whereas it is His Majesty's most gracious wish to rescue His faithful and loyal subjects from the cruel tyranny under which they have groaned for several years, I have thought proper to issue the proclamation to invite all such faithful and loyal subjects to repair without loss of time . . . to the royal standard . . . AND I do hereby assure them that I am ready to concur with them in effectual measures for suppressing the remains of rebellion in this province and for re-establishment of good order and constitutional government."[1]

In other words, game over, or so Cornwallis would have the people of North Carolina believe. Similarly, the campaign's British chroniclers through their histories tried to cast the American retreat in a favorable light, though their enthusiasm seems forced. Stedman could only manage: "Lord Cornwallis, having thus driven general Greene out of the province of North Carolina, returned by easy marches from the banks of the Dan to Hillsborough."[2] With a bit more enthusiasm, Tarleton manages: "The continentals being chased out of North Carolina, and the militia being awed and impeded from collecting, Earl Cornwallis thought the opportunity favourable for assembling the King's friends."[3]

More soon will be revealed about these "favourable" opportunities. For now, our narrative returns to the north bank of the Dan, where far from behaving as if they had just been pushed from the Carolinas in disgraceful defeat, leaving a subjugated South in their wake, the Continental army—cold, wet, hungry, and weary in their tattered clothes and with bleeding feet—was celebrating as if they had just won the World Series. In prose too purple to resist, we shall let Greene's biographer and great-grandson, George Washington Greene, describe the celebratory scene:

> Officer and soldier met with radiant smile and beaming eye. Around every watch-fire there were tales of risks run, feats performed, and privations endured. Loud were the praises of Williams and his gallant light troops; earnest the commendations of Carrington, who had done staff duty and field duty through those anxious days, and done both so well. But louder and more earnest still were the expressions of their admiration for Greene, who had foreseen every danger, provided for every contingency, and inflicted upon the British arms the severest blow which they had received in the whole course of the Southern war.[4]

Of course, that last bit about the "severest blow" is pure hyperbole, but the rest rings true, in spirit if not actual detail. Most of it was paraphrased from Lee, who wrote similarly, "In the camp of Greene, joy beamed in every face . . . the subsequent days to the reunion of the army on the north of the Dan were spent in mutual gratulations."[5]

The American chroniclers could hyperbolize as effectively as the British, but clearly the Patriots celebrated their feat, if not their defeat. And why not? Through Greene's brilliant orchestration and his soldiers' resiliency, the stalwart leadership of his officers, the Southern Army had been pre-served, without any significant loss of his enlisted troops. True, the militia had deserted them, but Greene knew they could be rallied again under more favorable circumstances. More importantly, he had preserved his wagons and most of his stores, which awaited him in Virginia. And the British pris-oners taken at Cowpens had been marched safely out of North Carolina, valuable currency for future prisoner exchanges. "The people of the Halifax County received us with the affection of brethren, mingled with admiration of the brave devotion to country just exhibited," observes Lee. "Volunteers began to tender their services, of which laudable enthusiasm Greene availed himself."[6]

While the Americans celebrated on one side of the Dan, the British fumed on the other. Their pursuit had led them 240 miles from their nearest base of supply, in Camden, South Carolina. They had burned most of their baggage and stores at Ramsour's Mill over two weeks before, and now their own clothes were almost as tattered and rotten as the Americans, the new leather soles their shoes had received at Ramsour's worn through by the interminable marching in horrid, wet weather. "The fatigue of our troops and hardships which they suffered were excessive," Cornwallis admitted to his confidant Rawdon.[7]

O'Hara with the British vanguard arrived at the Dan about twelve hours after Lee and the last of the American light corps crossed. As at the Yadkin, they could do nothing but stare across the swollen river at the celebrating Americans on the other side. This time, however, they lacked the wrathful spirit to launch a cannonade. According to Charles Stedman, in their last desperate attempt to catch the Americans before they crossed the river, the British had marched forty miles in the previous twenty-four hours, only to have their quarry escape once again. "The hardships suffered by the British troops, for want of their tents and usual baggage, in this long and rapid pursuit, through a wild and unsettled country, were uncommonly great."[8]

True, the state of North Carolina now lay undefended before them, but the ever-fickle Cornwallis seemed no longer sure he even wanted it. "The immense extent of this country, cut with numberless rivers and creeks, and with the total want of internal navigation, which renders it impossible for our army to remain long in the heart of the country, will make it very dif-ficult to reduce this province to obedience by a direct attack upon it," he would eventually write to Germain, an opinion surely influenced by his futile pursuit of Greene.[9] In essence, this was the epitaph for the Southern

Strategy, which had always been based on faulty conjecture about the South's people and her landscapes.

Cornwallis's despondency didn't prevent Greene from preparing defenses for another attack or contemplating his own. As usual, he found time to correspond and strategize among the celebrations. Informing his mentor George Washington of the narrow escape, Greene paused to congratulate the men he considered to be its true heroes, Edward Carrington and Otho Holland Williams. "Our Army are in good Spirits notwithstanding their suffering and excessive fatigue," he observed, before quickly returning to his strategic deliberations. "The enemy are on the other side of the river and it is falling. . . . I expect it will be fordable by night."

Greene expected Cornwallis to head for the Virginia town of Halifax. "That position would greatly awe Virginia and almost totally subject N. Carolina." To prepare for that contingency, he dispatched his engineer Thaddeus Kosciuszko along with 345 Maryland and Delaware Continentals to prepare a fortification for the town.[10] Meanwhile, Greene did what he had done so many times before during his administration of the Southern Army and what he would continue to do long after: solicit troops, militia, and supplies. In a blur of correspondence, Greene cast his nets far and wide, trying to raise militia both in Virginia and North Carolina, while pleading with his fellow Continental officers to either send him troops or raise new ones.

As usual, most of these efforts would fail, but Cornwallis had no appetite for pushing across the Dan. The "favourable opportunity" he foresaw for "assembling the King's friends" was in Hillsboro, North Carolina, not Virginia. With his own army run down and depleted from their pursuit, Cornwallis felt his force "ill suited to enter . . . so powerful a province as Virginia." And by now he was receiving reports of Patriot militia gathering in North Carolina: General Andrew Pickens had raised seven hundred militia in the state and was threatening his left flank; North Carolina militia general Richard Caswell was raising militia on his right. Eager to establish a presence in North Carolina, Cornwallis left the vicinity of the Dan River on February 17. He marched the sixty-two miles from Boyd's Ferry to Hillsboro in three days, arriving there on February 20, after crossing two branches of the Hycotee River and three creeks along the way—the rivers of North Carolina would forever be a plague on Cornwallis's soul.[11]

At Hillsboro, Cornwallis finally set about raising the Loyalist hordes long rumored to inhabit the state, issuing the proclamation that invited them "to repair . . . to the royal standard now erected at Hillsborough."[12] And for a time, the friends did come. Tarleton reported "many hundred inhabitants of the surrounding districts rode into the British camp."[13] By now, Lee was back across the Dan with his Legion, scouting the Hillsboro vicinity, and to Greene he reported the Loyalists "swarm to the town."[14]

But such "friendships" didn't last long in the North Carolina interior, for soon the Loyalists' arrival diminished, then slackened, then came to a suspicious stop. Cornwallis would quickly learn the reason why: on February 22, Greene had recrossed the Dan with his main army.[15] By then Lee's Legion was already campaigning in conjunction with Pickens against Loyalist militia, and the "Light Corps," again under the command of Otho Holland Williams, was approaching Cornwallis from the north. The Race to the Dan may have been over, but the campaign which would culminate at the Battle of Guilford Courthouse on March 15 had already begun.

THAT THE RACE TO THE DAN was better known in its own time than now is not surprising. Then, like now, the American public was addicted to news, though it was the newspaper that fed this addiction then, not the Internet. When the American Revolution began in 1775, there were thirty-eight newspapers printed on fifty presses in the American colonies. Because of the long process involved in laying out type, most newspapers published weekly. Often the "news" they printed about the conflict with England was letters from important military figures, not correspondents' reports. But no matter the source, or the delay, these newspapers were consumed by a rapt public, just as frequently read aloud in the taverns and on the street as in the privacy of the home.

And though the news cycle was considerably longer, with accounts appearing weeks, sometimes months, after the fact, the American public devoured news about the great race across North Carolina. The *Connecticut Journal* in New Haven published a copy of Nathanael Greene's February 9 letter to George Washington on March 15, 1781. Written directly after the council of war, this letter includes accounts of the actions at Cowan's Ford and the escape across the Yadkin at Salisbury, along with news of General Morgan's departure from the army. On September 13, 1781, the Boston paper *Massachusetts Spy* published Cornwallis's account of the chase to Lord Germain, which was reprinted from a Charleston, South Carolina, paper that ran the letter on July 26.[16] So, for a time, the Race to the Dan was "hot news," its circumstances familiar, if not famous. But then, as now, attention spans waned, and the public's interest in Greene's miraculous escape was soon replaced by accounts of the Battle at Guilford Courthouse on March 15, 1781, followed not long afterward by Cornwallis's stunning surrender at Yorktown on October 19.

If Greene felt spurned by the public's fickle attention, he at least had the adulation of his fellow Continental officers. "You may be assured that your Retreat before Lord Cornwallis is highly applauded by all Ranks and reflects much honor on your military Abilities," congratulated George Washington.[17] Congress, for its part, preferred to reward battlefield victories, not strategic evacuations, awarding the gold medal to Daniel Morgan for his victory at Cowpens in a proclamation dated March 9, 1781, but mentioning nothing about Greene's assiduously executed retreat.

After long years of stalemate, the war was nearing an end, and it's not surprising the Race to the Dan was eventually forgotten by the American public. Cornwallis's surrender at Yorktown undoubtedly sealed its fate, but contributing to this obscurity was that no major member of its Continental officer corps left a memoir. Neither Greene, who died tragically from heat stroke in 1786, just forty-three years old, nor Morgan ever attempted one. Otho Holland Williams started a memoir but never published it.

None, that is, until Henry Lee, who first published his Revolutionary War memoirs in 1812, more than thirty years after the Race to the Dan. But better late than never. Like this account, many of Nathanael Greene's nineteenth-century biographers—men like William Johnson, who first published his two-volume biography of Greene in 1822, and Greene's grandson, George Washington Greene, who published his three-volume biography between 1867 and 1871—borrowed heavily from Lee.

We leave it to Light Horse Harry, therefore, to offer some perspective on the Race to the Dan. Writing with his usual flair, Lee surmises: "No operation during the war more attracted the public attention than this did: not only the toils and dangers encountered by a brave general and his brave army interested the sympathy of the nation, but the Safety of the South, hanging on its issue, excited universal concern. The danger of this contingency alarmed the hearts of all, especially the more reflecting, who deemed the integrity of the Union essential to American liberty and happiness, and indispensable to our future safety and strength."[18]

A bold summation, no doubt, though perhaps one written by Otho Holland Williams was more accurate: "The retreat of the southern army to the

Dan River, though now forgotten, was, in my estimation, one of the most masterly and fortunate manoeuvres of our beloved Greene."[19]

And if the Race to the Dan was eventually forgotten in its own time, today it is virtually unknown. Despite the plethora of books on the American Revolution available today, popular and enduring ones, like John Ferling's *Almost A Miracle*, provide a broad overview of the conflict, its political machinations, and major events such as Bunker Hill, Valley Forge, and Yorktown. Both Ferling and his predecessor, Christopher Ward, devote but a few short pages to Greene's strategic retreat to the Dan out of tomes that approach one thousand pages.

A notable exception is the monumental *Road to Guilford Courthouse* by John Buchanan, first published in 1997, which brought a renewed focus to the southern campaign, including long overdue attention to the Race to the Dan. Many twenty-first-century writers, including this one, are heavily indebted to Buchanan and his work, which is required reading for any serious enthusiast of the southern campaigns.

Another relatively recent development contributing to renewed interest in the southern campaigns, including the Race to the Dan, is the publication of Nathanael Greene's collected papers. Started in 1976 and completed only in 2005, this thirteen-volume series is both a blessing to southern campaign enthusiasts and a national treasure. Indeed, a work like this one could not be written without it. Any University of North Carolina alumni should be proud this landmark collection was published by our own University of North Carolina Press.

But time marches on, and as one of the editors of Greene's papers laments, wars aren't taught in American schools anymore.[20] If this shift away from the study of a white-male dominated history of warfare and conflict to a more holistic focus on cultures and political movements is understandable in today's diverse world, it's too bad the legacies of men like Nathanael Greene, Daniel Morgan, and Otho Holland Williams have been lost in the transformation. What's sadder still is that today's grade school curriculums hardly teach history at all, preferring to focus on the more "practical" fields of science and math. What review there is on the American Revolution tends to focus on the leadership of George Washington, along with side notes on curiosities such as the Marquis de Lafayette and Betsy Ross.

But that doesn't mean new and important works about the southern campaigns aren't out there for those curious enough to seek them. Recent biographies have been published on the South Carolina partisans Andrew Pickens and Francis Marion. And even Continental officers such as Daniel Morgan, Otho Holland Williams, John Eager Howard, and William Washington now have full-length biographies. Independent publishers and university presses still publish quality, beautiful books about individual campaigns and issues within the American Revolution, like this one. Meanwhile, the Internet and advances in print-on-demand technologies make historical texts such as William Johnson's biography of Nathanael Greene and Charles Stedman's account from the British army perspective available to anyone with a Visa card. Plenty of information about the Race to the Dan and other elements of the little-known southern campaigns, such as King's Mountain, Camden, and Cowpens, is out there, for those with the curiosity to seek it.

GREENE'S SECOND ATTEMPT to raise a militia army to fight Cornwallis in North Carolina was more successful than his first. In Virginia, he had been rejoined by General Edward Stevens and six hundred Virginia riflemen. Though his trusted militia general Andrew Pickens now begged leave to return to South Carolina with his force of about 450 South Carolinians and Georgians, Greene was soon joined by several regiments of North Carolina and Virginia militia after recrossing the Dan and marching toward Hillsboro.[21]

During the first ten days of March, Greene maneuvered tirelessly around Cornwallis's position in an attempt to keep the British guessing his intentions while continuing to assemble his militia force. Cornwallis also was on the move, the food and forage around Hillsboro soon exhausted by his hungry army. Meanwhile, the Royal "friends" he called to the king's standard either disappeared back into the North Carolina wilderness after gawking at the British camp or never materialized at all.

"I am certain that in our March of near a Thousand miles, almost in as many directions, thro' every part of North Carolina, tho every means possible was taken to persuade our Friends as they are called, and indeed as they call themselves, to join us, we never had with us at any one time One Hundred Men in Arms," lamented the irascible O'Hara, never a fan of the British strategy to rely on Loyalist support. "When will Government see these People thro' proper medium? I am persuaded never."[22]

Complicating matters was Henry's Lee's slaughter of some of these "Friends." On the afternoon of February 25, while campaigning as an advance force on the outskirts of the British position, Lee and his green-jacketed dragoons encountered a party of four hundred Loyalist militia under the command of Colonel John Pyle on a road between the Haw and Deep Rivers in central North Carolina. To Pyle's misfortune, he and his men had been searching for the camp of Banastre Tarleton's Legion, which also wore green jackets. Taking advantage of their misunderstanding, Lee and his men fell on Pyle's column in a brutal massacre, killing ninety and seriously wounding many more. Like the slaughter at Hammond's Store, it was another manifestation of the southern campaign's "dirty war," the Americans no less guilty of barbarity than the British, though the butchery served its purpose: after "Pyle's Massacre," as the encounter is most commonly known, Loyalist support for the British army withered.[23]

By the middle of March, Greene's total militia and volunteer infantry had swelled to 2,600. Added to this were two new regiments of Continentals, recently recruited from Virginia. His regular Continental infantry now numbered 1,600, though only 630 of those were his battle-tested veterans from Maryland and Delaware, the heart of his army. With William Washington and Henry Lee's cavalry, along with about sixty artillerists, his total force was approximately 4,400 troops.

Further delay could provide no benefit. With most of his militia enlisted only for a six-week term, and the supply of food and forage exhausted in central North Carolina, Greene marched once more to Guilford Courthouse, where he turned and offered Cornwallis battle. Cornwallis's force numbered only 1,900. Though his army was considerably weaker than it had been when he marched from South Carolina with 2,400 back in early January, Cornwallis also believed battle was now his best, perhaps only, opportunity for success. With his supplies exhausted and the Loyalist support he'd been promised vanished, his only other option was to admit defeat and march toward his depots in Wilmington. Cornwallis, the warrior, chose battle.[24]

The two armies met each other on the fields and forests around Guilford Courthouse on March 15. As Morgan had at Cowpens, Greene placed much of his militia in a forward line, ordering them to fire twice before quitting the field. But on the battlefield, Greene was no Morgan, and with his lines spread out across a much greater distance than at Cowpens, too far in fact for Greene to observe or adequately command from his position behind the main Continental line, the Patriot militia mostly scattered in disarray at the approach of the British regulars. Though his Continentals held firm, Greene was too much the strategist to risk them in an all-out assault. After a bloody and obstinate fight that lasted almost three hours, Greene quit the field.

Cornwallis finally had defeated Greene in battle during the North Carolina campaign. But at what cost? His casualties were ninety-three dead and 439 wounded, almost a quarter of his army, and included in that number were twenty-nine British and Hessian officers either killed or wounded. Greene's casualties were seventy-eight killed and 183 wounded, not including the militia that ran away. Though the result of Guilford Courthouse was devastating, Greene was only four months into his administration of the Southern Army, and his efforts to combine local militia with the core of his Continental army were starting to show results. Never an ideal concoction, this mixture of regulars and militia, it would eventually prove an effective one.

Cornwallis, however, failed to exhibit similar accomplishments. Call it unrealistic expectations. Call it impatience. Call it aristocratic hauteur. Whatever you call it, the earl was no "man of the people," nor did he show much inclination toward pretending to be one. "The principal reasons for undertaking the winter's campaign were the difficulty of a defensive war in South Carolina and the hopes that our friends in North Carolina, who were said to be very numerous, would make good their promises of assembling and taking an active part with us in endeavoring to reestablish His Majesty's Government," Cornwallis would complain to Germain. "Our experience has shewn that their numbers are not so great as had been represented and their friendship was only passive."

His interest in North Carolina now diminished, Cornwallis set his sights on Virginia, where he believed "successful operations might not only be attended with important consequences" but also "would tend to the security of South Carolina and ultimately to the submission of North Carolina."[25] If Virginia was subdued, Patriot sentiment in the colonies to its south would wither on the vine, or so he hoped and claimed to believe. Based on Cornwallis's experiences in North and South Carolina thus far, it is generous to call this assumption wishful thinking. With Greene's army still intact, it bordered on lunacy.

Still, Cornwallis was in no mood for self-reflection . . . or waiting. Writing to both Germain and Clinton from Wilmington, North Carolina, where he had marched his army following the Pyrrhic victory at Guilford Courthouse, Cornwallis would await response from neither of them to commence the invasion of Virginia he believed was the only remaining viable option left to him in the South. It would result in his doom.

In Virginia, he was reinforced with approximately three thousand troops under Benedict Arnold, along with other British troops sent south by Clinton from New York. With an army now exceeding seven thousand men, he spent the summer campaigning in Virginia, including a series of indecisive skirmishes with Continental forces under the Marquis de Lafayette, before establishing camp at Yorktown on the Williamsburg neck. This location was to serve as the base for planned operations in Virginia's Chesapeake Bay that fall.

While Cornwallis awaited reinforcement from the British navy for the planned invasion, George Washington skillfully moved his troops into position, trapping Cornwallis on the Chesapeake Peninsula. And when the British navy was stymied by the French fleet in late August and early September, and forced to return to New York, the trap was set. On September 28, 1781, a combined force of over 16,000 men, including 7,800 French troops, started the siege of Cornwallis's position at Yorktown. Without the naval support he expected, Cornwallis was helpless, and on October 17, he surrendered his army.[26]

This surrender, of course, was decisive, an iconic moment in American history, the world turned upside down, but the war was far from over. Nathanael Greene received the news on the outskirts of Charleston after spending the spring and summer of 1781 systematically removing the British from the South Carolina interior. In the interim, he had successfully modified his tactics of winter 1781, forming light partisan corps with the militia of South Carolina, often acting in conjunction with Henry Lee's Legion, to attack the British supply chain, while reserving his Continental regulars for major actions at Hobkirk's Hill outside Camden, the siege of the British outpost at Ninety Six, and a bloody slugfest with the last remnants of the British occupation force at a place called Eutaw Springs on the road to Charleston.

Greene won none of these engagements. As in the Race to the Dan and Guilford Courthouse, Greene in South Carolina relied on the strategic retreat, withdrawing rather than attacking in the campaign's decisive moments because he understood the presence of the Continental army was more important than any battlefield victory. Clearly he longed for the kind of glory Washington achieved at Yorktown, though from his position out-side Charleston's heavy fortifications, his army as hungry and destitute as ever, he could only acknowledge the irony of his achievements.

"We have been beating the bush and the General has come to catch the bird," he wrote to his friend General Henry Knox, as Washington prepared his siege of Yorktown in late September 1781. "The General is a most for-tunate Man, and may success and laurels attend him. We have fought fre-quently and bled freely, and little glory comes to our share."[27]

The narrative thread that it was Greene, Morgan, and the Southern Army that "beat" Cornwallis into Virginia, allowing Washington to "catch the bird," is a complicated one, far beyond the attention span of modern America. For most of us, the story of the American Revolution is of George Washington and the minutemen, Valley Forge and Yorktown. That a retreat through a wilderness of swamps and rivers, marched through thick, frozen mud with bleeding feet, with narrow, last-minute escapes made possible by plans months in the making, played an important, even critical role, in this narrative is just too much plotline for our selfie-sodden brains.

Not surprisingly, Henry Lee's lively prose best explains this complicated narrative for posterity's sake: "Destroy the army of Greene, and the Car-olinas with Georgia, inevitably become members of the British empire. Vir-ginia, the bulwark of the South, would be converted first into a frontier, then into a theater of war. . . . The stoutest heart trembles lest the Potomac should become the boundary of British dominion on the east of the Blue Ridge.

"Happily for these States, a soldier of consummate talents guided the destiny of the South. . . . The difficulty of the retreat from South Carolina with an inferior army, and that army acting necessarily in two divisions at a great distance from each other . . . presented in themselves impediments great and difficult. When we add the comfortless condition of our troops in point of clothing, the rigor of the season, the inclemency of the weather, our short stock of ammunition, and shorter stock of provisions . . . we have abundant cause to honor the soldier whose mental resources smoothed every difficulty, and ultimately made good a retreat of two hundred and thirty miles."[28]

If the "favourable" opportunities lost by Cornwallis in western South Carolina and central North Carolina during the winter of 1780-81 were eventually found by Washington at Yorktown in September 1781, it was their orchestration by Greene that enabled both. Though history may remember the Race to the Dan as a retreat, it was one by definition only. In spirit, in function, it was the masterful victory of a man whom history remembers as having none, executed under extraordinary circumstances by a small but determined army and its talented officers, a remarkable story of human courage and resilience that deserves a place in American history.

CHAPTER 16

FAREWELL TO THE SOUTHERN GENTLEMEN

AT A PLACE CALLED EUTAW SPRINGS, Nathanael Greene fought the last remnants of the British army's South Carolina occupation force on September 8, 1781. By now, Cornwallis had established his base on the Williamsburg neck, where he would soon be trapped at Yorktown. Instead of following Cornwallis into Virginia, Greene had turned to South Carolina, losing the Battle of Hobkirk's Hill outside Camden on April 25, 1781, and unsuccessfully sieging the British outpost at Ninety Six during May and June. But on June 5, the British outpost at Augusta was captured by a combined Patriot force under Henry Lee, Andrew Pickens, and the Georgia militia leader Elijah Clarke. And even as they were defeating Greene in battle, the British were losing their supply lines to Greene's partisan detachments.

Now in command of the South Carolina occupation force was Francis, Lord Rawdon, Cornwallis's twenty-six-year-old confidant, who would prove Greene's match in battle at Hobkirk's Hill. However, with his supply lines and civic support eroding, Rawdon showed little taste for holding the South Carolina interior. Before chasing Greene away from Ninety Six, Rawdon would order Camden evacuated, then also Ninety Six after the failed siege, before eventually retreating to Orangeburg, South Carolina, where he would be relieved of command due to malaria.

By September, the British occupation force was commanded by Lt. Colonel Alexander Stewart, who had moved his army of approximately two thousand men to Eutaw Springs, located on a main route to Charleston. There he set up camp in an open field. Greene and his combined force of approximately 2,800—1,775 Continental regulars and about one thousand militia—surprised Stewart on the morning of September 8 but were unable to overtake his position. In a battle that lasted over three hours, Greene lost 138 killed, 378 wounded, and 41 missing. Stewart lost 84 killed and 351 wounded.[1]

When Stewart abandoned the field later that day, seeing little sense in another round of battle, Greene declared victory by technicality only. Today, most historians agree the battle was yet another loss for Greene, though thanks to Stewart's retreat, Greene was awarded the congressional gold medal for his "victory" at Eutaw Springs, the same medal won previously by Daniel Morgan at Cowpens and awarded to only five others throughout the entire American Revolution.[2]

For the rest of the fall, Greene continued to push the British toward Charleston until eventually surrounding them there. But the British would not evacuate the city until December 14, 1782, leaving Greene and his weary Continentals little to do for the next year and a half except skirmish with the occasional British raiding party and slowly starve. Even then, the war was not technically over, and Greene did not dismiss his men until June 21, 1783, departing Charleston himself on August 11.

If these last days of Nathanael Greene's war are now largely forgotten, they were not inconsequential. The supply lines he and Washington contemplated in November 1780 had never been successfully implemented, and as Greene's weary army waited for the British to leave Charleston, and their long years of Continental service to end, they continued to suffer. Desperate for supplies, Greene entered into a complicated financing scheme with a merchant named John Banks, assured by the Continental Congress he would eventually be reimbursed for these debts. But after the war, Banks died and the reimbursement promised Greene were delayed by interminable bureaucracy, leaving Greene hounded by Banks's creditors.

With his father's family enterprise diminished by eight long years of war, and his wartime investments now virtually worthless, Greene was desperate for capital. Luckily, he had been given some in recognition of his valiant service during the war. In 1781, the South Carolina General Assembly had gifted Greene ten thousand guineas in thanks for his service to the state, and this money had been used to purchase a 6,600-acre estate on the Edisto River called Boone's Barony. The North Carolina and Georgia assemblies would soon follow suit, gifting to Greene estates of twenty-five thousand and two thousand acres respectively.[3]

The North Carolina property would eventually be sold. But Greene's scheme to pay his wartime debts hinged on a transformation from Yankee merchant and Continental general to southern plantation master. For revenue, he would use Boone's Barony and Mulberry Grove, the Georgia plantation. (Eventually he would be awarded another eleven thousand acres on Georgia's Cumberland Island, a property that will play a later role in our story.) A successful transformation it was not. Managing his southern plantations mostly in absentia, Greene was plagued by bad advice and bad luck. Meanwhile, his creditors pursued him relentlessly. "I tremble at my own situation when I think of the enormous sums I owe and the great difficulty of obtaining money," Greene lamented in a 1785 letter to Caty. "I seem to be doomed to a life of slavery and anxiety."[4]

Sadly, that doom was not for a troubling life but an early death. After a June 1786 meeting in Savannah to refinance some debt, Greene and Caty stopped at the plantation of their neighbor William Gibbons Jr. on the way back to Mulberry Grove. Greene spent the visit touring Gibbons's plantation in the hot sun, and shortly after he and Caty departed, his health began to fail. Diagnosed with heat stroke, Greene's condition deteriorated rapidly. On the morning of June 19, 1786, the forty-three-year-old Greene died in his bed.[5]

We have already acknowledged the historian's folly of "what if," but the prodigious talents of Nathanael Greene draw us inevitably into this game: what if Greene had lived and eventually taken a role in the Washington administration? The question is not unreasonable. Washington trusted him implicitly; no man was more aware of Greene's unique aptitudes. Greene had already declined an opportunity to serve as secretary of war in 1781,[6] and his wartime debts were eventually reimbursed by the United States government, as promised. Alas, we can only speculate on this hypothetical legacy.

What if Nathanael Greene could be remembered not only as an important American general but also a brilliant partisan officer? That question fate still may decide. In Greene's time, ideas about warfare were shifting to recognize the martial power of a nimble mind. Always attuned to intellectual wavelengths, Greene was usually in the right place at the right time, at least when it came to strategy. Yes, one of his legacies is that of the Continental general who never won a battle, and it's true he was no genius as a battlefield tactician. Yet his strategies extended beyond the battlefield, always focused on the endgame, or at least several moves ahead. This is the type of legacy that doesn't translate well in history books, where the focus tends toward wins and losses. However, the still relatively recent publication of his collected papers allows us to view Greene with more insight and contemplate the scope of his more unusual decisions. In that light, the breadth of his partisan tactics become more focused; their outcomes, like the narrative thread there would be no Yorktown without the Race to the Dan, more defined. I'm not suggesting Greene practiced the maxims of Frederick the Great; his mind was more complex than that. Greene didn't reflect the intellectual currency of the day so much as he embodied it. You can have your Saxe and Jeney; I'll take Nathanael Greene any old day.

One Greene admirer (albeit a reluctant one) who needed no further occasion to recognize his genius was Charles, Lord Cornwallis. Having fallen into Greene's trap in the Race to the Dan, then exhausted his North Carolina invasion at Guilford's Courthouse, before trapping himself at Yorktown, Cornwallis returned to England in January 1782 a "parolee," ineligible for further military service until officially exchanged.

You might think the career of the American Revolution's "loser" would be in tatters, but Cornwallis's reputation was buffered by public awareness of the overall failures of Britain's war policy and his still rock-solid relationship with King George III. Cornwallis was always too much the nobleman to "dirty" himself in the American South, though his fiery moment of resolution at Ramsour's Mill and daring at Cowan's Ford were exceptions to the rule. But we can't blame him for it; the British army was built on such class distinctions. He was a warrior, yes, but his commitment to the American Revolution was never total; there was always some accountability he could . . . and did . . . blame on others. That the American army was more innovative, their commitment more total, is no surprise; they were more desperate. Given all these contingencies, we begin to realize Cornwallis never truly had a chance.

Except for a bitter public feud with Henry Clinton, played out in the fashion of the times, through a series of published pamphlets and rebuttals, Cornwallis was able to successfully resurrect his career. Notably, he was able to shape the lessons he learned in America into more successful adaptations, proving he was no mediocre mind himself. This career resurrection began in 1786, when he was appointed governor general in India. Learning from England's mistakes in America, Cornwallis took the job on the condition he also be appointed commander in chief, uniting political and military control. The move allowed him to test the limits of a newfound enthusiasm for political pragmatism in India but back up his policies with force when necessary.

Cornwallis's Indian administration was distinguished by his fight against the corruption that undermined previous British ones. He instituted a new system of courts, reformed the criminal justice system, and established a land taxation system that stabilized British support among the Indian land-owning class. When forced to wield the sword, as in his campaign against Tippoo Sahib, Sultan of Mysore, who invaded the British protectorate of Travancore in 1791, he did so with a newfound respect for preparation and logistics. Never again would he risk his armies on ill-conceived missions into unknown country.

Returning to England in 1793, Cornwallis was awarded a marquessate, the English rank of nobility under duke, thereafter becoming the 1st Marquess Cornwallis. In 1795, with fears of a French invasion looming, he was named master general of the ordnance, a cabinet position with responsibility for overseeing England's home defenses. But duty soon called him abroad again, this time to Ireland. Threats of an Irish uprising, aided by the French, called for a cool-headed administrator, and with his newfound reputation for expedience, Cornwallis was named Lord Lieutenant of Ireland, its chief governor.

In Ireland, Cornwallis believed his primary duty was to craft a peaceful coexistence with England, requiring some conciliation with Ireland's Catholic population. Again and again, Cornwallis pushed measures of Catholic emancipation, only to be perpetually dismayed by the intransigence of both Irish loyalists and King George. This obstinacy stretched the limits of Cornwallis's patience, undermining his authority. Eventually, Cornwallis found England's Irish Catholic policy untenable. "No consideration could induce me to take a responsible part with any administration who can be so blind to the interest, and indeed to the immediate security of their country, as to persevere in the old system of proscription and exclusion in Ireland," he wrote in a letter explaining his 1801 resignation.

After brief service as an English diplomat, negotiating the treaty of Amiens with France, Cornwallis agreed to a second tenure as India's governor general in 1805. But England's best warrior during the American

Revolution soon fell ill during a diplomatic mission to the Indian up-country. The sixty-seven-year-old Cornwallis died on October 5, 1805.

Today, Cornwallis's legacy is mostly ignored in England. No British historian has ever attempted a comprehensive biography, an oversight the writer John Bey attributes to Cornwallis's lack of a signature victory. Yet his post-American Revolution career was easily the most successful of any of England's major military figures from that conflict, and his intellectual capacities as administrator during his later career show marked improvement from his not inconsiderable lapses during the southern campaigns. But if British historians neglect his complicated legacy, he is at least remembered in America as the general Washington defeated at Yorktown. And despite his weaknesses, he forever earned the respect and loyalty of his troops, with one notable exception.[7]

According to his biographers at the *Oxford Dictionary of National Biography*, Banastre Tarleton's "prevaling foible" was "vanity," and he showed a fair bit of it in his memoir, *History of the Campaigns of 1780 and 1781, in the Southern Provinces of North America*, published in 1787. Critical of Cornwallis, the work drew the wrath of Cornwallis devotees like Roderick Mackenzie, who published his rebuttal later that same year. The memoir is certainly self-serving, particularly in his defense of his actions at Cowpens, along with glossed accounts of other brutalities. "The author appears every where, forward, on the canvas," complained one reviewer, "and, when his importance is estimated by the weight of his own remarks, we are tempted to frequently remove him to the background."[8]

Cornwallis himself wrote of the book: "Tarleton's is a most malicious and false attack; he knew and approved the reasons for the measures which he now blames . . . I know it is very foolish to be vexed about these things, but yet it touches me in a tender point."[9]

Of Tarleton's reaction to such criticisms, his biographer Robert Bass does not explain, noting only that Tarleton's ally British major Charles Hanger published a defense of *History of the Campaigns* in response to Mackenzie that "set the friends of the disputant chuckling."[10] And as self-serving as *History of the Campaigns* can be, it is nevertheless a valuable account of the southern campaigns, often the sole primary source from a British perspective when Stedman or O'Hara are mute. It is referenced extensively in this work and many others on the subject, though it must be read and used critically.

After the war, Tarleton enjoyed a life of notoriety, adopting the persona of the dashing rogue. For a time, he was close friends with the Prince of Wales, the future King George IV, and it was from this period the famous portrait by Sir Joshua Reynolds was painted, now in London's National Gallery. Also during this period Tarleton began an affair with Mrs. Mary Robinson, a famous actress, poet, and former mistress of the prince, who was rumored to have passed her off to his friend Tarleton. Often referred to by her nickname "Perdita," from her most famous role in Shakespeare's *Winter's Tale*, Robinson and Tarleton lived extravagantly, reportedly spending £2,500 per year, financed partially by Tarleton's gambling. The pair were together for fifteen years, though separated in 1797 allegedly over Tarleton's designs on Robinson's daughter, who was only twenty-one.

Tarleton married in 1798 and settled down to a life of politics and military service, if increasing obscurity. First elected to the House of Commons in 1790, he stayed in office until 1812, with one brief interval between 1806 and 1807. He remained in the army, becoming major general in 1794, lieutenant general in 1801, and full general in 1812. He briefly held an independent command in Portugal in 1798 but did not see active service again after the American war. He died on January 15, 1833.[11]

Daniel Morgan was approximately forty-five years old at the time of Cowpens (his actual birth date lost to time),[12] certainly no "old soldier" by today's standard, though frontier life had left him physically depleted. Still, Cowpens and the Race to the Dan would not be his curtain call: after recuperating at his "Soldier's Rest" home in Frederick County, Virginia, Morgan raised and led a local militia that campaigned in Virginia during the summer of 1781 without seeing major action.

But after this limited service Morgan's war was essentially over, and ill-suited for a job in the new federal administration, though he maintained a close and cordial relationship with George Washington, he "retired" to the life of a country squire. Morgan biographer Albert Louis Zambone notes there were four ways for Virginia gentry to establish status for themselves and their families: acquiring land, financial instruments, livestock, and slaves. Morgan leveraged his wartime reputation to pursue all four. Owning several hundred acres at the close of the war, he eventually accumulated 250,000 acres in Virginia, Ohio, Kentucky, and Tennessee.

Morgan prospered and built a fine new home he named "Saratoga." He and his wife, Abigail, married their daughters, Nancy and Betsey, to Continental officers. From this period also emerges an illegitimate son named

Willoughby, born probably to a resident of Winchester but sent to Kentucky or South Carolina at an early age. In the 1790s, Morgan returned prominently to public life, running for Congress twice, losing in 1794 and winning in 1797. He was a strong supporter of George Washington and participated vigorously in the emerging debate between the "Federalists" supporting a strong central government and "Republicans," such as Thomas Jefferson and James Madison, who advocated for more limited federal control. He continued to serve as a general of Virginia militia, and in 1794 he led a small army during the "Whiskey Rebellion" in western Pennsylvania, though he saw no fighting there.

Once more suffering infirmities, and scared of a yellow fever epidemic sweeping through Philadelphia, Morgan resigned from Congress in 1798 and returned not to his new "Saratoga" mansion but to his more modest abode at Traveler's Rest. There he lived out the last of his days, becoming an ardent Christian near the end, and dying on July 6, 1802. His illegitimate son Willoughby returned to Winchester by 1812 and eventually went on to a successful career in the United States Army, rising to the rank of colonel by his death in 1832.[13]

Otho Holland Williams continued to serve loyally with Nathanael Greene throughout the southern campaigns, fighting with distinction at Guilford's Courthouse, Hobkirk's Hill, and Eutaw Springs. As the Continental army settled into their defenses around Charleston, Williams was finally relieved of his duties and permitted to return to his Maryland home in 1782. With him he carried a letter from Greene recommending Williams promotion to brigadier general, which was finally granted on May 9, 1782.

Just thirty-three years old at the time of his promotion, Williams's postwar life was plagued by bad health—rheumatism and perhaps other maladies. Not that such infirmities interrupted his love life. "Many women seemed to feel solicitious about his well being as though they were caring for a beloved younger brother," writes his biographer John Beakes.

With opportunities in the army declining after the war, Williams accepted an appointment on January 15, 1783, by the state of Maryland to the post of naval officer of the port of Baltimore, responsible for collecting custom duties for goods passing through the busy harbor. When that post was set to be absorbed into the federal government, Williams lobbied old friends like Henry Lee to make sure he retained the appointment, which he received in August 1789.

Meanwhile the bachelor Williams finally married in 1785 to Mary Smith, a member of a prominent Baltimore business family. He took an active role in the establishment of the Society of Cincinnati, a fraternal order of former Continental officers, and dabbled in politics. In 1788, he became judge of the Baltimore Criminal Court, a political appointment made by his old comrade, John Eager Howard, now the governor of Maryland. A strong pro-Federalist, he considered a run for governor himself in 1792 but eventually declined to run, worried about his poor health and losing a profitable federal job. Much of his later life was spent traveling to spas and treatments, seeking some relief from the health issues that continued to plague him. He never found it and died on July 15, 1794, at the age of forty-five.[14]

After Greene's failed siege of the British outpost at Ninety Six in June 1781, Edward Carrington requested leave for an opportunity to take command of the 4th Continental Artillery Regiment, a position he deserved by rank and service, but due to congressional bureaucracy, the promotion due Carrington was never approved. After the surrender at Yorktown, he eventually returned to service as Greene's quartermaster general, traveling to Philadelphia under orders from Greene to lobby for supplies. He rejoined Greene in 1782 and continued to serve with him until the British departed Charleston and the Southern Army was eventually disbanded.

From 1785 to 1787, Carrington served in Congress as a Virginia delegate but then disappeared from public life until 1798. That year, Congress authorized the post of quartermaster general for the army, with the rank and pay of a major general. Alexander Hamilton nominated Carrington for the job, though President Washington never authorized the appointment. In 1807, Carrington served on the jury that acquitted Aaron Burr of treason. He died three years later, in 1810, at the age of sixty-one. "A man to be better remembered for his varied services in the Continental army," eulogizes historian Mark M. Boatner III, "perhaps his epitaph should be the words of Greene: 'No body ever heard of a quarter Master, in History.'"[15]

Everybody's heard of George Washington, of course, though the legacy of his cousin, William Washington, a hero of Cowpens, has today slipped into obscurity. Perhaps with good reason. "His occupation and his amusements applied to the body, rather than the mind," recalled his fellow cavalryman, Henry Lee, suggesting William was not suited to the life of public service his second-cousin-once-removed, George, pursued.[16]

William Washington was seriously wounded and captured at the Battle of Eutaw Springs and spent the rest of the war as a prisoner in Charleston. There he met and married Jane Riley Elliot, gaining through the marriage Sandy Hill plantation and other properties in St. Paul's Parish. The couple also purchased a Charleston home at 8 South Battery in 1785. "In temper he was good-humored; in disposition amiable; in heart upright, generous, and friendly; in manners lively, innocent, agreeable," Lee continues,[17] and perhaps it was due to this disposition that he prospered and thrived in the role of low country gentry. But his political aspirations were modest: he served in the South Carolina General Assembly from 1787 to 1804 but declined an opportunity to run for governor because he was not born a Carolinian and "could not make a speech."

In 1794 he accepted a post as brigadier general in the South Carolina state militia and in 1798, during anticipated hostilities with France, received a commission as brigadier general in the US Army, commanding South Carolina and Georgia until 1800. He died on March 16, 1810, having led his final days as a planter and gentleman. If history has only begun to conduct serious scholarship about the atrocities committed under William Washington's command at Hammond's Store, it is fair to say the incident appears to be an anomaly in his Revolutionary War career.[18]

And these were brutal times, difficult for the modern mind to contemplate. The career of Andrew Pickens proves as much. Though Pickens fought with distinction at Cowpens, and earned Nathanael Greene's devout trust and admiration during the Race to the Dan and later in the South Carolina campaign, his 1782 campaigns against the Cherokee make for uncomfortable reading. By the winter of 1782, many Loyalists fleeing from Patriot persecution had taken refuge with the Cherokee, where they incited the Cherokee into reprisals on Patriot settlers for encroachments on their negotiated territory. In response, Andrew Pickens led a militia detachment against the Native American nation, killing forty Cherokee, taking many prisoners, and burning thirteen towns. Later that year, Pickens teamed with the Georgia militia commander Elijah Clarke for another punitive expedition against the Cherokee, forcing them to surrender claim to all land south of the Savannah River and east of the Chattahoochee River to Georgia.

But Pickens is revered today as a hero of the American Revolution and one of South Carolina's great partisan militia leaders, not for his brutalities against the Cherokee. Following the war, Pickens served in the South Carolina legislature from 1783 until 1788, returning in 1796-1799 and 1812-

1813. He served in the state senate from 1790 to 1791 and from 1793 to 1795 in the United States Congress. In 1794, he was named major general of the South Carolina militia and for many years was engaged in dealing with Indians on boundary policies, where he favored a more peaceful approach than that he adopted in 1782. He died on August 11, 1817.[19]

The "American Diomed," Robert Kirkwood, was another southern gentleman who became engaged in Indian affairs after the war, with tragic results. According to Henry Lee, Kirkwood risked his life in battle thirty-three times, including at Long Island, Trenton, Princeton, Camden, Cowpens, Guilford Courthouse, Hobkirk's Hill, and Eutaw Springs, among many more. Yet as we have noted, due to the limited size of the Delaware regiment after their decimation at Camden, "Kirkwood never could be promoted in regular routine." He retired from the army a mere captain, despite his heroic service, though he received a brevet, or honorary, promotion to major on October 30, 1783.[20]

Only the state of Virginia recognized his service, awarding him a grant of two thousand acres in 1787 in what is now southeastern Ohio. Moving there, he was made a justice of the peace in 1790. On March 4, 1791, Kirkwood was commissioned a captain in the Second Regiment of US infantry to fight under General Arthur St. Clair in the Indian uprising of the Miami, Delaware, and Shawnees in the Northwest Territory. According to his eighteenth-century biographer, Kirkwood was killed in battle against the Native American confederation near Fort Recovery, when he refused to retreat and "died with his face to the foe on the 4th of November, 1791, at the age of forty-five."[21]

Three of Greene's "Southern Gentlemen" went on to become governors, perhaps the most successful post-war careers of any in his officer corps. John Eager Howard served as governor of Maryland from 1788 to 1791. He also served as delegate to the Continental Congress (1788) and United States senator (1796-1803). He declined an offer to serve as secretary of war in 1795 and was the Federalist Party's unsuccessful candidate for vice president in 1816. Born to a prominent Maryland planter family, Howard's social and financial status only increased with his 1787 marriage to Peggy Oswald Chew, daughter of Pennsylvania Supreme Court chief justice Benjamin Chew. He died a wealthy man in 1827, his funeral attended by President John Quincy Adams. The line "Remember Howard's warlike thrust" in Maryland's state song, "Maryland, My Maryland," is in tribute to his valiant service in the American Revolution, of which his heroics at Cowpens will always be best remembered.[22]

We come now to the post-war career of Henry Lee, our chief correspondent, whose *Revolutionary War Memoirs* made this work possible, especially in its account of the last, desperate days of the Race to the Dan. "Lee was not always a reliable storyteller," notes the historian Charles Royster, in an introduction to the *Memoirs*, "but he made his narrative irresistible. For many dramatic episodes his account is the only surviving one or the one with the most vivid detail."

Royster notes the difficulties in Lee's personality, both during and after the war: "He expected to be obeyed by soldiers and honored by citizens because he was braver, smarter, and better than they were." Such arrogance does not make for popularity, although for a time after the war, Henry Lee seemed to thrive. He married advantageously, speculated prodigiously, and achieved political success, representing Virginia first in the Continental Congress, then as its governor from 1791 to 1794, before serving in the US House of Representatives from 1799 to 1801.

However, his avarice and spendthrift practices began to catch up with him in the 1790s. Several of his investment schemes collapsed, leading his creditors and critics to label him corrupt. Royster disagrees: "If Lee was a swindler, he was not a good one, and he paid a high price for his crimes." By 1809, Lee was broke, though not insolvent, because he refused to declare himself such. Doing so would have surrendered control of his property, if not the final shreds of his dignity, though it would have saved him from debtor's prison, where he soon landed. He turned to writing, ostensibly as a scheme to pay his bills, though Royster believes it was as much a psychological escape to a more glorious time, a chance to live again among his Continental comrades.

Much of the *Memoirs* were written in the Spotsylvania County jail between 1809 and 1810, where Lee was imprisoned. Though they were received favorably when published in two volumes in 1812, their literary success did little to relieve his crushing debt.

An ardent Federalist, Lee attended a Baltimore rally in 1812 against America's declaration of war with Britain, which the Federalists opposed. The rally turned into a brawl, and Lee was severely beaten, never again to regain his health. He spent the last five years of his life in a self-imposed exile. In March 1818, returning from a visit to the Caribbean Islands, Lee asked to be put ashore on Cumberland Island, and went to Dungeness, a home on Nathanael Greene's property there. Following Greene's death, his wife, Caty, had built Dungeness in 1803, and the estate was now in the care of Greene's daughter Louisa. At Dungeness Lee died on March 25, 1818 and was interred there. He was sixty-two-years old.[23]

For last we turn to William Richardson Davie, only a minor character in the Race to the Dan, relegated to service as Greene's commissary officer, though far from minor in the history of North Carolina. Trained as an attorney, Davie served on the "Grand Committee," which sought to address balancing government representation between the larger and smaller states, and cast North Carolina's vote for the "Great Compromise" establishing the Constitution's legislative representation in two houses of Congress. Though active in drafting the United States Constitution, he had to leave the convention to attend court in North Carolina, preventing him from signing it. Back in North Carolina, he was instrumental in the state's ratification of the Constitution at the Fayetteville Convention in 1789.

That same year, as a state representative from Halifax County, North Carolina, where he settled after marrying into a prominent Halifax family, Davie introduced legislation to establish the University of North Carolina. He would join the university's board of trustees later that year, a role he continued in until 1807. Today, Davie is considered the founding father of the University of North Carolina at Chapel Hill, recognized for his active role in establishing the institution.

Meanwhile he served as governor of North Carolina from 1798 to 1799 and then (briefly simultaneously) a minister to France from 1799 to 1800. An ardent Federalist, like Greene's other officers, the *rage militaire* transforming into support for a strong Federal government, Davie's political fortunes waned after the inauguration of President Thomas Jefferson in 1801. Losing a campaign for the US House of Representative in 1803 to a Democratic opponent, Davie renounced politics, retiring to an estate near Lancaster, South Carolina, where he devoted his days to farming, writing, and developing the university he loved. Though he lacked the literary talents of Henry Lee, he penned his own *Revolutionary War Sketches*, though not particularly relevant to the period covered in this book. Today he is considered one of North Carolina's most distinguished citizens, revered not only for his spectacular service during the American Revolution but also for his influence on North Carolina government and the University of

North Carolina at Chapel Hill, your author's alma mater.[24] In our university motto, *Lux Libertas*, meaning "Light and Liberty," surely the spirit of Nathanael Greene and his southern gentlemen endures.

NOTES

INTRODUCTION

1. Charles Heaton, "The Failure of Enlightenment Military Doctrine in Revolutionary America: The Piedmont Campaign and the Fate of the British Army in the Lower South," *North Carolina Historical Review*, Vol. 87, No. 2 (April 2010).
2. William B. Willcox, *Portrait of a General: Sir Henry Clinton in the War of Independence* (New York: Alfred A. Knopf, 1962), 442.

PROLOGUE: *ALEA IACTA EST*

1. Franklin and Mary Wickwire, *Cornwallis and the War of Independence* (London: Faber and Faber, 1971), 114.
2. In the parlance of the times, Lord Frederick North was better known as England's "first" or "chief" minister; though occasionally used in the eighteenth century, the term "prime minister" was not widely adopted until the nineteenth. For the clarity of modern readers, North is described as the "prime minister" here.
3. "Clinton to Cornwallis," December 13, 1780, *The Cornwallis Papers* (East Sussex, England: Naval & Military Press, 2010), arranged and edited by Ian Saberton, vol. 3, 32. Hereafter cited as *CP* with appropriate volume and page numbers, i.e., *CP*, 3:32.
4. Henry Clinton, *The American Rebellion: Sir Henry Clinton's Narrative of His Campaigns, 1775-1782, with an Appendix of Original Documents* (New Haven: Yale University Press, 1954), edited by William B. Willcox, 262.
5. John S. Pancake, *This Destructive War: The British Campaign in the Carolinas, 1780-1782* (Tuscaloosa: University of Alabama Press, 2003), 150-151.
6. "British Orderly Book, 1780-1782," *North Carolina Historical Review*, Vol. 9, No. 3 (July 1932), edited by A.R. Newsome, 286.
7. Charles O'Hara, "Letters of Charles O'Hara to the Duke of Grafton," *South Carolina Historical Magazine*, Vol. 65, No. 3 (July 1964), edited by George C. Rogers, Jr., 174.
8. "Earl Cornwallis to Lord George Germain," March 17, 1781, *Correspondence of Charles, First Marquis Cornwallis* (London: John Murray), edited by Charles Ross, 1:503.
9. O'Hara, "Letters of Charles O'Hara to Duke of Grafton," 174.

CHAPTER ONE: RIVERS AND ROADS

1. George Washington Greene, *The Life of Nathanael Greene, Major-General in the Army of the Revolution*, Volume 1 (Boston: Houghton Mifflin, 1890), 9-21.

2. Ibid., 168-169.

3. *The Papers of General Nathanael Greene*, Richard K. Showman, general editor (Chapel Hill: University of North Carolina Press, 1991), Volume 6, xvii. Note 4 on page 431 of Volume 6 describes Greene's other traveling companions as aides Major Ichabod Burnet and Colonel Lewis Morris Jr. Greene's collected papers and their notes hereafter are referenced as *NG*, with volume and page number, as in *NG*, 6:431.

4. Don Higginbotham, *The War of the American Independence: Military Attitudes, Policies, and Practice, 1763-1789* (Bloomington: Indiana University Press paperback edition, 1978), 211-212. Higginbotham cites Philadelphia doctor Benjamin Rush and Continental general Thomas Mifflin as two prominent critics of Greene's influence on Washington.

5. Ibid.

6. "Nathanael Greene (hereafter NG) to George Washington," November 19, 1780, *NG*, 6:486.

7. This brief overview of the economic pressures facing Congress and the colonial administrations is informed by H. James Henderson, "The Structure of Politics in the Continental Congress," from *Essays on the American Revolution*, edited by Stephen G. Kurtz and James H. Hutson (Chapel Hill: UNC Press, 1973), 157-196; and Higginbotham, *The War of American Independence*, 288-296.

8. Christopher Ward, *The War of the Revolution* (New York: Skyhorse Publishing, 2011), 698, 703. Ward writes 5,466 "Continentals, militia, and armed citizens" were taken prisoner at Charleston's surrender, though only 2,650 of those who remained were Continental soldiers. Other sources differ on these numbers.

9. Charles Royster, *A Revolutionary People at War: The Continental Army & American Character, 1775-1783* (Chapel Hill: University of North Carolina Press, 1979), 315.

10. "Nathanael Greene to Samuel Blachley Webb," December 21, 1779, quoted in Royster, *A Revolutionary People at War*, 317.

11. M. F. Treacy, *Prelude to Yorktown: The Southern Campaign of Nathanael Greene, 1780-1781* (Chapel Hill: University of North Carolina Press, 1963), 58.

12. Theodore Thayer, *Nathanael Greene: Strategist of the American Revolution* (New York: Twayne, 1960), 228-229.

13. Ibid., 222-223.

14. Greene had first solicited Washington for command of the Southern Army in 1779 and had solicited it in a letter to South Carolina congressman John Mathews as recently as October 3, 1780, contradicting Greene's later assertions that the role had been thrust upon him. See "NG to John Mathews, October 3, 1780" and note 9 to this letter, *NG*, 6:335-337.

15. "George Washington to NG," November 8, 1780, *NG*, 6:469-470. Italics from original text.

16. "George Washington to NG," October 22, 1780, *NG*, 6:425.

17. Ibid.

18. "Thomas Jefferson to NG," November 26, 1780, *NG*, 6:506. Also *NG*, Note 2, 6:471. This note describes Jefferson's additional correspondence on the subject, aside from that he sent to Greene.

19. Ward, *The War of the Revolution*, 582.

20. *NG*, Note 2, 6:517. Also Mark M. Boatner, *Encyclopedia of the American Revolution* (Me-

chanicsburg, PA: Stackpole Books, 1994), 184.

21. "Edward Carrington to Horatio Gates," September 23, 1780, Documenting the American South webpage, University Library, University of North Carolina at Chapel Hill (https://docsouth.unc.edu/csr/index.php/document/csr14-0540, accessed on July 15, 2018).

22. "Edward Carrington to Horatio Gates," November 27, 1780, Documenting the American South webpage, University Library, University of North Carolina at Chapel Hill (https://docsouth.unc.edu/csr/index.php/document/csr14-0675, accessed on July 15, 2018). In this letter, Carrington assures Gates of Greene's sympathies regarding the debacle at Camden: "Your successor, General Greene, is my Friend, & I have been made happy, in my ride with him to this place, to find his opinion of the Matter results from having duly weighed all the circumstances which has attended your Situation, & he has generously represented them to such persons as we have fallen in Company with who were blindly led away by having only considered events. I have communicated to him the instructions you have been pleased to honor me with, which have met with his entire approbation."

23. "NG to Thomas Jefferson," November 20, 1780, *NG*, 6:493.

24. "NG to George Washington," November 19, 1780, *NG*, 6:486.

25. "NG to General Edward Stevens," December 1, 1780, *NG*, 6:512.

26. *NG*, Note 2, 6:545.

27. Parke Rouse, Jr., *The Great Wagon Road: How Scotch-Irish and Germanics Settled the Uplands* (Richmond, VA: Dietz Press, 1995), 70.

28. NG, Note 1, 6:513-514.

29. "NG to General Edward Stevens," December 1, 1780, *NG*, 6:513.

30. "NG to Thaddeus Kosciuszko," December 3, 1780, *NG*, 6:515.

31. "NG to Captain John Thompson," December 3, 1780, *NG*, 6:515. *Also* Note 1 to this letter, *NG*, 6:515.

32. "NG to Edward Carrington," December 4, 1780, *NG*, 6:516.

33. "NG to Thomas Jefferson," December 6, 1780, *NG*, 6:531.

34. "Edward Carrington to NG," December 6, 1780, *NG*, 6:537.

35. "Captain John Smith to NG," December 25, 1780, *NG*, 6:614.

36. "NG to North Carolina Board of War," December 14, 1780, *NG*, 6:574.

37. William R. Davie, *The Revolutionary War Sketches of William R. Davie* (Raleigh: N.C. Department of Cultural Resources, 1976), 13-14.

38. Boatner, *Encyclopedia of the American Revolution*, 318.

39. Davie, *Revolutionary War Sketches of William R. Davie*, 39.

40. George F. Scheer and Hugh Rankin, *Rebels & Redcoats: The American Revolution Through the Eyes of Those Who Fought and Lived It* (New York: Da Capo Press, 1957), 436.

41. "NG to Edward Carrington," December 29, 1780, *NG*, 7:15.

42. "Edward Carrington to NG," January 28, 1780, *NG*, 7:209-210. Also Note 3 to this letter, *NG*, 7:210.

CHAPTER TWO: CORNWALLIS CONQUERS THE SOUTH

1 Thomas Pinckney, "Thomas Pinckney and the Last Campaign of Horatio Gates," Robert Scott Davis, Jr., ed., *South Carolina Historical Magazine*, Vol. 86, No. 2 (April 1985), 75-99.

2. "Cornwallis to Germain," August 21, 1780, *CP*, 2:11-14.

3. Boatner, *Encyclopedia of the American Revolution*, 168-169.

4. Ward, *The War of the Revolution*, 2:715-718. Also Mark M. Boatner, *Encyclopedia of the American Revolution*, 158.

5. Otho Holland Williams, "A Narrative of the Campaign of 1780," appearing in Appendix B of *Sketches of the Life and Correspondence of Nathanael Greene* by William Johnson, 1:486.

6. William Johnson, *Sketches of the Life and Correspondence of Nathanael Greene* (Charleston, SC: A.E. Miller, 1822), 1:294.

7. Ward, *The War of the Revolution*, 722-723.

8. Williams, "A Narrative of the Campaign of 1780," in Johnson, 1:493.

9. Ibid.

10. Ward, *The War of the Revolution*, 726-730.

11. Williams, "A Narrative of the Campaign of 1780," in Johnson, 1:499.

12. James Cook, "A map of the province of South Carolina with all the rivers, bays, inlets, islands, inland navigation, soundings, time of high water on the sea coast, roads, marshes, ferrys, bridges, swamps, parishes, churches, towns, townships, county, parish, district, and provincial lines," 1773. Library of Congress website, https://www.loc.gov/item/74692124/; accessed on May 14, 2019.

13. Williams, "A Narrative of the Campaign of 1780," in Johnson, 1:497.

14. Ibid., 1:501.

15. John Fiske, *The American Revolution* (Boston: Houghton Mifflin, 1902), 2:197.

16. John Marshall, *The Life of George Washington: commander in chief of the American forces, during the war which established the independence of his country, and first president of the United States* (New York: Citizens Guild of Washington's Boyhood Home, 1926), 1:405.

17. "Cornwallis to Cruger," August 18, 1780, *CP*, 2:19.

18. Ward, *The War of the Revolution*, 733.

19. John W. Gordon, *South Carolina and the American Revolution: A Battlefield History* (Columbia: University of South Carolina Press, 2003), 109.

20. Clinton, *The American Rebellion*, 225.

21. Ibid., 186. Italics are Clinton's.

22. John Buchanan, *The Road to Guilford Courthouse: The American Revolution in the Carolinas* (New York: John Wiley & Sons, 1997), 26.

23. Wickwire, *Cornwallis and the War of Independence*, 15-16. The proceeding biographical sketch of Cornwallis is based on the Wickwires' fine biography.

24. Ibid., 18-19.

25. Ibid., 24-26.

26. Ibid., 28-29.

27. Ibid., 38-46.

28. Buchanan, *Road to Guilford Courthouse*, 77. The remark about Clinton's "tortuous personality" is from Boatner, *Encyclopedia of the American Revolution*, 240.

29. Wickwire, *Cornwallis and the War of Independence*, 95-97.

30. Armstrong Starkey, *War in the Age of Enlightenment, 1700-1789* (Westport, CT: Praeger, 2003), 20-21. Also Wickwire, *Cornwallis and the War of Independence*, 77-78.

31. Wickwire, *Cornwallis and the War of Independence*, 60.

32. This analysis of British military administration was informed by Amstrong Starkey, *War in the Age of Enlightenment*, 41-63.

33. Wickwire, *Cornwallis and the War of Independence*, 75.

34. Ibid., 107-109.

35. Ibid., 113.

36. Ibid., 124

37. Pancake, *This Destructive War*, 27.

CHAPTER THREE: THAT RASCAL RUGELEY

1. Robert Stansbury Lambert, *South Carolina Loyalists in the American Revolution* (Columbia: University of South Carolina Press, 1987), 117. Also *CP*, 1:128, note 11.

2. Higginbotham, *The War of American Independence*, 240-241. Also Pancake, *This Destructive War*, 5-7.

3. Pancake, *This Destructive War*, 7.

4. Ibid., 27.

5. Ibid., 26.

6. Ibid., 26.

7. Lambert, *South Carolina Loyalists*, 117. Also "Rawdon to Cornwallis, June 22, 1780," *CP*, 1:189.

8. "Rawdon to Cornwallis," July 27, 1780, *CP*, 1:217-218.

9. Patrick O'Kelley, *Nothing But Blood and Slaughter: The Revolutionary War in the Carolinas* (Blue House Taven Press, 2004), 2:191-233. Also Boatner, *Encyclopedia of the American Revolution*, 456-457, for casualty figures on Hanging Rock.

10. Walter Edgar, *Partisans & Redcoats: The Southern Conflict That Turned the Tide of the American Revolution* (New York: William Morrow, 2001), 31-34.

11. "Cornwallis to Clinton," June 30, 1780, from *Correspondence of Charles, First Marquis Cornwallis*, edited by Charles Ross (London: John Murray, 1859), 1:487.

12. "Cornwallis to Clinton," August 6, 1780, *CP*, 1:177.

13. Wickwire, *Cornwallis and the War of Independence*, 134.

14. Banastre Tarleton, *A History of the Campaigns of 1780 and 1781 in the Southern Provinces* (London: T. Caddell, 1787), 155.

15. Ward, *The War of the Revolution*, 706. The Wickwires put the figure at closer to four thousand "present and fit for duty." (Wickwire, *Cornwallis and the War of Independence*, 136).

16. "Cornwallis to Germain," August 21, 1780, *CP*, 2:12.

17. "Cornwallis to Clinton," August 29, 1780, *CP*, 2:42.

18. Ibid., 171-172.

19. "Proclamation By the Right Honorable Charles Earl Cornwallis, Lieutenant-general of His Majesty's forces, September 6, 1780," appearing in *A History of the Campaigns of 1780 and 1781 in the Southern Provinces* by Tarleton, 186-187.

20. Starkey, *War in the Age of the Enlightenment*, 165-167. Starkey attributes the Rawdon quote to Great Britain, *Historical Manuscripts Commission, Report on the Manuscripts of the Late Reginald Rawdon-Hastings*, 4 vols. (London, 1934), 3:185. The Tarleton quote is attributed to Tarleton, *A History of the Southern Campaigns*, 90.

21. "Introduction to the rest of Part Five," *CP*, 2:25-27.

22. Pancake, *This Destructive War*, 117.

23. Ward, *The War of the Revolution*, 167.

24. Born in Hungary, his given name was Mihály Lajos Jeney.

25. Albert Louis Zambone, *Daniel Morgan: A Revolutionary Life* (Yardley, PA: Westholme Publishing, 2018), 118.

26. Starkey, *War in the Age of Enlightenment*, 54, 61.

27. Zambone, *Daniel Morgan*, 119.

28. Ibid., 119.

29. Pancake, *1777: The Year of the Hangman* (Tuscaloosa: University of Alabama Press, 1977), 184-186. Also Zambone, *Daniel Morgan*, 145.

30. Boatner, *Encyclopedia of the American Revolution*, 735-736.

31. Ibid., 1173-1174.
32. "Cornwallis to Clinton," August 6, 1780, *CP*, 1:175.
33. Williams, "A Narrative of the Campaign of 1780," in *Sketches of the Life and Correspondence of Nathanael Greene* by William Johnson, 1:508.
34. "Cornwallis to Balfour," September 13, 1780, *CP*, 2:82; also "McArthur to Cornwallis, September 30, 1780," *CP*, 2:281.
35. Davie, *The Revolutionary War Sketches of William R. Davie*, 23.
36. Ibid., 24.
37. Buchanan, *The Road to Guilford Courthouse*, 188-190. Also Tarleton, *A History of the Campaigns of 1780 and 1781*, 160. Cornwallis's quote about the "hornet's nest" appears in the NCPedia web page, https://www.ncpedia.org/charlotte-battle, accessed on July 17, 2018.
38. Ward, *The War of the Revolution*, 744.
39. Tarleton, *A History of the Campaigns of 1780 and 1781*, 166.
40. Clinton, *The American Rebellion*, 228.
41. Ward, *The War of the Revolution*, 745.
42. Zambone, *Daniel Morgan*, 210-213. Also Seymour, *A Journal of the Southern Expedition, 1780-1783* (Wilmington: Historical Society of Delaware, 1896), 9.
43. Starkey, *War in the Age of Enlightenment*, 51.
44. "Turnbull to Rawdon," October 31, 1780, *CP* 2:265.
45. Seymour, *Journal of the Southern Expedition*, 9.
46. "Rawdon to Cornwallis," November 17, 1780, *CP*, 3:153.
47. James Graham, *The Life of General Daniel Morgan: Of the Virginia Line of the Army of the United States, With Portions of His Correspondence* (New York: Derby & Jackson, 1859), 248.
48. Seymour, *Journal of the Southern Expedition*, 10.
49. Graham, *The Life of General Daniel Morgan*, 248.
50. Williams, *A Narrative of the Southern Campaign of 1780*, 508.
51. "Cornwallis to Rawdon," December 2, 1781, *CP*, 3:189-190.
52. "Rawdon to Cornwallis," December 3, 1780, *CP*, 3:192.
53. "Cornwallis to Rawdon," December 3, 1780, *CP*, 3:191.
54. "Cornwallis to Balfour," December 5, 1780, *CP*, 3:99.

CHAPTER FOUR: THE SOUTHERN GENTLEMEN

1. Williams, "A Narrative of the Campaign of 1780," appearing as Appendix B in *Sketches of the Life and Correspondence of Nathanael Greene* by William Johnson, 1:508.
2. "Rawdon to Cornwallis," December 3, 1780, *CP*, 3:192.
3. Johnson, *Sketches of the Life and Correspondence of Nathanael Greene*, 1:338.
4. Lee, *The Revolutionary War Memoirs of General Henry Lee*, 220-221.
5. George Washington Greene, *The Life of Nathanael Greene, Major General in the Army of the Revolution* (Boston: Houghton Mifflin, 1890), 1:8.
6. Ibid., 1:4-5.
7. *NG*, 1:4, Note 2. Also Greene, *The Life of Nathanael Greene*, 1:5.
8. Johnson, Nathanael Greene, 1:7; also "NG to Samuel Ward," October 9, 1772, *NG*, 1:47-49; also Greene, *The Life of Nathanael Greene*, 1:11.
9. Ibid., 1:8.
10. Ibid., 1:12.
11. Buchanan, *The Road to Guilford Courthouse*, 262.

12. Quote about "abstruse discussions" is from Greene, *The Life of Nathanael Greene*, 1:12. For this very brief study of John Locke and his *Essay Concerning Human Understanding* I referenced James MacGregor Burns, *Fire and Light: How the Enlightenment Transformed Our World* (New York: St. Martin's Press, 2013), 35; also Anthony Pagden, *The Enlightenment and Why It Still Matters* (New York: Random House, 2013), 78-79.

13. *NG*, 1:69-70, Note 2. According to the minutes of the East Greenwich Society of Friends Monthly Meeting on July 5, 1773, Greene and his cousin Griffin were suspended for being at "a Place in Connecticut of *Publick Resort* where they had No Proper Business." Greene's early biographer William Johnson interpreted *Publick Resort* as a "grand parade," or military exercise. The editors of Greene's papers, however, state that, at the time, "public resort" was a common term for a tavern or alehouse.

14. Terry Golway, *Washington's General: Nathanael Greene and the Triumph of the American Revolution* (New York: Henry Holt, 2006), 41-42.

15. "NG to Deputy Governor Nicholas Cooke of Rhode Island," June 18, 1775, *NG*, 1:88. Also Golway, *Washington's General*, 29.

16. "NG to Colonel James M. Varnum," October 31, 1774, *NG*, 1:75-76.

17. Golway, *Washington's General*, 56.

18. Boatner, *Encyclopedia of the American Revolution*, 388.

19. "Quartermaster General Nathanael Greene to General George Washington," April 24, 1779, NG, 3:427.

20. Summary information about Greene's career as quartermaster was taken primarily from *Washington's General* by Terry Golway.

21. "NG to George Washington," October 16, 1780, reprinted in *Sketches of the Life and Correspondence of Nathanael Greene* by William Johnson, 1: 219-220.

22. Pancake, *This Destructive War*, 49.

23. Ward, *The War of the Revolution*, 734.

24. Boatner, *Encyclopedia of the American Revolution*, 12. From the entry on *Adjutants*.

25. Ibid.; selection from Lee appears on pages 519-520.

26. Boatner, *Encyclopedia of the American Revolution*, 584-585.

27. Johnson, *Sketches of the Life and Correspondence of Nathanael Greene*, 1:443.

28. Lee, *The Revolutionary War Memoirs of Henry Lee*, note, 185.

29. This sketch of Henry Lee is taken primarily from Charles Royster's "Introduction" to Lee's Memoirs. A biographical note in *NG*, 6:430-431 (Note 1), also proved helpful, as did a sketch in Buchanan's *The Road To Guilford Courthouse*, 352-354.

30. Boatner, *Encyclopedia of the American Revolution*, 617. Much of this profile of William Washington is taken from Boatner, 1169.

31. Lee, *The Revolutionary War Memoirs of Henry Lee*, 589.

32. Ibid.

33. Boatner, *Encyclopedia of the American Revolution*, 1013.

34. Ibid., 532-533. Also Buchanan, *Road to Guilford Courthouse*, 62; and biographical note in *NG*, 10:535-536.

35. Biographical sketches of Seymour, Anderson, and Beatty from Lieutenant Colonel John Moncure, *The Cowpens Staff Ride and Battlefield Tour* (Fort Leavenworth, KS: 1996), 99-102, 139.

36. Starkey, *War in the Age of Enlightenment*, 164.

37. "NG to George Washington," December 7, 1780, *NG*, 6:543.

38. "NG to Catherine Greene," December 7, 1780, *NG*, 6:542.

39. Johnson, *Sketches of the Life and Correspondence of Nathanael Greene*, 1:349.

40. Ibid.

CHAPTER FIVE: FLYING ARMY

1. William Gordon, *The History of the Rise, Progress, and Establishment of the Independence of the United States of America*, (London: printed for the author, 1788), 4:27.

2. Elkanah Watson, *Men and the Times of the Revolution: or, Memoirs of Elkanah Watson, Including His Journals of Travel in Europe and America from the Year 1772 to 1842*, 2nd Ed., Winslow C. Watson, ed. (New York: Dana and Company, 1857), 297.

3. "NG to Thomas Jefferson," December 6, 1780, *NG*, 6:530.

4. "NG to Alexander Hamilton," January 10, 1780, *NG*, 7:90.

5. M.F. Treacy, *Prelude to Yorktown*, 64.

6. "NG to Thomas Jefferson," December 6, 1780, *NG*, 6:531.

7. "NG to General Edward Stevens," December 1, 1780, *NG*, 6:512-513.

8. "NG to Chevalier de la Lucerne," December 29, 1780, *NG*, 7:20.

9. "NG to Col. Thaddeus Kosciuszko," December 8, 1780, *NG*, 6:554.

10. Sydney G. Fisher, *The Struggle for American Independence* (Philadelphia: Lippincott, 1908), 2:377. Quoted by Ward, *The War of the Revolution*, 2:751.

11. "NG to Samuel Huntington," November 2, 1780, *NG*, 6:459.

12. Jay Luvaas, *Frederick the Great and the Art of War* (New York: Free Press, 1966), 336.

13. Ward, *The War of the Revolution*, 751.

14. Johnson, *Sketches of Nathanael Greene*, 1:488.

15. Boatner, *Encyclopedia of the American Revolution*, 1009.

16. "William Davidson to NC Board of War," November 27, 1780, State Records of North Carolina, Walter Clark, ed. (Winston, NC: M.I. and J.C. Stewart), 14:759-760. Quoted from William Lee Anderson, *Camp New Providence: Large Encampment of Southern Continental Army and Militia on Providence Road at Six Mile Creek, October–December 1780*, https://elehistory.com/amrev/MecklenburgDuringAmericanRevolution.pdf, originally accessed and downloaded October 12, 2018 (as of June 2019, this work unfortunately was not available online; it is an excellent and thoroughly researched article on the Continental camps in Charlotte).

17. "NG to Thomas Sumter," December 15, 1780, *NG*, 6:581. Greene writes to Sumter in reference to their meeting on December 8 and Sumter's proposal to detach Morgan west of Winnsboro toward Ninety Six: "The measure you wish I have been preparing for Ever since I was with you, and shall have the troops in readiness in a day or two at the farthest."

18. Gordon, *History*, 4:27.

19. "NG to Daniel Morgan," December 16, 1780, NG, 6:589-590. The troop numbers of Greene and Morgan's forces are from Gordon, *History*, 4:32, and Buchanan, *Road to Guilford Courthouse*, 296, respectively.

20. Herman Maurice de Saxe, *Reveries on the Art of War* (New Delhi, India: Pentagon Press, 2017), 104.

21. Michel de Jeney, *The Partisan: Or, the Art of Making War in Detachment* (London: R. Griffiths, 1760), 6.

22. "NG to an Unidentified Person," January 1-23, 1781, *NG*, 7:175. Includes quote about "discipline and spirits of my men" in paragraph above.

23. Buchanan, *The Road to Guilford Courthouse*, 294. Also William Gordon, *History*, 4:32.

24. Lee F. McGee, "The Better Order of Men: Hammond's Store and Fort Williams,"

Southern Campaigns of the American Revolution (hereafter *SCAR)*, Vol. 2, No. 12, December 2005.

25. Johnson, *Sketches of the Life and Correspondence of Nathanael Greene*, 1:347-349.

26. Greene, *The Life of Nathanael Greene*, 1:344. Quoted from Boatner, *Encyclopedia of the American Revolution*, 615.

27. "NG to Thomas Sumter," February 3, 1781, *NG*, 7:245-246.

28. Seymour, *A Journal of the Southern Expedition, 1780-1783*, 12.

29. Joseph Johnson, *Traditions and Reminiscences Chiefly of the American Revolution in the South: Including Biographical Sketches, Incidents and Anecdotes* (Charleston, SC: Walker & James, 1851), 484. Background on Robert Cunningham also taken from William T. Graves, *Backcountry Revolutionary: James Williams (1740-1780) with source documents* (Lugoff, SC: Southern Campaigns of the American Revolution Press, 2012), 24; and Edward McCrady, *The History of South Carolina in the Revolution: 1780-1783* (New York: Macmillan, 1902), 24-25.

30. Walter Edgar, *Partisans & Redcoats*, 71. For this account Edgar references Rachel N. Klein, *Unification of a Slave State: The Rise of the Planter Class in the South Carolina Backcountry, 1760-1808* (Chapel Hill: University of North Carolina Press, 1990), 100.

31. Robert Stansbury Lambert, *South Carolina Loyalists in the American Revolution* (Columbia: University of South Carolina Press, 1987), 211-212.

32. Lawrence E. Babits, *A Devil of a Whipping: The Battle of Cowpens* (Chapel Hill: University of North Carolina Press, 1998), 48.

33. Boatner, *Encyclopedia of the American Revolution*, 291-296, 866; Biographical information about Pickens also comprised from Buchanan, *The Road to Guilford Courthouse*, 299-301; and *NG*, 8:33 (note 3).

34. McGee, "The Better Order of Men: Hammond's Store and Fort Williams," *SCAR*, 2:12.

35. "William Washington to NG," December 24, 1780, *NG*, 6:611.

36. LMcGee, "The Better Order of Men," *SCAR*, 2:12. McGee admits there is no direct evidence linking this intelligence to Washington, though Washington was campaigning in this vicinity.

37. "Daniel Morgan to Nathanael Greene," December 31, 1780, *NG*, 7:30.

38. "Daniel Morgan to NG," December 31, 1780, *NG*, 7:30.

39. Thomas Young, "Memoir of Major Thomas Young," *Orion Magazine*, November 1843. (Accessed online at http://www.carolinamilitia.com/memoir-of-major-thomas-young/ on October 6, 2018).

40. "Daniel Morgan to NG," December 31, 1780, *NG*, 7:30.

41. Ward, *The War of the Revolution*, 708, 741.

42. TYoung, "Memoir of Major Thomas Young."

43. Lyman Draper, *King's Mountain and Its Heroes* (Cincinnati, OH: Peter G. Thomson, Publisher, 1881), 69.

44. "Isaac Allen to Charles Cornwallis," December 31, 1780, *CP*, 3:290.

45. "Cornwallis to Robert Cunningham," November 22, 1780, *CP*, 3:391-392. Account of Cunningham at Williams Fort from "Cornwallis to Balfour," January 3, 1781, *CP*, 3:121.

46. Murtie June Clark, *Loyalists in the Southern Campaign of the Revolutionary War* (Baltimore, MD: Genealogical Publishing, 1981), 1:260-264.

47. McGee, "The Better Order of Men," *SCAR*, 2:12.

48. Ibid.

49. "Archibald McArthur to Cornwallis," January 1, 1781, *CP*, 3:330-331.

50. "Daniel Morgan to NG," January 4, 1781, *NG*, 7:50-51.
51. "Daniel Morgan to NG," December 31, 1780, *NG*, 7:30.
52. "NG to Daniel Morgan," January 8, 1780, *NG*, 7:72.
53. Johnson, *Sketches of the Life and Correspondence of Nathanael Greene*, 1:363.
54. David Schenck, *North Carolina, 1780-'81: Being a History of the Invasion of the Carolinas by the British Army Under Lord Cornwalls in 1780-'81* (Raleigh, NC: Edwards & Broughton, 1889), 202-203.
55. McGee, "The Better Order of Men," *SCAR*, 2:12.

CHAPTER SIX: PERFECT INTENTIONS

1. "Cornwallis to Rawdon," December 26, 1780, *CP*, 3:226-227.
2. "Cornwallis to Rawdon," December 30, 1780, *CP*, 3:232-233. Also Harry Shenawolf, "The British Brigade of Guards in the American Revolution," Revolutionary War Journal website (http://www.revolutionarywarjournal.com/british-brigade-of-guards/, accessed on October 2, 2019).
3. William B. Willcox, *Portrait of a General: Sir Henry Clinton in the War of Independence* (New York: Alfred A. Knopf, 1964), 350.
4. "Cornwallis to Clinton," December 22, 1780, *CP*, 3:28-19; also Boatner, *Encyclopedia of the American Revolution*, 1038.
5. Tarleton, *A History of the Campaigns of 1780 and 1781*, 208.
6. "Cornwallis to Rawdon," December 28, 1780, *CP*, 3:229.
7. "NG to Francis Marion," December 24, 1780, *NG*, 6:607.
8. Ward, *War of the Revolution*, 753.
9. "NG to Robert Howe," December 28, 1780, *NG*, 7:18.
10. Tarleton, *A History of the Campaigns of 1780 and 1781*, 208-209.
11. "Cornwallis to Lt. Colonel Balfour," December 29, 1780, *CP*, 3:118. Responding to reports the French were going to attack the Cape Fear region, Cornwallis wrote, "If this French account does not interfere, I shall pursue the plan I originally intended. Tarleton will march up Broad River on Wednesday, and I shall move up the middle road on Thursday, Leslie going at the same time up the road by the Wateree."
12. "Cornwallis to Balfour," January 1, 1781, *CP*, 3:119.
13. "Haldane to Tarleton," December 27, 1781, *CP*, 3:357.
14. Buchanan, *Road to Guilford Courthouse*, 58-60. Also Boatner, *Encyclopedia of the American Revolution*, 1097.
15. Boatner, *Encyclopedia of the American Revolution*, 115. Boatner reports the soldiers of the British Legion were put on "Regular Establishment" in June 1881 at the same time Tarleton's lieutenant colonel commission was adopted into the regular army.
16. Ibid., 634.
17. Ibid., 115.
18. Charles Stedman, *The History of the Origin, Progress, and Termination of the American War* (London, 1794), 2:183.
19. "Cornwallis to Rawdon," July 15, 1780, CP, 1:205-206.
20. Buchanan, *Road to Guilford Courthouse*, 63.
21. Lawrence E. Babits and Joshua B. Howard, "Continentals in Tarleton's British Legion: May 1780 to October 1781," appearing in *Cavalry of the American Revolution*, edited by Jim Piecuch (Yardley, PA: Westholme Publishing, 2012), 182-202. Extract from Alexander Chesney's *Journal* is also taken from this article.

22. Buchanan, *Road to Guilford Courthouse*, 255-257.

23. "Cornwallis to Tarleton," November 8, 1781, *CP*, 3:334.

24. Saberton, *CP*, 3:11.

25. Robert D. Bass, *The Green Dragoon: The Lives of Banastre Tarleton and Mary Robinson* (Orangeburg, SC: Sandlapper Publishing, 1973), 141.

26. "George to Cornwallis," December 30, 1781, Letter One and Two, *CP*, 3:417-418.

27. "Cornwallis to Rawdon," January 3, 1781, *CP*, 3:239.

28. Tarleton, *A History of the Campaigns of 1780 and 1781*, 210.

29. "Cornwallis to Tarleton," January 2, 1781, from Tarleton's *Campaigns*, 244.

30. "Tarleton to Cornwallis," January 4, 1781, from Tarleton's *Campaigns*, 245-246.

31. "Cornwallis to Tarleton," January 5, 1781, from Tarleton's *Campaigns*, 246-247.

32. For returns of British troop strength before Cowpens, I relied on Ian Saberton, *The Cornwallis Papers*, Volume 3. For Cornwallis's pre-Cowpens invasion force strength, I used figures provided in the "Introduction," pages 11-12. For figures of the British occupation force under Rawdon, I used the returns provided in the table titled "Return of troops remaining in South Carolina under Rawdon, 15th January 1781," on pages 255-264. For Continental troop strength at this time I relied on Gordon, *The History of the Rise, Progress, and Establishment of the United States of America*, 4:27-28.

33. "Cornwallis to Tarleton," January 5, 1781, from Tarleton's *Campaigns*, 246-247.

34. Stedman, *The History of the Origin, Progress, and Termination of the American War*, 2:320.

35. "Cornwallis to Leslie," January 6, 1781, *CP*, 3:369.

36. Quoted in Buchanan, *Road to Guilford Courthouse*, 311. Buchanan cites his reference as Bass, *The Green Dragoon*, 148-149.

37. "Cornwallis to Leslie," January 12, 1781, *CP*, 3:371; also "Cornwallis to Rawdon," January 12, 1781, *CP*, 3:249.

38. Buchanan, *Road to Guilford Courthouse*, 311.

39. "Cornwallis to Tarleton," January 14, 1781, *CP*, 3:364-365.

40. "Pension Application of William Hillhouse," Southern Campaigns American Revolution Pension Statements & Rosters, transcribed by Will Graves; annotated by Charles B. Baxley, http://revwarapps.org/s7008.pdf, accessed on October 10, 2018. "The British Commander in Chief Lord Cornwallis on his march to Virginia in January 1781 made my plantation his place of rendezvous from Tuesday till Friday (January 16-19, 1781), stripping me of all my possessions except the land which he could not destroy," Hillhouse reported.

41. BTarleton, *A History of the Campaigns of 1780 and 1781*, 212-213.

42. "Cornwallis to Tarleton," January 16, 1781, *CP*, 3:365.

43. Clinton, *The American Rebellion*, 246.

44. "NG to Daniel Morgan," December 16, 1780, *NG*, 6:589.

45. Johnson, *Sketches of the Life and Correspondence of Nathanael Greene*, 1:362-363.

46. Schenck, *North Carolina, 1780-'81*, 200.

47. Babits, *A Devil of a Whipping*, 49.

48. "Daniel Morgan to NG," December 31, 1780, *NG*, 7:31.

49. "NG to Daniel Morgan," December 26, 1780, *NG*, 6:589.

50. "Daniel Morgan to NG," January 15, 1781, *NG*, 7:127.

51. For more on the Greene/Sumter feud, see *The Quaker and the Gamecock* by the author (Philadelphia, PA: Casemate Publishers, 2019).

52. Treacy, *Prelude to Yorktown*, 79.

53. "NG to Daniel Morgan," January 8, 1781, *NG*, 7:72-73.

54. Treacy, *Prelude to Yorktown*, 85.

55. "Daniel Morgan to NG," January 15, 1780, *NG*, 7:128.

CHAPTER SEVEN: BANNY IS COMING

1. North Callahan, *Daniel Morgan: Ranger of the Revolution* (New York: Holt, Rinehart and Winston, 1961), 202-203.

2. Seymour, *A Journal of the Southern Expedition, 1780-1783*, 12.

3. "NG to Daniel Morgan," January 13, 1781, *NG*, 7:106.

4. "Daniel Morgan to NG, January 15, 1781," *NG*, 7:128. For a fascinating discussion of the modern-day location of Burr's Mill, see John A. Robertson, "Burr's Mill Found," *Southern Campaigns of the American Revolution*, Vol. 2, No. 12, accessed online at http://www.southerncampaign.org/newsletter/v2n12.pdf on June 12, 2019.

5. Graham, *The Life of Daniel Morgan*, 281.

6. Babits, *A Devil of a Whipping*, 62.

7. For this analysis of Morgan's interior deliberations, I relied on Graham, *The Life of General Daniel Morgan*, 283-284. Also Treacy, *Prelude to Yorktown*, 89-91.

8. Graham, *The Life of Daniel Morgan*, 283-284.

9. Robert Kirkwood and Joseph Brown Turner, *The Journal and Order Book of Captain Robert Kirkwood of the Delaware Regiment of the Continental Line in Two Parts* (Wilmington: Historical Society of Delaware), 13.

10. BTarleton, *Campaigns of 1780 and 1781*, 214.

11. Burke Davis, *The Cowpens-Guilford Courthouse Campaign* (New York: J.B. Lippincott, 1962), 19.

12. This description of the Cowpens plain is adapted with gratitude from Babits, *A Devil of a Whipping*, 62-76.

13. Graham, *The Life of General Daniel Morgan*, 289.

14. Young, "The Memoir of Thomas Young," *Orion Magazine*, 1843.

15. Howard's recollection appears in a footnote on page 226 of Lee's *Revolutionary War Memoirs*.

16. Graham, *The Life of General Daniel Morgan*, 291.

17. Babits, *Devil of a Whipping*, 73.

18. Don Higginbotham, *Daniel Morgan: Revolutionary Rifleman* (Chapel Hill: University of North Carolina Press, 1961), 133-134.

19. Buchanan, *The Road to Guilford Courthouse*, 316.

20. Treacy, *Prelude to Yorktown*, 96.

21. Young, "Memoir of Thomas Young."

22. Babits, *A Devil of a Whipping*, 56.

23. Graham, *The Life of General Daniel Morgan*, 292.

24. Samuel Hammond, "Notes on the Battle of Camden," in Joseph Johnson, *Traditions and Reminiscences, Chiefly of the American Revolution in the South* (Charleston, SC: Walker & James, 1851), 527.

25. Babits, *A Devil of a Whipping*, 55-56.

26. Young, "Memoir of Major Thomas Young."

27. Nathanael Greene also employed mounted troops at Eutaw Springs on September 8, 1781.

28. Tarleton, *Campaigns of 1780 and 1781*, 213-214.

29. Ibid., 214.

30. Ibid., 215.
31. Ibid.
32. Lee, *The Revolutionary War Memoir of Henry Lee*, 226.
33. Callahan, *Daniel Morgan: Ranger of the Revolution*, 210.
34. Babits, *Devil of a Whipping*, 72.
35. Ibid., 72-75.
36. Ibid., 73.
37. Ibid., 33.
38. Ibid., 77.
39. Ibid., 78.
40. "Daniel Morgan to Nathanael Greene," January 19, 1781, *NG*, 7:155.
41. Ward, *War of the Revolution*, 755.
42. Tarleton, *Campaigns of 1780 and 1781*, 216.
43. LBabits, *Devil of a Whipping*, 150-152. Babits's estimate includes an extrapolation based on the number of pension applications from soldiers who claimed to be in the battle collected many decades later.
44. Graham, *The Life of General Daniel Morgan*, 297-298.
45. Treacy, *Prelude to Yorktown*, 100.
46. Saberton, *CP*, 3:11.
47. Tarleton, *Campaigns of 1780 and 1781*, 216.
48. Ibid.
49. "Daniel Morgan to NG," January 19, 1781, *NG*, 7:154.
50. Young, "Memoir of Major Thomas Young."
51. James Potter Collins, *Autobiography of a Revolutionary Soldier*, John M. Roberts, ed. (Clinton, LA: Feliciana Democrat Printing, 1859), 56-57.

CHAPTER EIGHT: VICTORY COMPLEAT

1. Roderick Mackenzie, *Strictures on Lt. Col. Tarleton's History of "Campaigns of 1780 and 1781, In the Southern Provinces of North America" in a Series of Letters to a Friend* (London: 1787), 108-109.
2. Ibid., 107-108.
3. Lee, *The Revolutionary War Memoir of Henry Lee*, 230-231.
4. Tarleton, *A History of the Campaigns of 1780 and 1781*, 216.
5. "Daniel Morgan to NG," January 19, 1781, *NG*, 7:154.
6. Young, "Memoir of Major Thomas Young."
7. WSeymour, *A Journal of the Southern Expedition*, 13.
8. Babits, *A Devil of a Whipping*, 92-93.
9. Thomas Anderson, "Journal of Lieutenant Thomas Anderson of the Delaware Regiment, 1780-1782," *Historical Magazine*, 2d ser., 1 (1867): 208-209.
10. "Daniel Morgan to NG," January 19, 1781, *NG*, 7:154.
11. Tarelton, *History of the Campaigns of 1780 and 1781*, 216.
12. Collins, *Autobiography of a Revolutionary Soldier*, 57.
13. Tarleton, *History of the Campaigns of 1780 and 1781*, 216.
14. HLee, *The Campaign of 1781 in the Carolinas* (Spartanburg, SC: Reprint Company, 1975), 97. Howard is quoted in a footnote on this page.
15. Ibid.
16. Anderson, "Journal of Lieutenant Thomas Anderson," 208-209.

17. Graham, *The Life of General Daniel Morgan*, 303-304. Includes quote from Morgan and Washington.

18. Howard quote in Lee, *The Campaign of 1781 in the Carolinas*, 97.

19. "Morgan to NG," January 19, 1781, *NG*, 7:154. Howard in Henry Lee, *The Campaign of 1781 in the Carolinas*, 97.

20. Anderson, "Journal of Lieutenant Thomas Anderson," 208-209.

21. Young, "Memoir of Major Thomas Young."

22. Anderson, "Journal of Lieutenant Thomas Anderson," 208-209.

23. Tarleton, *History of the Campaigns of 1780 and 1781*, 217.

24. Stedman, *The History of the Origin, Progress, and Termination of the American War*, 2:322.

25. Babits and Howard, "Continentals in Tarleton's British Legion: May 1780 to October 1781," 182-202.

26. "Daniel Morgan to NG," October 19, 1781, *NG*, 7:154.

27. "Daniel Morgan to NG," October 19, 1781, *NG*, 7:153.

28. Howard quote in Lee, *The Campaign of 1781 in the Carolinas*, 98.

29. The account of Washington's duel with Tarleton was taken from Lee, *Revolutionary War Memoirs*, 229, and Buchanan, *Road to Guilford Courthouse*, 326. Information about the actual identity of Washington's opponent, including the Howard quote, is from Babits, *A Devil of a Whipping*, 130.

30. Ward, *War of the Revolution*, 762.

31. "Daniel Morgan to NG," January 19, 1781, *NG*: 7:155. Also Note 14 to this letter, *NG*, 7:160-161.

32. Babits, *Devil of a Whipping*, 105, 151.

33. "Daniel Morgan to NG," January 19, 1781, *NG*, 7:152.

34. Higginbotham, *Daniel Morgan: Revolutionary Rifleman*, 142. Higginbotham lists the source of the quote to Snickers as "Morgan to Snickers," January 25, 1781, Gates Papers, N.Y. Historical Society.

35. Lee, *Revolutionary War Memoirs*, 230.

36. Buchanan, *Road to Guilford Courthouse*, 329.

37. Boatner, *Encyclopedia of the American Revolution*, 298.

38. Stedman, *The History of the Origin, Progress, and Termination of the American War*, 2:325.

39. Ibid., 324.

40. Mackenzie, *Strictures*, 89.

41. Lee, *Revolutionary War Memoirs*, 230.

42. Mackenzie, *Strictures*, 108.

43. Lee, *Revolutionary War Memoirs*, 231.

44. Stedman, *The History of the Origin, Progress, and Termination of the American War*, 2:321.

45. Mackenzie, *Strictures*, 109-110.

46. Tarleton, *History of the Campaigns of 1780 and 1781*, 217.

47. Stedman, *History of the Origin, Progress, and Termination of the American War*, 2:322.

48. Mackenzie, *Strictures*, 100.

49. Tarleton, *History of the Campaigns of 1780 and 1781*, 218.

50. Clinton, *The American Rebellion*, 247-248.

51. Mackenzie, *Strictures*, 88.

52. Stedman, *History of the Origin, Progress, and Termination of the American War*, 2:324.

53. Howard in Lee, *The Campaign of 1781 in the Carolinas*, 96-99.

54. William Moultrie, *Memoirs of the American Revolution: So Far as It Relates to the States*

of North and South Carolina, and Georgia (New York: David Longworth, 1802), 2:256-257.

55. "Otho Holland Williams to Daniel Morgan," January 25, 1781, from *The Cowpens Papers*, edited by Theodorus Bailey Myers (Charleston: The News & Courier, 1881), 33.

56. "The Gratitude of Congress," March 9, 1781, from *The Cowpens Papers*, 37. Information about Congressional Gold Medals was taken from Gary Shattuck, "Seven Gold Medals of America's Revolutionary Congress, *Journal of the American Revolution* Website, https://allthingsliberty.com/2015/04/7-gold-medals-of-americas-revolutionary-congress/. Accessed on February 17, 2019.

57. Lee, *The Revolutionary War Memoir of Henry Lee*, 226-227.

58. Johnson, *Sketches of the Life and Correspondence of Nathanael Greene*, 376.

59. Babits, *A Devil of a Whipping*, 132.

CHAPTER NINE: TO THE END OF THE WORLD

1. Babits, *A Devil of a Whipping*, 143.

2. Graham, *The Life of General Daniel Morgan*, 307.

3. Tarleton, *History of the Campaigns of 1780 and 1781*, 218.

4. Johnson, *Sketches of the Life and Correspondence of Nathanael Greene*, 1:384-385.

5. Young, "Memoir of Major Thomas Young."

6. Higginbotham, *Daniel Morgan: Revolutionary Rifleman*, 147. Higginbotham lists as his source the memoir of Joseph McJunkin, *Draper Papers*, 23VV193, State Historical Society of Wisconsin.

7. Graham, *The Life of General Daniel Morgan*, 325. Also Babits, *A Devil of a Whipping*, 143. It is Babits who reports Morgan crossed at Island Ford.

8. Graham, *The Life of General Daniel Morgan*, 326.

9. Ibid.

10. Schenck, *North Carolina, 1780-'81*, 228.

11. Graham, *The Life of General Daniel Morgan*, 325.

12. Buchanan, *The Road to Guilford Courthouse*, 334-335

13. "Cornwallis to Clinton," January 18, 1781, from Tarleton, *History of the Campaigns of 1780 and 1781*, 250-252.

14. "Cornwallis to Clinton," January 18, 1781, *CP*, 3:36.

15. "Cornwallis to Germain," March 17, 1781, *CP*, 4:12.

16. Wickwire, *Cornwallis: The American Adventure* (Boston: Houghton Mifflin, 1970), 274.

17. O'Hara, "Letters of Charles O'Hara to thr Duke of Grafton," 173.

18. Tarleton, *Campaigns of 1780 and 1781*, 222.

19. "Cornwallis to Rawdon," January 21, 1780, *CP*, 3:251.

20. Wickwire, *Cornwallis and the War of Independence*, 98-99.

21. Johnson, *Sketches of the Life and Correspondence of Nathanael Greene*, 1:387-388.

22. Ibid., 387.

23. Charles Heaton, "The Failure of Enlightenment Military Doctrine in Revolutionary America: The Piedmont Campaign and the Fate of the British Army in the Lower South," *North Carolina Historical Review*, Vol. 87, No. 2 (April 2010), 128.

24. Clinton, *The American Rebellion*, 247.

25. O'Hara, "Letters of Charles O'Hara to the Duke of Grafton," 173-174.

26. John Morgan, "Making Bricks Without Straw: Nathanael Greene's Southern Campaigns and Mao Tse-Tung's Mobile War," *Military Affairs*, Vol. 47, No. 3 (October 1983), 115-121.

27. Orders for December 26, 1780, January 2 and 18, 1781, in A. R. Newsome, ed., "A British Orderly Book 1780-1781," *North Carolina Historical Review*, 3:183, 274, 284.

28. Marching orders for British campaigns in 1776 and 1777 can be found in "Order Book of Lieut. Col. Stephen Kemble, Adjutant General and Deputy Adjutant General to the British forces in America, 1775-1778," *Collections of the New-York Historical Society* (New York: NYHS, 1883), 251-585. Many authors exaggerate the load carried by British soldiers; the data given here is based on weights of original and reproduction items, and orders for the items that soldiers carried on various campaigns in America.

29. Treacy, *Prelude to Yorktown*, 122.

30. Graham, *The Life of General Daniel Morgan*, 327.

31. Tarleton, *Campaigns of 1780 and 1781*, 223.

32. Graham, *The Life of General Daniel Morgan*, 327. Also Seymour, *A Journal of the Southern Expedition, 1780-1783*, 15.

33. Higginbotham, *Daniel Morgan*, 143.

34. "Daniel Morgan to Nathanael Greene," January 23, 1781, from Graham, *The Life of General Daniel Morgan*, 329-330.

35. "Daniel Morgan to NG," January 24, 1781, *NG*, 7:190-191.

36. Information about the mileage of Cornwallis's marches came from Treacy, *Prelude to Yorktown*, 122. Also Lawrence E. Babits and Joshua Howard, *Long, Obstinate, and Bloody: The Battle of Guilford Courthouse* (Chapel Hill: UNC Press, 2009), 15; Babits and Howard report Cornwallis marched 30 miles from January 22-25.

37. Stedman, *History of the Origin, Progress, and Termination of the American War*, 2:326.

38. Treacy, *Prelude to Yorktown*, 125. David Schenck writes, "At Ramsour's Mill some fatuity overshadowed his [Cornwallis's] reason and caused him to stop two more days." Schenck, *North Carolina, 1780-1781*, 231.

39. "Daniel Morgan to NG," second letter that date, January 25, 1781, *NG*, 7:201.

40. "Daniel Morgan to NG," first letter that date, January 25, 1781, *NG*; also Footnote 1 to this letter; *NG*, 7:199-200.

41. For this portrait of Ramsour's Mill I referenced the map titled "A map of North Carolina: from the best authorities," by William Harrison, et. al., originally published in 1794, found online at the Library of Congress website, https://www.loc.gov/resource/g3900.ct006849/?r=0.08,0.15,0.282,0.154,0, accessed on February 22, 2019. Also referenced is John Buchanan, *The Road to Guilford Courthouse*, 106-109.

42. "Brigade Orders, 24th January, 1781," in Newsome: "A British Orderly Book" 3:287.

43. "Cornwallis to Rawdon," January 25, 1781, *CP*, 3:252.

44. Stedman, *History of the Origin, Progress, and Termination of the American War*, 2:326.

45. Ibid.

46. Orders for January 28, 1781, in Newsome, "A British Orderly Book 1780-1781," 3:289.

47. "Earl Cornwallis to Lord George Germain," March 17, 1781, *Correspondence of Charles, First Marquis Cornwallis*, edited by Charles Ross, 1:503.

48. O'Hara, "Letters of Charles O'Hara to the Duke of Grafton," 174.

CHAPTER TEN: HORSES IN DEEP WATER

1. Newsome, "A British Orderly Book," 3:289-290.

2. "Cornwallis to Germain," March 17, 1781, *CP*, 4:13.

3. "A British Orderly Book," 3:289. Also "Daniel Morgan to NG," January 29, 1781, *NG*, 7:215.

4. "Cornwallis to Germain," March 17, 1781, *CP*, 4:13.

5. Stedman, *The History of the Origin, Progress, and Termination of the American War*, 2:326

6. Tarleton, *A History of the Campaigns of 1780 and 1781*, 223.

7. Ibid., 222.

8. "Cornwallis to Tarleton," January 30, 1781, from Tarleton, *History of the Campaigns of 1780 and 1781*, 252.

9. Wickwire, *Cornwallis: The American Adventure*, 271.

10. "NG to Major Edmund M. Hyrne," January 25, 1781, *NG*, 7:194.

11. Johnson, *Sketches of the Life and Correspondence of Nathanael Greene*, 1:394; also "NG to Francis Marion," January 25, 1781, *NG*, 7:194-195.

12. "NG to General Isaac Huger," January 30, 1781. Greene's specific orders to Huger have not been found. In a letter dated February 1, 1781, Huger reports to Greene, "Agreeable to your orders of the 28th ultimo, I put the army into motion about 3 o'clcock the following afternoon;" *NG*, 7:232.

13. Buchanan, *The Road to Guilford Courthouse*, 342.

14. Johnson, *Sketches of the Life and Correspondence of Nathanael Greene*, 1:403.

15. "NG to Thomas Sumter," January 8, 1781, *NG*, 7:74-75.

16. "NG to Colonel James Emmett," April 3, 1781, *NG*, 8:33.

17. Zambone, *Daniel Morgan: A Revolutionary Life*, 246.

18. "Daniel Morgan to NG," January 24, 1781, *NG*, 7:190-191; and "Daniel Morgan to NG," January 28, 1781, *NG*, 7:211.

19. "Daniel Morgan to NG," January 24, 1781, 7:192.

20. Graham, *General Joseph Graham and His Papers*, 286.

21. This portrait of William L. Davidson is taken from the article "Davidson, William Lee," by Chalmers G. Davidson, NCpedia.org, https://www.ncpedia.org/biography/davidson-william-lee, accessed on February 25, 2019.

22. "Daniel Morgan to NG," December 28, 1781, *NG*, 7:211. Also Joseph Graham, *General Joseph Graham and His Papers*, 288.

23. Boatner, *Encyclopedia of the American Revolution*, 442. Also Max R. Williams, "Graham, Joseph," Ncpedia.org, https://www.ncpedia.org/biography/graham-joseph, accessed on February 24, 2019.

24. Graham, *General Joseph Graham and His Papers*, 287.

25. Graham, *General Joseph Graham and His Papers*, 288. Also "Daniel Morgan to NG," January 29, 1781, *NG*, 7:225.

26. Graham, *General Joseph Graham and His Papers*, 288-289.

27. Zambone, *Daniel Morgan: A Revolutionary Life,* 217.

28. "NG to Isaac Huger," January 30, 1781, *NG*, 7:219-220.

29. Johnson, *Sketches of the Life and Correspondence of Nathanael Greene*, 1:407.

30. This portrait of Benedict Arnold in Virginia taken from "Benedict Arnold in Richmond, January, 1781," introduction by George Green Shackleford, *Virginia Magazine of History and Biography*, Vol. 60, No. 4 (October 1952), 591-599. Also M.F. Treacy, *Prelude to Yorktown*, 132-133. Also "Balfour to Cornwallis," January 7, 1781, *CP*, 3:132, for background on Craig's expedition to Wilmington. Greene quote from "NG to General Issac Huger," January 30, 1781, *NG*, 7:219.

31. Graham, *General Joseph Graham and His Papers*, 289-290.

32. "Nathanael Greene to the Officer Commanding the Militia in the Salisbury District of North Carolina," January 31, 1781, *NG*, 7:227-228.

33. Johnson, *Sketches of the Life and Correspondence of Nathanael Greene*, 1:414.

34. "Cornwallis to Germain," March 17, 1781, *CP*, 4:13.

35. Tarelton, *A History of the Campaigns of 1780 and 1781*, 224. Also "Cornwallis to Germain, March 17, 1781," *CP*, 4:13.

36. Tarleton, *A History of the Campaigns of 1780 and 1781*, 224.

37. Robert Henry, *Narrative of the Battle of Cowan's Ford, February 1st, 1781* (Greensboro, NC: David Schenck, 1891). My copy was purchased on Amazon without publication information or page numbers.

38. Graham, *General Joseph Graham and His Papers*, 290-291.

39. Henry, *Narrative of the Battle of Cowan's Ford*.

CHAPTER ELEVEN: PEALS OF THUNDER

1. "Cornwallis to Germain," March 17, 1781, *CP*, 4:13.

2. O'Hara, "Letters of Charles O'Hara to the Duke of Grafton," 175.

3. Graham, *General Joseph Graham and His Papers*, 291-292.

4. Roger Lamb, *An Original and Authentic Journal of Occurrences During the Late American War, From Its Commencement to the Year 1783* (Dublin: Wilkinson & Courtney, 1809), 343.

5. Charles Stedman, *History of the Origin, Progress, and Termination of the American War*, 2:327.

6. Henry, *Narrative of the Battle of Cowan's Ford*. Again, my edition of Henry has no page numbers.

7. Lamb, *An Original and Authentic Journal of Occurrences*, 343.

8. Stedman, *History of the Origin, Progress, and Termination of the American War*, 2:327.

9. Graham, *General Joseph Graham and His Papers*, 292-293.

10. Lamb, *An Original and Authentic Journal of Occurrences*, 344.

11. O'Hara, "Letters of Charles O'Hara to the Duke of Grafton," 175.

12. Graham, *General Joseph Graham and His Papers*, 293.

13. Henry, *Narrative of the Battle of Cowan's Ford*.

14. Graham, *General Joseph Graham and His Papers*, 294.

15. Henry, *Narrative of the Battle of Cowan's Ford*.

16. Graham, *General Joseph Graham and His Papers*, 293-294.

17. Chalmers G. Davidson, "Davidson, William Lee," Ncpedia.org, https://www.ncpedia.org/biography/davidson-william-lee, accessed on March 2, 2019.

18. "Cornwallis to Germain," March 17, 1781, *CP*: 4:14; also Stedman, *History of the Origin, Progress, and Termination of the American War*, 2:329.

19. Henry, *Narrative of the Battle of Cowan's Ford*.

20. Graham, *General Joseph Graham and His Papers*, 298.

21. Ibid., 295.

22. Thomas Anderson, "Journal of Lieutenant Thomas Anderson," *Historical Magazine*, 2d Ser., 1 (1867), 209.

23. Seymour, *A Journal of the Southern Expedition*, 15-16.

24. "Cornwallis to Germain," March 17, 1781, *CP*: 4:14.

25. "NG to the Militia Officers Posted on the Catawba River and Marching to Camp," February 1, 1781, *NG*, 7:231.

26. Schenck, *North Carolina, 1780-'81*, 251.

27. Graham, *General Joseph Graham and His Papers*, 295-296.

28. Ibid., 297-298; Also Tarleton, *A History of the Campaigns of 1780 and 1781*, 225-226.

29. "After Orders, February 2, 1781," *A British Orderly Book, 1780-1781*, 3:294.

30. Schenck, *North Carolina 1780-'81*, 251.

31. Maurice de Saxe, *Reveries on the Art of War*, 104.

32. Johnson, *Sketches of the Life and Correspondence of Nathanael Greene*, 1:417; Also William Read, "Reminiscences of Dr. William Read, Arranged from His Notes and Papers," appearing in *Documentary History of the American Revolution*, 1776-1782, edited by R.W. Gibbes (New York: D. Appleton, 1857), 274.

33. Wickwire, *Cornwallis and the War of Independence*, 172.

34. Tarleton, *A History of the Campaigns of 1780 and 1781*, 226.

35. Graham, *General Joseph Graham and His Papers*, 299-300.

36. Davie, *The Revolutionary War Sketches of William R. Davie*, 23.

37. "Orders, February 2, 1781," *A British Orderly Book, 1780-1781*, 3:293.

38. Graham, *General Joseph Graham and His Papers*, 300.

39. "Orders, February 5, 1781," *A British Orderly Book, 1780-1781*, 3:296.

40. Rouse, *The Great Wagon Road*, 70-71.

41. "NG to General Edward Stevens," December 1, 1780, *NG*, 6:512-513.

42. Johnson, *Sketches of the Life and Correspondence of Nathanael Greene*, 1:418.

43. "NG to Baron Steuben," February 3, 1781, *NG*, 7:243.

44. Babits and Howard, *Long, Obstinate, and Bloody*, 25.

45. "NG to Thaddeus Kosciuszko," January 1, 1781, *NG*, 7:35.

46. "NG to an Unidentified Person," January 1-23, 1781, *NG*, 7:175; also "NG to General Isaac Huger," January 30, 1781, *NG*, 7:219.

47. Ward, *The War of the Revolution*, 771.

48. "General Isaac Huger to NG," February 1, 1781, *NG*, 7:233.

49. "NG to General Isaac Huger," February 5, 1781, and also Footnote 8 to this letter, *NG*, 7:252.

50. Graham, *The Life of General Daniel Morgan*, 350.

51. Buchanan, *The Road to Guilford Courthouse*, 349.

52. Tarleton, *A History of the Campaigns of 1780 and 1781*, 227.

CHAPTER TWELVE: CAPITAL MISFORTUNES

1. Graham, *General Joseph Graham and His Papers*, 300-301.

2. O'Hara, *Letters of Charles O'Hara to the Duke of Grafton*, 175.

3. Johnson, *Sketches of the Life and Correspondence of Nathanael Greene*, 1:419. This quote from William Read appears there.

4. Read, "Reminiscences of Dr. William Read," from *Documentary History of the American Revolution*, 3:277

5. "NG to Abner Nash," February 3, 1781, *NG*, 7:241.

6. "NG to Andrew Pickens," February 3, 1781, *NG*, 7:241-242.

7. "NG to Thomas Sumter," February 3, 1781, *NG*, 7:245-246.

8. "NG to Baron Steuben," February 3, 1781, *NG*, 7:242-243. Also Note 13 to this letter, *NG*, 7:245.

9. "NG to Thomas Sumter," February 3, 1781, *NG*, 7:246; Also "General Isaac Huger to General Alexander Lillington, February 2, 1781," *NG*, 7:235.

10. "NG to Captain Joseph Marbury," February 2, 1781, *NG*, 7:235.

11. "Cornwallis to Germain," March 17, 1781, *CP*, 4:14-15.

12. Clinton, *The American Rebellion*, 261-262.

13. "NG to Isaac Huger," February 5, 1781, *NG*, 7:251-252.

14. Greene quote taken from Zambone, *Daniel Morgan*, 217. Zambone's attribution is "To George Washington from Major Nathanael Greene," May 31, 1779.

15. "NG to Isaac Huger," February 5, 1781, *NG*, 7:251-252.

16. For insight into Greene's strategies at this time, see "NG to Baron Steuben," February 3, 1781, *NG*, 7:242-243; also "NG to Thomas Sumter," February 3, 1781, *NG*, 7:245-246, and "NG to General Isaac Huger," February 5, 1781, *NG*, 7:252.

17. Tarleton, *History of the Campaigns of 1780 and 1781*, 227-228.

18. "NG to General Isaac Huger," February 5, 1781, *NG*, 7:251.

19. Sallie W. Stockard, *The History of Guilford County, North Carolina* (Knoxville, TN: Gaut-Ogden, 1902). Information about the courthouse building and Martinsville community was also taken from the article "A History of Martinsville, North Carolina" from the Carolana website, http://www.carolana.com/NC/Towns/Martinville_NC.html; accessed on March 7, 2019.

20. Stockard, *The History of Guilford County, North Carolina*. Also Davis, *The Cowpens-Guilford Courthouse Campaign*, 98.

21. "NG to Christopher Greene," January 29, 1776, *NG*, 1:189.

22. "NG to Members of the New Garden Monthly Meeting near Guilford Courthouse," March 26, 1781, *NG*, 7:469-470.

23. Higginbotham, *Daniel Morgan*, 152-153. Also "Daniel Morgan to NG," February 6, 1781, *NG*, 7:254.

24. Benson J. Lossing, *The Pictorial Field-Book of The Revolution* (New York: Harper & Brothers, 1860), 2:408.

25. "NG to General Isaac Huger," February 5, 1781, *NG*, 7:251-252. Greene's orders for Huger to join him at Guilford Courthouse appear to have been made in a letter Greene sent to Huger on February 4, 1781. This letter is referenced in "NG to General Isaac Huger," February 5, 1781, but has not been found.

26. Johnson, *Sketches of the Life and Correspondence of Nathanael Greene*, 1:421.

27. Ibid., 1:425.

28. "NG to Commanding Officer of the Guilford Militia," February 5, 1781, *NG*, 7:253.

29. William S. Powell and Michael Hill, *The North Carolina Gazetteer: A Dictionary of Tar Heel Places and Their History*, 2nd Edition (Chapel Hill: UNC Press, 2010), 3.

30. "NG to General Isaac Huger," February 7, 1781, *NG*, 7:255.

31. Ward, *War of the Revolution*, 772. Also Greene, *The Life of Nathanael Greene*, 3:161.

32. "NG to Colonel James Emmett," April 3, 1781, *NG*, 8:33.

33. "To the Officer Commanding the Militia in the Rear of the Enemy," *NG*, 7:254.

34. "British Orderly Book, 1780-1781," 3:297.

35. Tarleton, *The Campaigns of 1780 and 1781*, 228. Tarleton's account makes the timing of this report unclear. He writes that he left for his "patrole" on February 6, the same day Cornwallis marched from Salisbury, but states that upon receiving his report, "Earl Cornwallis directed General O'Hara to quit his position at the Trading ford, and return to head quarters; which being accomplished, the royal army marched from Salisbury." Since Tarleton was not in Salisbury, and is sometimes prone to hyperbole, I believe Cornwallis had already departed Salisbury and received Tarleton's report on the march.

36. Newsome, "A British Orderly Book, 1780-1781," 3:295.

37. Davis, *The Cowpens-Guilford Courthouse Campaign*, 99.

38. Newsome, "A British Orderly Book, 1780-1781," 3:297.

39. "NG to General Isaac Huger," February 7, 1781, *NG*, 7:255.

40. Graham, *General Joseph Graham and His Papers*, 308-309. Graham reports this encounter as occurring on the evening of February 6, but I believe his recollection is off by one day; he also reports Cornwallis marched out of Salisbury on February 5, when in fact, Cornwallis left Salisbury on February 6.

41. Accounts differ as to what day Cornwallis crossed the Yadkin at Shallow Ford. In *Long, Obstinate, and Bloody*, Babits and Howard report he crossed on February 7 (p. 27). Buchanan, in *The Road to Guilford Courthouse*, reports Cornwallis crossed at Shallow Ford on February 9 (p. 354). According to the British Orderly Book, Cornwallis camped at a place called Lindsays Plantation on the night of February 8: and the editors of Greene's paper report Cornwallis camped at Lindsays "after crossing the Yadkin River (NG, 7:265, Note 2). The orderly book reports Cornwallis ordered "one days Rum will be Issued to the Troops" on February 8. Why would Cornwallis reward his men with a day's rum ration if not for finally crossing the Yadkin? Graham's account also supports this date, which is the one I have reported here.

42. Graham, *General Joseph Graham and His Papers*, 309-310.

43. "From the Residents of Salem, North Carolina," February 8, 1781, *NG*, 7:260.

44. Newsome, "British Orderly Book," February 8, 1781, 3:297. Greene would describe the camp at Lindsays as "three miles on this side of the ford," in a letter to North Carolina governor Abner Nash written on February 9, *NG*, 7:263.

45. "General Isaac Huger to Nathanael Greene," February 8, 1781, *NG*, 7:259.

46. Ibid.

47. Seymour, *A Journal of the Southern Expedition*, 16.

48. Ward, *The War of the Revolution*, 772. Also reacy, *Prelude to Yorktown*, 146-147, and Johnson, *Sketches of the Life and Correspondence of Nathanael Greene*, 1:426-427.

49. "Baron Steuben to NG," February 3, 1781, *NG*, 7:249-250.

50. Graham, *The Life of General Daniel Morgan*, 353.

CHAPTER THIRTEEN: COUNCIL OF WAR

1. "NG to Alexander Hamilton," January 10, 1781, *NG*, 7:90.

2. "NG to Henry Lee," February 8, 1781, *NG*, 7:257.

3. Golway, *Washington's General*, 254.

4. "Proceedings of the Council of War," February 9, 1781, *NG*, 7:261.

5. "NG to Captain Joseph Marbury," February 2, 1781, NG, 7:235.

6. Johnson, *Sketches of the Life and Correspondence of Nathanael Greene*, 1:428-429.

7. Lee, Jr., *Campaign of 1781 in the Carolinas*, 116-117. Carrington is quoted in this passage.

8. Lee, *The Revolutionary War Memoirs of Henry Lee*, 236.

9. Ibid., 261-262.

10. "NG to Colonel Alexander Hamilton," January 10, 1781, *NG*, 7:90.

11. "NG to Governor Abner Nash of North Carolina," February 9, 1781, *NG*, 7: 263-264.

12. This portrait of North Carolina's Moravian settlements taken primarily from C. Daniel Crews, "Moravians," 2006, NCPedia.org website, https://www.ncpedia.org/moravians, accessed on March 8, 2019. Quote about "barely a hundred adults" from "From the Residents of Salem, North Carolina," February 8, 1781, *NG*, 7:260.

13. Tarleton, *History of the Campaigns of 1780 and 1781*, 228.

14. Buchanan, *Road to Guilford Courthouse*, 354-355.

15. Johnson, *Sketches of the Life and Correspondence of Nathanael Greene*, 1:423.

16. "Daniel Morgan to NG," January 24, 1781, *NG*, 7:192.

17. Graham, *The Life of General Daniel Morgan*, 307.

18. Lee, *The Revolutionary War Memoirs of Henry Lee*, 237.

19. "NG to Colonel Francis Lock and Others in the Rear of the Enemy," February 9, 1781, *NG*, 7:262.

20. Buchanan, *The Road to Guilford Courthouse*, 351.

21. Graham, *The Life of General Daniel Morgan*, 358.

22. John Beakes, *Otho Holland Williams in the American Revolution* (Mount Pleasant, SC: Nautical and Aviation Publishing, 2015), 4-5. Other elements of Williams's life and military career depicted here are also from Beakes's work.

23. Washington quote from Beakes, *Otho Holland Williams*, 38.

24. Lee, *The Revolutionary Memoirs of Henry Lee*, 595-596; Washington quote in this paragraph from Beakes, *Otho Holland Williams*, 316.

CHAPTER FOURTEEN: TO THE DAN

1. "NG to Thomas Sumter," February 9, 1781, *NG*, 7:266; also "NG to Thomas Jefferson," February 10, 1781, *NG*, 7:271. Quote is from "NG to Sumter."

2. "NG to Colonel Otho H. Williams," February 13, 1781, *NG*, 7:285.

3. "NG to George Washington," February 9, 1781, *NG*, 7:268.

4. Greene, *The Life of Nathanael Greene*, 3:168.

5. Johnson, *Sketches of the Life and Correspondence of Nathanael Greene*, 1:431.

6. Ibid., 1:429.

7. Ibid. Also Greene, *The Life of Nathanael Greene*, 168.

8. Lee, *Revolutionary War Memoir*, 237-238.

9. Buchanan, *Road to Guilford Courthouse*, 355.

10. Johnson, *Sketches of the Life and Correspondence of Nathanael Greene*, 1:431.

11. Greene, *The Life of Nathanael Greene*, 169.

12. Newsome, "A British Orderly Book," 3:297-298 and 4:366.

13. Johnson, *Sketches of the Life and Correspondence of Nathanael Greene*, 1:430.

14. "NG to Colonel John Gunby," February 11, 2019, *NG*, 7:280. All three letters to Gunby dated this day appear on this page.

15. Lee, *Revolutionary War Memoir*, 237-238.

16. "Colonel Otho Holland Williams to NG," February 11, 1781, *NG*, 7:282.

17. Lee, *Revolutionary War Memoir*, 239.

18. Ibid., 240-242.

19. Seymour, *Journal of the Southern Expedition*, 17.

20. "Colonel Otho Holland Williams to NG," February 11, 1781, *NG*, 7:283; also Lee, *Revolutionary War Memoir*, 242-243, and Tarleton, *History of the Campaigns of 1780 and 1781*, 228.

21. "Colonel Otho Holland Williams to NG," Sunday, February 11, 1781, *NG*, 7:283.

22. Lee, *Revolutionary War Memoir*, 244-245.

23. Greene, *The Life of Nathanael Greene*, 166.

24. "NG to George Washington," February 15, 1781, *NG*, 7:293.

25. Seymour, *Journal of the Southern Expedition*, 17.

26. Greene, *The Life of Nathanael Greene*, 3:165.

27. Lee, *Revolutionary War Memoir*, 248.

28. Thayer, *Nathanael Greene: Strategist of the American Revolution*, 317. Thayer lists as his source a Greene letter to Samuel Ward, written December 23, 1782. Also "NG to Colonel Otho H. Williams," February 13, 1781, *NG*, 7:287.
29. Greene, *The Life of Nathanael Greene*, 165-166.
30. Babits and Howard, *Long, Obstinate, and Bloody*, 36.
31. Lee, *Revolutionary War Memoir*, 243-244.
32. "NG to John Butler," February 12, 1781, *NG*, 7:284.
33. "NG to Colonel Otho Holland Williams," February 13, 1781, *NG*, 7:285.
34. Newsome, "British Orderly Book," 4:366-367.
35. "NG to Colonel Otho H. Williams," February 13, 1781, *NG*, 7:285.
36. "Cornwallis to Germain," March 17, 1781, *CP*, 4:15.
37. Tarleton, *Campaigns of 1780 and 1781*, 229.
38. "Otho H. Williams to Greene," February 13, 1781, *NG*, 7:285-286.
39. Lee, *Revolutionary War Memoir*, 245-246.
40. "NG to Colonel Otho Holland Williams," February 14, 1781, *NG*, 7:287.
41. Buchanan, *The Road to Guilford Courthouse*, 358.
42. Lee, *Revolutionary War Memoir*, 247.

CHAPTER FIFTEEN: FAVOURABLE OPPORTUNITIES

1. "Proclamation, 20th February, 1781, By the Rt Hon Charles Earl Cornwallis, Lt. General of His Majesty's forces, etc., etc., etc.," *CP*, 4:55.
2. Stedman, *History of the Origin, Progress, and Termination of the American War*, 2:332.
3. Tarleton, *History of the Campaigns of 1780 and 1781*, 229.
4. Greene, *The Life of Nathanael Greene*, 3:174
5. Lee, *Revolutionary War Memoir*, 251.
6. Ibid.
7. "Cornwallis to Rawdon," February 21, 1781, *CP*, 4:45.
8. Stedman, *History of the Origin, Progress, and Termination of the American War*, 332.
9. "Earl Cornwallis to Lord George Germain," April 18, 1781, *Correspondence of Charles, First Marquis Cornwallis*, edited by Charles Ross, 1:90.
10. "NG to George Washington," February 15, 1781, *NG*, 7:293-294; also "NG to Thaddeus Kociuszko," February 16, 1781, *NG*, 7:296-297. Also Ward, *War of the Revolution*, 778.
11. Clinton, *The American Rebellion*, 263. Also "Colonel Henry Lee to NG, February 18, 1781," *NG*, 7:313. Lee reported Cornwallis had departed the Dan on February 17 at "5 oclock" in the morning and was headed toward Hillsborough.
12. "Proclamation by the Rt. Hon. Charles Earl Cornwallis," February 20, 1781, *CP*, 4:55.
13. Tarleton, *Campaigns of 1780 and 1781*, 230.
14. "Henry Lee to NG," February 23, 1781, *NG*, 7:336.
15. Buchanan, *Road to Guilford Courthouse*, 365.
16. Todd Andrlik, *Reporting the Revolutionary War: Before It Was History, It Was News* (Naperville, IL: Sourcebooks, 2012), ix-x, and 308-311.
17. "George Washington to NG," March 21, 1781, *NG*, 7:458.
18. Lee, *Revolutionary War Memoir*, 247.
19. Lee, Jr., *The Campaigns of 1781 in the Carolinas*, 125-126.
20. Larry G. Aaron, *Race to the Dan: The Retreat That Rescued the American Revolution* (Halifax, VA: Halifax County Historical Society, 2007), 125. The comment comes from Dennis Conrad, editor of Greene's papers, taken from remarks made at the Crossing of the Dan

River Memorial dedication on February 13, 1999, which are included in this book.

21. Ward, *War of the Revolution*, 780.

22. O'Hara, *Letters to the Duke of Grafton*, 177.

23. Buchanan, *Road to Guilford Courthouse*, 363.

24. Ward, *War of the Revolution*, 784-785.

25. "Cornwallis to Germain," April 18, 1781, *CP*, 4:106.

26. This brief portrait of the Yorktown campaign was taken primarily from various sections of Boatner's *Encyclopedia of the American Revolution* and Ward, *War of the Revolution*, 885-887.

27. "NG to General Henry Knox," September 29, 1781, *NG*, 9:411.

28. Lee, *Revolutionary War Memoirs*, 247-248.

CHAPTER SIXTEEN: FAREWELL TO THE SOUTHERN GENTLEMEN

1. For troop and casualty figures from Eutaw Springs, I relied on the article "Nathanael Greene and the Battle of Eutaw Springs" by Jim Piecuch, appearing in the excellent collection *General Nathanael Greene and the American Revolution in the South*, Columbia: University of South Carolina Press, 2012.

2. Gary Shattuck, "7 Gold Medals of America's Revolutionary Congress," *Journal of the American Revolution Website*, https://allthingsliberty.com/2015/04/7-gold-medals-of-americas-revolutionary-congress/, accessed on September 18, 2019.

3. Notes 1 and 2 from "Hugh Rutledge, Speaker of the House of Representatives, to NG," February 26, 1781, *NG*, 10:411-412. Also Gerald M. Carbone, *Nathanael Greene* (New York: Palgrave Macmillan, 2008), 218.

4. "NG to Catherine Littlefield Greene," April 14, 1785, *NG*, 13:493.

5. Gregory D. Massey, "The Transformation of Nathanael Greene," from *General Nathanael Greene and the American Revolution in the South*, 254-257.

6. Golway, *Washington's General*, 291.

7. This portrait of Cornwallis's later career was drawn primarily from the following sources: C.A. Bayly and Katherine Prior, "Cornwallis, Charles, first Marquess Cornwallis," *Oxford Dictionary of National Biography* (online edition), article first published September 23, 2004, revised September 22, 2011; John Bew, "The Case for Cornwallis," *National Interest*, Nov/Dec 2014, Issue 134, pp. 58-66; and Buchanan, *The Road to Guilford Courthouse*, 389-390.

8. Bass, *The Green Dragoon*, 257. Bass attributes this excerpt to the *Critical Review*.

9. Ibid., 259. Bass quotes a letter dated December 12, 1787, from Cornwallis to his brother, the Rev. Doctor James Cornwallis.

10. Ibid., 260.

11. This profile of Banastre Tarleton was drawn primarily from Stephen Conway, "Tarleton, Sir Banastre, baronet," *Oxford Dictionary of National Biography* (online edition), article first published September 23, 2004, revised January 5, 2012.

12. James Graham, *The Life of General Daniel Morgan*, 19.

13. For this portrait of Daniel Morgan's later years I sourced primarily from Zambone's *Daniel Morgan: A Revolutionary Life*, 282-303.

14. Portrait of Otho Holland Williams's later years compiled from Beakes, *Otho Holland Williams in the American Revolution*, 287-322.

15. Boatner, *Encyclopedia of the American Revolution*, 185-186.

16. Lee, *Revolutionary War Memoirs*, 588. For the analysis of the family connection between

George and William Washington, I am indebted to Boatner's *Encyclopedia of the American Revolution*, 1169.

17. Ibid., 588.

18. In addition to Lee and Boatner, the entry for William Washington in the South Carolina Encyclopedia (http://www.scencyclopedia.org/sce/entries/washington-william/, accessed on September 23, 2019) by Samuel K. Fore was influential in writing this brief post-war biography.

19. "Pickens, Andrew," Encyclopedia.com (https://www.encyclopedia.com/history/encyclopedias-almanacs-transcripts-and-maps/pickens-andrew, accessed on September 24, 2019). Also Boatner, *Encyclopedia of the American Revolution*, 866-867.

20. Lee, *Revolutionary War Memoirs*, 185. Also Boatner, *Encyclopedia of the American Revolution*, 585.

21. Rev. Joseph Brown Turner, editor, "Introduction" to *Papers of the Historical Society of Delaware. LVI. The Journal and Order Book of Captain Robert Kirkwood of the Delaware Regiment of the Continental Line* (Wilmington: Historical Society of Delaware, 1910), 5-6.

22. Boatner, *Encyclopedia of the American Revolution*, 520. A biography of Howard titled *Cool Deliberate Courage: John Eager Howard in the American Revolution* by Jim Piecuch and John Beakes was published in 2009 but is, sadly, already out of print. I gleaned a few facts about Howard from a review of that book by Charles P. Niemeyer that appeared in *Journal of Military History*, Jan 2012, Vol. 76, Issue 1, 234-236.

23. Charles Royster, "Introduction" to *The Revolutionary War Memoirs of General Henry Lee* (New York: De Capo Press edition, 1998), iv-ix.

24. William R. Davie profile taken primarily from the article "Davie, William Richardson," by Blackwell P. Robinson (1986) for the NCPedia website (https://www.ncpedia.org/biography/davie-william-richardson, accessed on September 25, 2019). NCPedia attributes the article to *Dictionary of North Carolina Biography*, 6 volumes, edited by William S. Powell (Chapel Hill: University of North Carolina Press, 1979-1996). Some information also came from the article "William R. Davie: UNC's Founding Father," by Jennifer L. Larson from the Documenting the American South website (https://docsouth.unc.edu/highlights/davie.html, accessed on September 25, 2019).

BIBLIOGRAPHY

PRIMARY AND CONTEMPORARY SOURCES

Anderson, Thomas. "Journal of Lieutenant Thomas Anderson of the Delaware Regiment, 1780-1782," *Historical Magazine*, 2d ser., Vol. 1 (1867).

Clinton, Henry, and William B. Wilcox, ed. *The American Rebellion: Sir Henry Clinton's Narrative of His Campaigns, 1775-1782.* New Haven: Yale University Press, 1954.

Collins, James Potter, and John M. Roberts, ed. *Autobiography of a Revolutionary Soldier.* Clinton, LA: Feliciana Democrat Printing, 1859.

Cornwallis, Charles, and Charles Ross, ed. *Correspondence of Charles, First Marquis Cornwallis.* London: John Murray, 1859. In three volumes, although only volume one pertains to the American Revolution.

Cornwallis, Charles, and Ian Saberton, ed. *The Cornwallis Papers: The Campaigns of 1780 and 1781 in the Southern Theatre of the American Revolutionary War.* East Sussex, England: Naval and Military Press, 2010. In six volumes.

Davie, William R. *The Revolutionary War Sketches of William R. Davie.* Raleigh: N.C. Department of Cultural Resources, 1976.

Greene, Nathanael, and Richard K. Showman, Margaret Cobb, and Robert E. McCarthy, eds. *The Papers of Nathanael Greene.* Chapel Hill: University of North Carolina Press for Rhode Island Historical Society, 1976-2005.

Hammond, Samuel. "Notes on the Battle of Camden," in Joseph Johnson, ed. *Traditions and Reminiscences, Chiefly of the American Revolution in the South.* Charleston, SC: Walker & James, 1851.

Henry, Robert. *Narrative of the Battle of Cowan's Ford, February 1st, 1781.* Greensboro, NC: David Schenck, 1891. My copy was purchased on Amazon without publication information or page numbers.

(de) Jeney, Michel. *The Partisan: Or, the Art of Making War in Detachment.* London: R. Griffiths, 1760.

Kirkwood, Robert, and Joseph Brown Turner, ed. *The Journal and Order Book of Captain Robert Kirkwood of the Delaware Regiment of the Continental Line in Two Parts.* Wilmington: Historical Society of Delaware, 1910.

Lamb, Roger. *An Original and Authentic Journal of Occurrences During the Late American War, From Its Commencement to the Year 1783.* Dublin: Wilkinson & Courtney, 1809.

Lee, Henry. *The Revolutionary War Memoirs of General Henry Lee.* Edited by Robert E. Lee with introduction by Charles Royster. New York: Da Capo Press, 1998; originally published in 1812.

Lee, Henry. *The Campaign of 1781 in the Carolinas.* Spartanburg, SC: Reprint Company, 1975. This is a revised edition of Henry Lee's memoir, originally published in 1824, and edited by Lee's son, Henry Lee, Jr. It is valuable for appendices and footnotes of original material not included in the original edition, such as an account collected from John Eager Howard about the Battle of Cowpens.

Mackenzie, Roderick. *Strictures on Lt. Col. Tarleton's History of "Campaigns of 1780 and 1781, In the Southern Provinces of North America" in a Series of Letters to a Friend.* London, 1787.

Moultrie, William. *Memoirs of the American Revolution: So Far as It Relates to the States of North and South Carolina, and Georgia.* New York: David Longworth, 1802, 2 volumes.

Myers, Theodorus Bailey, ed. *The Cowpens Papers.* Charleston, SC: News & Courier, 1881. A useful collection of primary documents, some found elsewhere, a few not.

Newsome, A.R. ed., "A British Orderly Book, 1780-1781," Volumes III and IV. *North Carolina Historical Review*, Volume III appears in Vol. 9, No. 3 (July 1932), 273-298; Volume IV appears in Vol. 9, No. 4 (October 1932), 366-392.

O'Hara, Charles, and George C. Rogers, Jr., ed., "Letters of Charles O'Hara to the Duke of Grafton." *South Carolina Historical Magazine*, Vol. 65, No. 3 (July 1964), 158-180.

Read, William. "Reminiscences of Dr. William Read, Arranged from His Notes and Papers." Appearing in *Documentary History of the American Revolution, 1776-1782*, edited by R.W. Gibbes. New York: D. Appleton, 1857.

(de) Saxe, Herman Maurice. *Reveries on the Art of War.* New Delhi, India: Pentagon Press, 2017.

Seymour, William. *A Journal of the Southern Expedition, 1780-1783.* Wilmington: Historical Society of Delaware, 1896.

Stedman, Charles. *The History of the Origin, Progress, and Termination of the American War*, in two volumes. London: published for the author, 1794. Stedman was an officer on Cornwallis's staff during the Race to the Dan, although his *History* covers the entire American Revolution.

Tarleton, Banastre. *A History of the Campaigns of 1780 and 1781, in the Southern Provinces of North America.* London, 1787.

Turner, Rev. Joseph Brown, editor. *Papers of the Historical Society of Delaware. LVI. The Journal and Order Book of Captain Robert Kirkwood of the Delaware Regiment of the Continental Line.* Wilmington: Historical Society of Delaware, 1910.

Watson, Elkanah, and Winslow C. Watson, ed. *Men and the Times of the Revolution: or, Memoirs of Elkanah Watson, Including His Journals of Travel in Europe and America from the Year 1772 to 1842.* 2nd Edition. New York: Dana and Company, 1857. The reminiscences of Gates's commissariat officer, Colonel Thomas Polk, are found here.

Williams, Otho Holland. "A Narrative of the Campaign of 1780," appearing in Appendix B of *Sketches of the Life and Correspondence of Nathanael Greene* by William Johnson. Charleston, SC: A.E. Miller, 1822.

Young, Thomas. "Memoir of Major Thomas Young," *Orion Magazine,* November 1843. (Accessed at http://www.carolinamilitia.com/memoir-of-major-thomas-young/.)

SECONDARY SOURCES

Aaron, Larry G. *Race to the Dan: The Retreat That Rescued the American Revolution.* Halifax, VA: Halifax County Historical Society, 2007.

Anderson, William Lee. "Camp New Providence: Large Encampment of Southern Continental Army and militia on Providence Road at Six Mile Creek, October-December 1780." Downloaded from https://elehistory.com/amrev/MecklenburgDuringAmericanRevolution.pdf on October 12, 2018. Sadly, this outstanding article about the Continental camps in Charlotte is no longer available online; a Google search suggests Mr. Anderson has passed away. Luckily, I made a paper copy.

Andrlik, Todd. *Reporting the Revolutionary War: Before It Was History, It Was News.* Naperville, IL: Sourcebooks, 2012.

Babits, Lawrence E. *A Devil of a Whipping: The Battle of Cowpens.* Chapel Hill: University of North Carolina Press, 1998. Groundbreaking battle documentary. Essential for study of Cowpens.

Babits, Lawrence E., and Joshua B. Howard. "Continentals in Tarleton's British Legion: May 1780 to October 1781," appearing in *Cavalry of the American Revolution,* edited by Jim Piecuch. Yardley, PA: Westholme Publishing, 2012.

Babits, Lawrence E. and Joshua Howard. *Long, Obstinate, and Bloody: The Battle of Guilford Courthouse.* Chapel Hill: UNC Press, 2009.

Bass, Robert D. *The Green Dragoon: The Lives of Banastre Tarleton and Mary Robinson.* Orangeburg, SC: Sandlapper Publishing, 1973.

Beakes, John. *Otho Holland Williams in the American Revolution.* Mount Pleasant, SC: Nautical and Aviation Publishing, 2015.

Bew, John. "The Case for Cornwallis," *National Interest,* Nov/Dec 2014, Issue 134.

Boatner, Mark M., III. *Encyclopedia of the American Revolution*. Mechanicsburg, PA: Stackpole Books, 1994. (Originally published in 1966 by David McKay.)

Buchanan, John. *The Road to Guilford Courthouse: The American Revolution in the Carolinas*. New York: John Wiley & Sons, 1997.

Burns, James MacGregor. *Fire and Light: How the Enlightenment Transformed Our World*. New York: St. Martin's Press, 2013.

Callahan, North. *Daniel Morgan: Ranger of the Revolution*. New York: Holt, Rinehart and Winston, 1961.

Carbone, Gerald M. *Nathanael Greene*. New York: Palgrave Macmillan, 2008.

Clark, Murtie June. *Loyalists in the Southern Campaign of the Revolutionary War*. Baltimore, MD: Genealogical Publishing, 1981.

Davis, Burke. *The Cowpens-Guilford Courthouse Campaign*. New York: J.B. Lippincott, 1962.

Edgar, Walter. *Partisans & Redcoats: The Southern Conflict That Turned the Tide of the American Revolution*. New York: William Morrow, 2001.

Fisher, Sydney G. *The Struggle for American Independence*. Philadelphia: Lippincott, 1908.

Fiske, John. *The American Revolution*, 2 vols. Boston: Houghton Mifflin, 1902.

Golway, Terry. *Washington's General: Nathanael Greene and the Triumph of the American Revolution*. New York: Henry Holt, 2006.

Gordon, John W. *South Carolina and the American Revolution: A Battlefield History*. Columbia: University of South Carolina Press, 2003.

Gordon, Wlliam. *The History of the Rise, Progress, and Establishment of the Independence of the United States of America*. 4 vols. London: printed for the author, 1788. I referenced only volume 4. Gordon's historical work is listed here as a secondary source, though he was in correspondence with many of the war's major figures during its writing, including Nathanael Greene and Otho Holland Williams. Williams once noted that Gordon's account of the Race to the Dan is almost a verbatim copy of the account Williams sent to the author for reference.

Graham, James. *The Life of General Daniel Morgan: Of the Virginia Line of the Army of the United States, With Portions of His Correspondence*. New York: Derby & Jackson, 1859.

Graves, William T. *Backcountry Revolutionary: James Williams (1740-1780) with Source Documents*. Lugoff, SC: Southern Campaigns of the American Revolution Press, 2012.

Greene, George Washington. *The Life of Nathanael Greene, Major-General in the Army of the Revolution*, 3 vols. The editions used for this work were Volume I, Boston: Houghton Mifflin, 1890; Volume 3, New York: Hurd and Houghton, 1871.

Heaton, Charles. "The Failure of Enlightenment Military Doctrine in Revolutionary America: The Piedmont Campaign and the Fate of the British Army in the Lower South," *North Carolina Historical Review*, Vol. 87, No. 2 (April 2010).

Henderson, H. James. "The Structure of Politics in the Continental Congress," from *Essays on the American Revolution*, edited by Stephen G. Kurtz and James H. Hutson. Chapel Hill: University of North Carolina Press, 1973.

Higginbotham, Don. *Daniel Morgan: Revolutionary Rifleman*. Chapel Hill: University of North Carolina Press, 1961.

Higginbotham, Don. *The War of American Independence: Military Attitudes, Policies, and Practice, 1763-1789*. Bloomington: Indiana University Press paperback edition, 1978.

Johnson, Joseph. *Traditions and Reminiscences Chiefly of the American Revolution in the South: Including Biographical Sketches, Incidents and Anecdotes*. Charleston, SC: Walker & James, 1851.

Johnson, William. *Sketches of the Life and Correspondence of Nathanael Greene*, 2 vols. Charleston, SC: A.E. Miller, 1822.

Lambert, Robert Stansbury. *South Carolina Loyalists in the American Revolution*. Columbia: University of South Carolina Press, 1987.

Lossing, Benson J. *The Pictorial Field-Book of The Revolution*, 2 volumes. New York: Harper & Brothers, 1860.

Luvaas, Jay. *Frederick the Great and the Art of War*. New York: Free Press, 1966.

Marshal, John. *The Life of George Washington: commander in chief of the American forces, during the war which established the independence of his country, and first president of the United States*. New York: Citizens Guild of Washington's Boyhood Home, 1926.

McCrady, Edward. *The History of South Carolina in the Revolution: 1780-1783*. New York: Macmillan, 1902.

McGee, Lee F. "The Better Order of Men: Hammond's Store and Fort Williams." *Southern Campaigns of the American Revolution*, Vol. 2, No. 12, December 2005. Essential reading on Hammond's Store. Luckily the Southern Campaigns of the American Revolution archive is still available online at: http://www.southerncampaign.org/.

Morgan, John. "Making Bricks Without Straw: Nathanael Greene's Southern Campaigns and Mao Tse-Tung's Mobile War," *Military Affairs*, Vol. 47, No. 3 (October 1983).

O'Kelley, Patrick. *Nothing But Blood and Slaughter: The Revolutionary War in the Carolinas*. Blue House Tavern Press, 2004. In four volumes, one for each year beginning in 1779.

Pagden, Anthony. *The Enlightenment and Why It Still Matters*. New York: Random House, 2013.

Pancake, John S. *1777: The Year of the Hangman*. Tuscaloosa, AL: University of Alabama Press, 1977.

Pancake, John S. *This Destructive War: The British Campaign in the Carolinas, 1780-1782*. Tuscaloosa: University of Alabama Press, 2003 (originally published 1985).

Peicuch, Jim, and Gregory D. Massey, eds. *General Nathanael Greene and the American Revolution in the South.* Columbia: University of South Carolina Press, 2012. A fine collection of essays about the life, legacy, and influence of Nathanael Greene.

Powell, William S., and Michael Hill, *The North Carolina Gazetteer: A Dictionary of Tar Heel Places and Their History*, 2nd Edition. Chapel Hill: UNC Press, 2010.

Rouse, Parke, Jr. *The Great Wagon Road: How Scotch-Irish and Germanics Settled the Uplands.* Richmond, VA: Dietz Press, 1995.

Royster, Charles. *A Revolutionary People at War: The Continental Army & American Character, 1775-1783.* Chapel Hill: University of North Carolina Press, 1979.

Royster, Charles. "Introduction" to *The Revolutionary War Memoirs of General Henry Lee.* New York: Da Capo Press, 1998.

Scheer, George F., and Hugh Rankin. *Rebels & Redcoats: The American Revolution Through the Eyes of Those Who Fought and Lived It.* New York: Da Capo Press, 1957.

Schenck, David. *North Carolina, 1780-'81: Being a History of the Invasion of the Carolinas by the British Army Under Lord Cornwallis in 1780-'81.* Raleigh, NC: Edwards & Broughton, 1889.

Shattuck, Gary. "Seven Gold Medals of America's Revolutionary Congress," *Journal of the American Revolution.* Website, https://allthingsliberty.com/2015/04/7-gold-medals-of-americas-revolutionary-congress/.

Starkey, Armstrong. *War in the Age of Enlightenment, 1700-1789.* Westport, CT: Praeger, 2003.

Stockard, Sallie W. *The History of Guilford County, North Carolina.* Knoxville, TN: Gaut-Ogden, 1902.

Thayer, Theodore. *Nathanael Greene: Strategist of the American Revolution.* New York: Twayne, 1960.

Treacy, M.F. *Prelude to Yorktown: The Southern Campaign of Nathanael Greene, 1780-1781.* Chapel Hill: University of North Carolina Press, 1963.

Ward, Christopher. *The War of the Revolution.* New York: Skyhorse Publishing, 2011.

Waters, Andrew. *The Quaker and the Gamecock: Nathanael Greene, Thomas Sumter, and the Revolutionary War for the Soul of the South.* Philadelphia, PA: Casemate Publishers, 2019.

Wickwire, Franklin and Mary. *Cornwallis and the War of Independence.* London: Faber and Faber, 1971.

Wickwire, Franklin and Mary. *Cornwallis: The American Adventure.* Boston: Houghton Mifflin, 1970.

Zambone, Albert Louis. *Daniel Morgan: A Revolutionary Life.* Yardley, PA: Westholme Publishing, 2018.

WEBSITES, MAPS, MISCELLANEOUS

Carolana.com webpage, "A History of Martinsville, North Carolina," http://www.carolana.com/NC/Towns/Martinville_NC.html, accessed on March 7, 2019.

Chalmers, G. Davidson, "Davidson, William Lee," Ncpedia.org, https://www.ncpedia.org/biography/davidson-william-lee, accessed on March 2, 2019.

Cook, James. "A map of the province of South Carolina with all the rivers, bays, inlets, islands, inland navigation, soundings, time of high water on the sea coast, roads, marshes, ferrys, bridges, swamps, parishes, churches, towns, townships, county, parish, district, and provincial lines," 1773. Library of Congress website, https://www.loc.gov/item/74692124/.

Crews, C. Daniel. "Moravians," NCPedia.org website, https://www.ncpedia.org/moravians, accessed on March 8, 2019.

Davidson, Chalmers G. "Davidson, William Lee." Biographical entry for William Lee Davidson on Ncpedia.org, https://www.ncpedia.org/biography/davidson-william-lee, accessed on March 2, 2019.

Documenting the American South webpage, University Library, University of North Carolina at Chapel Hill, https://docsouth.unc.edu.

Encyclopedia.com. "Pickens, Andrew." https://www.encyclopedia.com/history/encyclopedias-almanacs-transcripts-and-maps/pickens-andrew, accessed on September 24, 2019.

Fore, Samuel K. "William Washington." South Carolina Encyclopedia online edition, http://www.scencyclopedia.org/sce/entries/washington-william/, accessed on September 23, 2019.

Hillhouse, William. "Pension Application of William Hillhouse," *Southern Campaigns American Revolution Pension Statements & Rosters*, transcribed by Will Graves; annotated by Charles B. Baxley, http://revwarapps.org/s7008.pdf, accessed on October 10, 2018.

Oxford Dictionary of National Biography (online edition): Bayly, C.A. and Katherine Prior. "Cornwallis, Charles, first Marquess Cornwallis," article first published September 23, 2004, revised September 22, 2011; also Conway, Stephen. "Tarleton, Sir Banastre, baronet," article first published September 23, 2004, revised January 5, 2012.

Robertson, John A. "Burr's Mill Found," *Southern Campaigns of the American Revolution*, Vol. 2, No. 12, http://www.southerncampaign.org/newsletter/v2n12.pdf, accessed on June 12, 2019.

Robinson, Blackwell P. "Davie, William Richardson." NCPedia website, https://www.ncpedia.org/biography/davie-william-richardson, accessed on September 25, 2019.

Shenawolf, Harry. "The British Brigade of Guards in the American Revolution," Revolutionary War Journal website, http://www.revolutionarywarjournal.com/british-brigade-of-guards/, accessed on October 2, 2019.

ACKNOWLEDGMENTS

———

First of all, I would like to thank my family for their unconditional love and support of my ambitions to be an author. This includes my beloved wife, Anne, and dear son, Eli; my father and step-mother, Charles Waters and Linda Moxley Waters; my sister Sara and her husband, Joe; my sister Emily and her family, Conan, Ian, Maya, and Forrest; and my precious aunts Bobbie Hastings and Jane Nielsen. I remember as a child playing on the floor of my living room, with my father's history books looking down from the shelves over me, and feeling strongly something awaited me there. To this feeling I must attribute the influence of my mother, Lee Waters, who instilled in me her love for books, among so many other things.

I've had so many wonderful teachers over the years who have encouraged me as a writer but in particular I would like to thank Beverly Russell, Tom Orr, William McCranor Henderson, and David Guy. I would like to thank Bruce H. Franklin and his talented crew at Westholme for believing in this project and publishing the most beautiful American Revolution books in the market today, and cartographer Tracy Dungan for making the story of the Race to the Dan come alive. Special thanks to Don N. Hagist at *Journal of the American Revolution* for publishing my first efforts at nonfiction historical writing and giving me and so many other American Revolution writers a forum for our work. Don also made a substantial editorial contribution to Chapter Nine, "To the End of the World." I am grateful to historian Jim Piecuch for reading the final draft manuscript and providing helpful feedback.

I would also like to thank Charles B. Baxley for his encouragement and support as well as Paul Wood. A special thanks to the great South Carolina historian Walter Edgar and his producer, Alfred Turner, for having me as a guest on NPR's *Walter Edgar's Journal.* Surely, this was the highlight of my writing career so far, and also a ripping good time. I have said before that reading John Buchanan's *The Road to Guilford Courthouse* was a revelation to me, and anyone familiar with that book will see its strong influence in this one. Thank you, Mr. Buchanan. The editors and anyone else associated with the landmark publication of *The Papers of General Nathanael Greene* also deserve my thanks, for this book would certainly not be possible without them.

INDEX